DISKI 316

DISKI

Dissertationen zur Künstlichen Intelligenz

Mit Unterstützung des Fachbereichs 1 „Künstliche Intelligenz" der Gesellschaft für Informatik e.V. herausgegeben von

Trust-Based Recommendations in Multi-Layer Networks

Claudia Heß

Claudia Heß
Auf der Höhe 29
91341 Röttenbach
Germany
E-mail: claudia.hess@uni-bamberg.de

Dissertation thesis submitted in a jointly supervised
German-French Cotutelle to obtain the degree of
Doktor der Naturwissenschaften (Dr. rer. nat.)
by the University of Bamberg, Germany,
Faculty for Information Systems and Applied Computer Science

and

Grade de Docteur Spécialité Informatique
by Paris-Sud 11 University, France,
Faculty of Sciences, Ecole Doctorale d'Informatique

Numéro d'ordre: 8957

Thesis examiners: Prof. Dr. Christoph Schlieder
                  Prof. Dr. Günther Görz
                  Prof. Dr. Mohand-Said Hacid

Defence of the thesis: 25. January 2008

Bibliographic information published by *Die Deutsche Bibliothek*
Die Deutsche Bibliothek lists this publication in the *Deutsche Nationalbibliografie*;
Detailed bibliographic data is available on the Internet at http://dnb.ddb.de.

"infix" is a joint imprint of Akademische Verlagsgesellschaft Aka GmbH and IOS Press
BV (Amsterdam)

Reproduced from PDF supplied by the author
Printed in the Netherlands

ISSN 0941-5769
ISBN 978-3-89838-316-5 (Aka)
ISBN 978-1-58603-854-0 (IOS Press)

Foreword of the Thesis Advisor

Recommendation services are widely found in today's web commerce, the most prominent example being the patented recommending technology used by Amazon. However, the example of Amazon also illustrates some of the limitations of current technology. In general, recommendations are computed with an item-similarity approach: if, for example, a customer buys a travel guide, the system generates the recommendation to buy a second travel guide of the same geographic region. Such results are of little utility in many application scenarios. As a consequence, personalization is the central concern in both academic and industrial research on recommender systems. The thesis of Claudia Heß makes a significant contribution to this issue focusing on the problem of text document recommendation.

So far, recommending approaches have treated text documents not differently from any other type of items. The basic idea that Claudia Heß explores in her thesis is that cross-references between texts (e.g. hyperlinks between web pages, citations between scientific papers) constitute a rich source of information that recommending should take into account. This observation connects document recommendations to the research field of information filtering in document networks. Techniques for quantifying and computing the visibility of a document in a network of other documents have been studied especially in the context of search engines with the patented Pagerank used by Google as the best known example of an algorithmic visibility measure.

Claudia Heß' innovative approach combines information filtering techniques based on document visibility with trust-based computations of recommendations. This is to say that two rather different types of networks act as basic sources of information: a network of trust relationships between readers (or authors) and a network of linked documents. Interestingly, the approach generalizes to cases where more than two types of networks act as information sources.

The major methodological contributions of the thesis consist in algorithmic approaches for measuring trust-enhanced document visibility and thus belong to AI research on semantic information processing. I will highlight some of the results that I personally think are of special interest.

- A first result is the requirement analysis based on two use cases of text document recommendation. Three types of requirements are identified relating to (1) the layering of the architecture, (2) the enhancement of visibility measures with trust, and (3) the problem of duplicate documents. Not just the requirements but also the uses cases themselves are of interest as they show novel applications for recommender systems.

- Especially interesting is the use case of recommendations dealing with retracted publications. Maybe even more important than the few spectacular cases of scientific fraud mentioned in the thesis are those many cases where the conclusions of a publication are no longer considered valid because of new evidence reported by subsequent publications. Clearly, any recommending service of a scientific digital library should be able to handle such cases.

- Claudia Heß proposes a recommending approach consisting of three elements: (1) a multi-layer architecture, (2) the computation of trust-enhanced document visibilities, and (3) a solution for the problem of duplicated documents. This architecture provides an elegant way to describe the basic propagation mechanisms, node-to-node and edge-to-edge propagation, independently of the type of networks considered.

- Two types of trust networks are analyzed in connection with the computation of trust-enhanced document visibilities: reviewer trust networks and author trust networks. The reviewer trust network helps to personalize document recommendations by making the impact of a review on a document's visibility dependent on the user's trust in the reviewer. Claudia Heß speaks of trust-review-enhanced visibility or TRE-visibility for short. A central result of the discussion and a major contribution of the thesis is the approximation of the integrated TRE-visibility by the efficiently computable review-propagating TRE-visibility.

- Results from simulation studies provide further evidence for the usefulness of the approach. The advantage of a simulation study over a field study is that the relevant parameters such as the size of the network can be systematically varied. For the TRE-visibility the most relevant findings relate to (1) the fine-tuning of the parameter settings for the distance-based TRE-visibility, (2) the comparison of different TRE-visibilities, and (3) the analysis of scenarios with competing scientific communities.

These results contribute to our understanding of the representation of information processing and knowledge representation in social networks. From an application perspective, however, the thesis also contributes to the field of digital libraries where the first document recommendation services are currently put into practice. It is little surprising that some of the thesis' results have been published at conferences on either semantic information processing or digital libraries. However, the thesis contains a number of original results that have not been previously published.

Even more important, what has been written as a thesis turns out to be a very readable book. Many readers will use the book to learn about the details of the trust-based approach to document recommendation that Claudia Heß has developed. Because of the comprehensive and knowledgeable survey of the state of the art, however, the book may also serve as an introductory text into the field of document recommendation.

Prof. Dr. Christoph Schlieder

Abstract

The huge interest in social networking applications – Friendster.com, for example, has more than 40 million users – led to a considerable research interest in using this data for generating recommendations. Especially recommendation techniques that analyze *social trust networks* were found to provide very accurate results. In this dissertation, I use trust information for personalizing document recommendations. I show the benefits of such trust-enhanced recommendations in the context of digital libraries and wikis. Documents are often linked by some reference mechanism, for example, citations between scientific publications or hyperlinks between websites. Measures for the visibility of documents use this *document reference network*. A document is considered the more important, the more often it is referenced by important documents. A recommendation based exclusively on citations, however, can be misleading: there exist articles, highly visible in terms of citation rank, which years after their publication are proven to rely on forged data – recall, for instance, the stem cell researcher Hwang whose most-cited publications have been revealed as faked. A trust-based recommender system would advise against a forged article if its author is distrusted. Evaluating the reliability of a document is also important in wikis. In Wikipedia, for example, the question on the accuracy of the information provided is central because millions of often anonymous users contribute.

I suggest a joint analysis of social trust networks and document reference networks. Actually, the idea can be extended to more networks, for example, organization networks. In such a *multi-layer architecture*, information can be propagated within and between the layers. Trust-based recommendations and reference-based visibilities can thus be integrated. Apart from the specification of the multi-layer framework, the focus of the dissertation is on the development of such *trust-enhanced visibility measures*. An important requirement for these measures is that they are efficiently computable at query time, i.e. in direct response to a user query. I present two sets of measures, namely for author and reviewer trust networks. The *trust-review-enhanced visibilities*, the so-called TRE-visibilities, integrate users' reviews into reference-based measures on documents. Reviews by highly trusted users considerably influence the recommendation because high trust means appreciating these users' reviews. *Author-trust-enhanced visibilities*, the so-called ATE-visibilities, connect an author trust network with the document reference network. The degree of trust refers now to an author's capabilities to produce new research results or to compile a survey article.

The reference-based visibilities of documents are modulated by the trust in their authors. With the TRE- and the ATE-visibility measures, I have defined functions for both basic types of two-layer networks.

The trust-enhanced visibility measures are evaluated in the simulation environment *Comte* which was designed for analyzing large communication processes, such as collaboratively authored wiki pages or scholarly publications. Both TRE- and ATE-visibilities are computed from the perspective of a user. Results show that they clearly reflect this user's personal preferences expressed in the trust statements and in the reviews. The impact of trust and distrust statements could be shown by comparing visibilities and rankings for two users with diverging trust statements. The TRE- and the ATE-visibility measures efficiently downgrade fraudulent papers in their visibility and thus in their position in a document ranking.

When ranking scientific papers provided by different digital libraries or webpages offered on several mirrors, duplicate documents have to be taken into consideration because they distort the results by visibility measures. I develop a *model of uncertainty* that permits dealing with uncertainty during the computation of trust-enhanced visibilities. As recommendations and rankings have to be generated very efficiently, I introduce an approximation approach and apply it to the TRE-visibility.

The trust-based Scientific Paper Recommender SPRec implements the two-layer architecture consisting of a reviewer trust network and a document reference network. While a reviewer trust network is established directly between the users, the document reference network is based on the metadata on academic papers provided by CiteSeer. SPRec generates personalized document recommendations and rankings with the TRE-visibility.

Zusammenfassung

Soziale Netzwerke mit Millionen von Nutzern – zum Beispiel sind mehr als 40 Millionen Benutzer auf Friendster.com registriert – haben zu einem großen Interesse an der Fragestellung geführt, wie die Informationen aus solchen sozialen Netzwerken in Empfehlungssystemen genutzt werden können. Aktuelle Forschungsarbeiten haben gezeigt, dass vor allem Techniken, die *soziale Vertrauensnetzwerke* zur Grundlage nehmen, sehr gute Ergebnisse liefern. In meiner Dissertation nutze ich die Informationen darüber, wer wem zu welchem Grad vertraut, um Empfehlungen für Dokumente zu personalisieren. Ich zeige die Vorzüge solcher vertrauensbasierten Empfehlungen in den Bereichen Digitale Bibliotheken und Wikis. Häufig verweisen Dokumente aufeinander: Referenzen sind beispielsweise Zitate zwischen wissenschaftlichen Publikationen oder Hyperlinks zwischen Webseiten. Maße für die Sichtbarkeit eines Dokumentes nutzen dieses *Dokumentennetzwerk*. Ein Dokument wird als umso wichtiger erachtet, je mehr wichtige Dokumente darauf verweisen. Eine Empfehlung, die nur auf der Verweisstruktur beruht, kann jedoch auch irreführend sein: es gibt Artikel, die hinsichtlich ihres Zitationsgrades als sehr sichtbar angesehen werden, bei denen sich aber – oft erst Jahre nach ihrer Veröffentlichung – herausstellt, dass sie auf gefälschten Daten beruhen. Ein solches Beispiel ist der Fall des Stammzellenforschers Hwang, dessen bahnbrechende Forschungsergebnisse sich als gefälscht herausgestellt haben. Ein vertrauensbasiertes Empfehlungssystem würde solche Dokumente nicht empfehlen, bzw. sogar davon abraten, wenn dem Autor misstraut wird. Eine derartige Analyse der Vertrauenswürdigkeit ist auch für Wikis von Bedeutung. In Wikipedia zum Beispiel stellt sich die Frage nach der Verlässlichkeit von Informationen, weil Millionen von häufig anonymen Nutzern die Artikel erstellen.

In dieser Arbeit schlage ich die gemeinsame Analyse von Vertrauensnetzwerken und Dokumentennetzwerken vor. Weitere Netzwerke, wie zum Beispiel Organisationsnetzwerke können noch hinzugefügt werden. In einer derartigen *mehrschichtigen Architektur* können Informationen innerhalb der einzelnen Schichten sowie zwischen den Schichten propagiert werden. Vertrauensbasierte Empfehlungen und Sichtbarkeiten, die auf der Verweisstruktur zwischen den Dokumenten basieren, können damit integriert werden. Neben der Spezifikation der mehrschichtigen Architektur liegt der Schwerpunkt der Dissertation auf der Entwicklung solcher *vertrauensbasierter Sichtbarkeitsmaße*. Eine wichtige Anforderung ist, dass diese Maße effizient zur Anfragezeit berechenbar sind und damit die Ergebnisse zu einer Anfrage direkt zurückzugeben werden können. Ich präsentiere zwei Arten von Maßen, nämlich für Vertrauensnetzwerke zwischen Autoren und zwischen Lesern, die die Dokumente bewerten. Letztere, nämlich die TRE (trust-review-enhanced)-Sichtbarkeitsmaße integrieren die Vertrauens- und die Dokumentenbewertungen (Reviews) in referenzbasierte Sichtbarkeitsmaße. Reviews von Nutzern, die als vertrauenswürdig eingestuft werden, haben einen starken Einfluss auf die Empfehlung, weil ein hohes Vertrauen bedeutet, dass die Reviews dieses Nutzers gut passen. Im Gegensatz dazu basieren die ATE (author-trust-enhanced)-Sichtbarkeitsmaße auf einem Autorennetzwerk kombiniert mit einem Dokumentennetzwerk. Der Grad des Vertrauens bezieht sich nun auf die Fähigkeit des Autors, gute Forschungsergebnisse zu erzielen oder einen guten Übersichtsartikel zu schreiben. Die referenzbasierten Sichtbarkeiten der Dokumente werden durch das Vertrauen in den Autor angepasst. Mit den TRE- und ATE-Sichtbarkeitsmaßen habe ich damit Funktionen für die beiden grundlegenden Arten von zweischichtigen Netzwerken definiert.

Die vertrauensbasierten Maße werden in der Simulationsumgebung *Comte* evaluiert. Comte ermöglicht die Analyse von umfangreichen (Massen-) Kommunikationsprozessen, wie es auch wissenschaftliche Publikationen sind. Sowohl TRE- als auch ATE-Sichtbarkeiten werden für einen bestimmten Nutzer berechnet. Die Ergebnisse der Simulationen zeigen, dass sich die Präferenzen des Nutzers, ausgedrückt in den Vertrauensbewertungen und den Reviews, deutlich in den personalisierten Sichtbarkeiten widerspiegeln. Der Einfluss der Vertrauens- und Mißtrauensbewertungen zeigt sich deutlich im Vergleich der Sichtbarkeiten für zwei Benutzer, die sich hinsichtlich dieser Bewertungen stark unterscheiden. Die TRE- und die ATE-Sichtbarkeitsmaßen mindern deutlich die Sichtbarkeit von betrügerischen Veröffentlichungen und setzen diese dadurch auch in einem Dokumentenranking herab.

Beim Ranking von wissenschaftlichen Artikeln, die aus verschiedenen digitalen Bibliotheken stammen oder von Webseiten, die auf mehreren Mirrors liegen, müssen Duplikate beachtet werden, weil diese die Ergebnisse von referenzbasierten Sichtbarkeitsmaßen verzerren. Ich entwickele daher ein *Modell für Unsicherheit*, das es erlaubt, mit Unsicherheit bei der Berechnung der vertrauensbasierten Sichtbarkeiten umzugehen. Um Empfehlungen und Rankings effizient zu berechnen führe ich einen Ansatz zur Approximation ein und wende ihn auf die TRE-Sichtbarkeit an.

Das vertrauensbasierte Empfehlungssystem für wissenschaftliche Publikationen, SPRec, implementiert die mehrschichtige Architektur bestehen aus einem Vertrauensnetzwerk zwischen Reviewern und einem Dokumentennetzwerk. Das Vertrauensnetzwerk besteht aus den explizit angegebenen Vertrauensbewertungen zwischen den Nutzern. Das Dokumentennetzwerk basiert auf Metadaten die CiteSeer für wissenschaftliche Veröffentlichungen bereitstellt. SPRec generiert personalisierte Empfehlungen für Dokumente und Rankings mit dem TRE-Sichtbarkeitsmaß.

Résumé

Durant les dernières années, nous avons pu constater le succès des réseaux sociaux d'Internet avec un nombre considérable d'utilisateurs. Friendster.com, par exemple, a plus de 40 millions d'utilisateurs. Récemment, ces réseaux sociaux sont utilisés comme base pour des systèmes de recommandation. Surtout les techniques de recommandation qui utilisent les réseaux de confiance ont donné des résultats très précis. Dans ma thèse, je propose d'utiliser les informations en provenance de réseaux de confiance pour améliorer les recommandations pour les documents. J'expose les avantages d'une telle approche à l'aide de deux domaines d'application : les bibliothèques électroniques et les wikis. Des systèmes de recommandation pour les documents exploitent souvent les réseaux de documents, c'est à dire les références entre les documents, par exemple les citations entre des publications scientifiques ou les liens entre les pages Web. La visibilité d'un document est définie en fonction des liens menant à lui. Un document est donc très visible s'il est cité par beaucoup de documents visibles. Le système de placement de Google, PageRank, par exemple, est basé sur cette idée. Cependant, recommander un document uniquement en fonction de sa visibilité peut être trompeur. Par exemple, il n'est pas approprié de recommander un document très visible, dont il est avéré qu'il s'agit d'un plagiat, ou d'un document faisant état d'expériences truquées, comme dans le cas des publications du professeur Hwang. Il était un expert en clonage avant que ses publications se révèlent être des manipulations. Un système de recommandation basé sur la confiance ne recommanderait plus le document manipulé si des utilisateurs dignes de confiance avaient indiqué leur méfiance vis-à-vis de l'auteur responsable de la supercherie. Une deuxième application dans laquelle l'analyse des réseaux de confiance aide à déterminer la fiabilité d'un document est les wikis. Cette question est importante, par exemple, dans le contexte de Wikipédia, une encyclopédie libre sur Internet, parce que les articles sont écrits par des millions d'internautes bénévoles dans un effort collaboratif.

Dans cette thèse, je propose l'analyse conjointe de réseaux de confiance et de réseaux de documents. Des réseaux supplémentaires peuvent aussi être considérés comme les réseaux d'organisations. Je spécifie donc une architecture structurée - un réseau à plusieurs strates - qui intègre les informations en provenance de différents types de réseaux. Dans une telle architecture, les informations peuvent être propagées indépendamment sur les différentes strates. De plus, les liens entre les strates permettent de propager l'information entre les strates. Les recommandations basées sur les relations de confiance et les mesures de visibilité sur le réseau de documents peuvent donc être combinées dans des mesures de visibilité renforcées par la confiance. A côté de la spécification de l'architecture à plusieurs strates, l'accent est mis sur le développement de telles mesures.

Je présente des mesures de visibilité renforcée par la confiance pour deux types de réseaux à deux strates. Le premier consiste en un réseau de confiance entre des lecteurs qui évaluent les documents qu'ils avaient lu et un réseau de documents. Ce groupe de mesures, la TRE (trust-review-enhanced)-visibilité, représente les mesures qui intègrent les notes données par les utilisateurs dans des mesures de visibilité sur les documents. Les conseils d'un utilisateur considéré comme très fiable ont une grande influence sur la visibilité parce que considérer quelqu'un comme fiable veut dire apprécier ses notes et ses rapports sur des documents. Le deuxième réseau à deux strates combine un réseau de documents avec un réseau de confiance entre les auteurs de ces documents. Ce groupe de mesures sont les mesures de ATE (author-trust-enhanced)-visibilité. Faire confiance à quelqu'un veut dire maintenant apprécier l'habilité de cette personne d'écrire des articles ou des pages Web intéressants, bien investigués, qui, par exemple, n'ont pas de liens à des pages spam. La visibilité d'un document qui était calculée sur la base des liens entrants peut être modifiée directement par la confiance dans l'auteur. Les mesures définies sur les réseaux à deux strates peuvent encore être améliorées en considérant d'autres types de réseaux. Je discute dans ma thèse comment intégrer un réseau d'organisation dans ces réseaux à deux strates et comment utiliser l'information en provenance de cette source d'information additionnelle dans les mesures de visibilité renforcée par la confiance.

Dans les collections de documents, il y a souvent des copies de documents, c'est-à-dire, il n'y a pas une seule version d'un document mais plusieurs qui probablement diffèrent minimalement dans leur contenu mais aussi dans les listes de citations. Si une collection de documents contient de telles copies, la qualité des recommandations peut être détériorée. J'introduis un modèle d'incertitude qui est capable de manier les copies en calculant les visibilités basées sur la confiance. Afin de calculer les recommandations d'une manière efficace, je développe une approximation.

Le système de recommandation SPRec (Scientific Paper Recommender) implémente l'architecture à deux strates consistant d'un réseau de confiance entre lecteurs et d'un réseau de publications scientifiques. Le réseau de documents est basé sur les metadonnées offertes par CiteSeer, une bibliothèque électronique pour les publications scientifiques surtout en informatique. Le réseau de confiance est construit explicitement par les utilisateurs : ils sont menés à indiquer des valeurs de confiance aux collègues afin de pouvoir utiliser les notes données par les collègues. Les recommandations et les rankings de documents sont générés avec la mesure de la TRE-visibilité. L'utilisateur peut comparer directement la recommandation calculée avec la TRE-visibilité, qui est certainement personnalisée, avec celle calculée avec PageRank.

Les mesures de visibilité renforcée par la confiance sont évaluées analytiquement
et dans l'environnement de simulation Comte qui permet de simuler des processus
de communication à grande échelle. Comte était élargi dans le cadre de cette thèse
avec des mesures de visibilité basée sur la confiance. Les mesures de TRE- et ATE-
visibilité sont calculées du point de vue d'un certain utilisateur. Les résultats montrent
que les visibilités sont personnalisées pour chaque utilisateur en fonction du réseau de
confiance. Les mesures de TRE- et ATE-visibilité baissent la visibilité d'un document
manipulé et sa position dans un placement.

Acknowledgements

First, I would like to thank Prof. Dr. Christoph Schlieder and Prof. Dr. Michel de Rougemont, my supervisors at the University of Bamberg and the University of Paris-Sud 11 who made it possible for me to write my dissertation thesis as a jointly supervised German-French cotutelle. I especially thank Christoph Schlieder for his encouragement and guidance throughout this work. I would also like to thank Michel de Rougemont for granting me insight into approximation algorithms on graphs.

Thanks as well to all the members of the jury for the attention they have paid to my work and for their constructive remarks and questions. I especially thank Prof. Dr. Günter Görz and Prof. Dr. Mohand-Said Hacid for their kind willingness to read and evaluate my dissertation. Prof. Dr. Ute Schmid gave me valuable input on modeling trust as seen from a psychological standpoint. Thanks to her and to Prof. Dr. Nicolas Spyratos for their participation in my thesis committee.

Two scholarships made it possible for me to spend a part of the last three years at the Laboratoire de Recherche en Informatique (LRI) at the Paris-Sud 11 University. First, the scholarship from the German Academic Exchange Service DAAD covered my stay in 2006 in France. Thanks to the scholarship from the Franco-German University, I was able to undertake a number of short research stays at the LRI during my whole dissertation.

I want wish to thank my colleagues for the warm and pleasant work atmosphere throughout these last years. To Klaus Stein I would like to convey my special thanks for always listening to me and for all our many fruitful discussions! He also co-authored some of the work that appears in chapter 5. Thanks as well to Cornelia Pickel and Stéphanie Druetta who supported me in Bamberg and Paris, respectively, with the many administrative tasks that came up due to the cotutelle and with the organization of the research stays in both countries.

My family has always been there for me. Thanks to my parents Karin and Günter Heß for their endless love, patience, and support at every stage of my life. Of course a special thanks to Markus Rieger for his support and understanding.

Contents

Contents

List of Figures

List of Tables

1 Introduction

Web-based social networks are one of the key elements of the Social Web, often called
Web 2.0, a concept which has been formed by O'Reilly (2005). Web 2.0 applications
differ from the applications that were en vogue during the Internet hype around 2000 in
the sense that they are social, i.e., users play an active role in providing content, such
as in Wikipedia, in writing reviews and comments that are used in personalized services, such as the book reviews written at Amazon.com and they participate actively,
e.g., by selling and buying at Ebay.com or by tagging photos at Flickr and websites
at del.icio.us. In social networks, users link themselves to people they know either
from the real world or from their interactions in the online world. Currently, very successful examples for web-based social networks are XING.com (formerly openBC.com)
and Facebook.com. In XING, users have a contact list with mainly business contacts.
Facebook, in contrast, does not focus on the business community, but rather on students. These social networking applications allow for browsing the networks in order
to find new friends, i.e. to get in contact with the friends of your friends, to revive old
friendships or make contact with new business partners.

Apart from browsing these social networks, more elaborate applications can be built.
The "collective intelligence" (O'Reilly, 2005) resulting from the activity of the web
users (who add content, create new links between webpages, participate by tagging
content or pictures) can be used to differentiate between reliable sources of information
and unreliable sources. This becomes feasible if more expressive social networks are
used, namely trust networks. They are more expressive because the relationships
expressed, that are the trust relationships, indicate varying degrees of trust, ranging
from absolute distrust to full trust. A user trusts another user, for instance, to provide
good recommendations about books. So we could look up each web resource that we
want to use to see whether it is reliable. For example, we could ask our friends whether
some seller at an auction platform is trustworthy. We could also ask whether some
information on a website is reliable. This can be achieved by looking in the trust
network to see if the author of this information can be considered as trustworthy or
whether a particular user that we trust considers the information as good. However,
carrying out these checks should be an automatic procedure and there should be no
need for manual efforts. Assessing automatically the trustworthiness of information
(or pieces of information, put together by agents) is the combined challenge for the
Social and the Semantic Web.

The Semantic Web aims to make the information on the Web machine-readable (Berners-Lee *et al.*, 2001). Therefore, webpages and any other content on the web are augmented with data that is machine-processable. XML and related technologies are used as the basis. In order to make machines understand the semantics, the data needs a well-defined meaning, which is provided with the help of RDF (Resource Description Framework) and ontology modeling languages such as OWL (Web Ontology Language). When the meaning of the information provided on a webpage is understood, individual pieces of information can be combined and new information can be inferred. This is possible, because inference procedures provided by ontology languages and rules allow for reasoning on the content and for proving facts. However, as everybody can make statements on the Semantic Web, and as these pieces of information are the basis for further computations or for answering user queries, it is necessary to be able to assess the trustworthiness of the information used. This is reflected in the famous "layer cake" by Tim Berners-Lee. The layers represent the different languages and techniques used in the context of the Semantic Web. My thesis relates to the highest layer, the trust layer. According to Swartz and Hendler (2001), digital signatures, which assure that the person who claims to be the author of a statement is actually the author, have to be complemented with a notion of social trust: in processing statements or making recommendations, it has to be clear whom to trust. This is to say that the user's "Web of Trust" (Swartz and Hendler), i.e., the people about whom the user has directly asserted a trust rating as well as the people who are rated by the direct acquaintances, is analyzed in order to predict the trustworthiness of some piece of information on the web. Such recommendations are therefore called trust-based recommendations.

This dissertation on trust-based recommendations, however, does not only use the trust network to generate recommendations, but jointly analyzes the trust network and the structure of the underlying network of interlinked webpages. Such document reference networks are not restricted to the Web, but paper citation networks, wikis or networks of interrelated statements on the Semantic Web can be analyzed, too. So the basic idea is to use the information from a trust network in order to enhance recommendations for documents and other interlinked information objects. The goal of this work is to develop an architecture for jointly analyzing different types of networks. As the architecture encompasses several interconnected networks, for example, an author network connected via is-author-relationships with a document network, I will speak of a multi-layer architecture. Functions for propagating information between the different layers of networks have to be defined. Having developed such framework for trust-based recommendations, the question arises as to how this approach can be used. I discuss several application scenarios and show the benefits of using trust-based recommendations. One of these scenarios, a trust-based recommender system for scientific publications, is implemented. By using social networks, this doctoral thesis is closely related to the technology and approaches promoted in the context of the Social Web. By providing trust-based recommendations, however, it goes a step further towards the realization of the Semantic Web.

1.1 Contributions

The central idea of my dissertation is to jointly analyze different types of networks, in particular social trust networks and document reference networks. I demonstrate that recommendations, such as the ranking of search engine results can be enhanced by integrating the information from such distinct networks. In order to accomplish this,

- I introduce a framework for the integration of different types of networks, the so-called multi-layer architecture.

- I define a set of trust-enhanced visibility measures for documents in two types of two-layer networks. These measures not only personalize document recommendations but are also able to deal with special cases in which classical recommendation techniques fail to provide appropriate results. An important aspect is that they must be efficiently computable in response to a user query. Moreover, I show how to use the information from an interorganizational trust network to improve the measures defined.

- I discuss a problem that arises when generating document recommendations: document collections often contain duplicate versions. I develop a model of uncertainty and I adapt the trust-enhanced visibility measures so that they are able to cope with the uncertainty introduced by the duplicates. An approximation allows for computing them efficiently.

In my thesis I present a set of use cases that benefit from these contributions. First of all, the trust-enhanced visibility measures developed can be used for ranking webpages, for generating personalized recommendations for academic publications, and for measuring the quality of wiki articles or of blogs. Moreover, following the multi-layer architecture and the basic mechanisms introduced for propagating information between layers, other types of networks can be integrated, leading to trust-based recommendations for various types of items, pieces of information or individuals.

1.2 Outline

In my dissertation, I have studied how to use social trust information in order to enhance document recommendations that are based on an analysis of the references between the documents. To this end, I have organized the different types of network-based information in a multi-layer architecture. Before introducing this architecture, chapter 2 will give the examples of two use cases to motivates the need for such trust-based recommendations. The first use case is taken from the area of digital libraries. In cases of scientific fraud, or simply diverging opinions between distinct research communities, a multi-layer-based recommender system assists users in deciding on the importance and the trustworthiness of scientific papers and other types of interlinked resources such as webpages. The second use case shows how trust-based recommendations can be used to assess the quality and the trustworthiness of the articles in a wiki. In both cases, such a multi-layer-based recommendation is personalized for the requesting user.

Generating recommendations based on different types of layers requires understanding as to how to evaluate separately the information presented in a particular layer. Chapter 3 therefore discusses related work, particularly on recommender systems, that is concerned with trust networks and document reference networks. Prominent examples are document rankings for search engine results on the basis of document reference networks, and trust-based recommendations for various types of items based on the social network between the participating users. I therefore discuss for both trust and document reference networks their basic characteristics as well as appropriate algorithms for their analysis.

The main contribution of my thesis is the specification of the multi-layer architecture and the development of appropriate mechanisms for jointly analyzing the different layers in order to generate personalized recommendations. Chapter 4 introduces the multi-layer architecture. I define how multi-layer networks are composed on the basis of independently collected networks and present basic mechanisms for propagating information between the distinct layers. In chapter 5, I then focus on two extensions of a multi-layer architecture. Firstly, an author trust network is coupled with a document reference network, and secondly, a reviewer trust network is connected with a document reference network. For both types of two-layer networks, I define several so-called trust-enhanced visibility functions for measuring the subjective visibility and trustworthiness of a document for any random user. I particularly emphasize that these measures must be efficiently computable because a possible application is the ranking of search engine results. The computation of trust-enhanced visibilities must thus be possible at query time. The two-layer networks are then extended to a multi-layer architecture by adding an organization network. I show how to integrate the information from such an organization network into the trust-enhanced visibility measures.

Duplicates in the document reference network are a main problem for the recommendation quality. Having duplicate versions of one and the same document with slight differences in the content and in the reference lists distorts the results of reference-based visibility measures. I address this problem in chapter 6 for the trust-enhanced visibility measures by introducing a model of uncertainty that allows for generating appropriate recommendations despite of the uncertainty introduced by the duplicates. In order to compute the trust-enhanced visibility measures efficiently, I develop an approximation on the uncertainty networks.

SPRec, the trust-based Scientific Paper Recommender system, realizes the two-layer architecture consisting of a reviewer trust network and a document reference network. This web application allows for users to establish their personal web of trust and for them to rating papers from the computer science literature. It also provides personalized document recommendations based on an implementation of one of the trust-enhanced visibility measures as defined in chapter 5. This application is presented in chapter 7.

In chapter 8, I analyze the trust-enhanced visibility measures analytically as well as in simulation studies. Apart from a thorough comparison of the different trust-enhanced visibility measures, I am particularly interested in the question of how the visibilities computed take into account personal views on the trust network, i.e. the users' subjective opinions on other users, and on the document reference network, i.e. their personal preferences for certain documents. I can show that this personal view is well reflected in the recommendations and rankings generated. Last but not least, I demonstrate that the trust-enhanced visibility measures are able to deal with papers considered as scientific fraud: their rank is effciently decreased by considering the information available in a multi-layer network

2 The Multi-Layer Architecture in Practice

By communicating and collaborating, humans establish social relationships, be they trustful, indifferent or depreciatory. These relationships are a rich source of information that can be used when generating recommendations. This chapter shows two application domains in which the consideration of social trust information enhances established recommendation approaches. The first use case is taken from the area of digital libraries. Trust-enhanced document recommendations and rankings provide a highly personalized view on some research area. Also they permit dealing with faked publications. A preliminary version of this use case was published in Hess (2005). The second use case deals with quality assurance in wikis. Trust-enhanced measures are of interest because the steadily growing number of collaboratively authored articles makes a manual assessment of the quality of the wiki articles impossible. In both application scenarios, it becomes evident that document reference networks are a basic type of information for recommender systems. Document reference networks and social trust networks can be combined in a multi-layer architecture. Based on both use cases, the requirements for a multi-layer framework and the recommendations generated in such a framework are defined.

2.1 Document Recommendations in Digital Libraries

Digital libraries provide access to a large number of digital documents. They offer elaborated search functions and additional services, such as personalized notification about new documents. Documents are either carefully selected by the digital library after peer-reviewing, or can be posted by the users without any prior quality control such as in the World Wide Web. The (preprint) server arXiv[1] is an example for a document collection in which scientists directly publish their articles. The ACM digital library[2], in contrast, contains only articles that passed the peer-reviewing of ACM

---

[1] http://arxiv.org
[2] http://portal.acm.org

conferences or journals. An ever-increasing amount of scholarly publications is nowadays available online, spread over diverse digital document collections. Recommender systems support users in searching these archives. Techniques from information retrieval are used to select the documents that match the search term(s) given by the user. The document ranking represents a recommendation: highly ranked documents are most likely to be relevant to the user's search query. The following sections discuss current document recommender systems. Motivated by various shortcomings of these approaches, a new approach is proposed that includes a measure of trust into classical document recommendations.

2.1.1 The Visibility of a Document

Scientists often have to decide whether an article is worth reading or whether a pay-per-view article is worth buying. Normally, the article's abstract is available so that users can decide on the relevance of the article for their research. However, the information provided by the abstract is often insufficient. In research fields such as computing, abstracts contain information about the problem solved but often do not provide algorithmical details. Document recommender systems therefore aim to provide users with additional information about the documents in question. Citation-based measures have gained much attention in the last few years for providing these recommendations. Document rankings are generated on the basis of the citation-based measure. The idea is to recommend users to read or to buy an article if the article is often cited. These citation-based measures assume that a citation conveys that the author who cites deems the cited document in some way important. Following Malsch and Schlieder (2002), I refer to such measures as measures of *social visibility*. These measures not only count how often a document is cited but may consider further criteria as discussed by Malsch *et al.* (2007). An important criterion is the visibility of the publications citing the paper, i.e., the more important the citing papers are, the more important is the cited paper itself. Another criterion is the author's visibility, for example, the one derived from his or her reputation in the scientific community. The key element of the citation-based measures is therefore to analyze document reference networks, i.e., networks in which documents are connected via references.

As Leydesdorff (1998) explains, such document reference networks can be established only for the scientific literature from around 1900 on. This is because the meaning of citations has changed over centuries (Leydesdorff, 1998; Leydesdorff and Wouter, 1999). In the Middle Ages, the only texts cited were those that were discussed. It was not usual to take citations from contemporary colleagues working on related topics. In modern science, any publication should, at least in principle, extend the existing scientific literature. This requires new citation modes. In 19th century science, references were attributed to the authors – other "learned gentlemen" – in the style of 'Monsieur

X said'. Not before the 20th century did the modern citation format become adopted. References without a date started to be used around 1890; they refer to a person's oeuvre, i.e. all works of this author. They have been replaced around 1900 with dated references that refer to a concept-symbol; the cited document now stands for a given idea. Citations to a distinct document by a certain author or by a group of authors permit the construction of document reference networks. In scientometrics, this is also referred to as *citation indexing*. According to Leydesdorff, citation indexing changed the system of reference for citation analysis from a historical model in which citations were only used to establish the historical background of some knowledge claim to an evolutionary model in which a document's authority is measured on the basis of the citations received from other documents. This enabled the development of visibility measures.

Visibility measures of documents exist in bibliometry, scientometrics, social network analysis, network physics and information retrieval. Citation-based measures are widely used. In the scientific domain, the impact factor exerts an immense influence on the evaluation of scientific achievement. Leydesdorff even states that citation analysis is used as an instrument for the managerial control of science. The impact factor, originally presented in Garfield (1972) (for more recent publications on the impact factor see e.g., Garfield (1999, 2003)) is provided by Thomson Scientific, formerly Thomson ISI (Institute for Scientific Information) and therefore also known as the ISI impact factor. The impact factor is part of the Journal Citation Reports that compare and rank journals. By indicating the status of a journal, the impact factor supports libraries in managing their journal subscriptions. It is also widely used to evaluate scientific careers: Scientists' achievements are measured by their publications in high impact journals. Therefore the impact factor often encourages scientists to submit their work to a particular journal. The impact factor of a journal is normally based on the previous two years. It divides the number of citations from current year articles to the articles that were published in the journal during the previous two years by all articles published in this journal in the same two years.

The impact factor is accused of being biased (e.g. Dong *et al.*, 2005; Seglen, 1997). An important aspect is the selection of the journals to be included in the citation index. For example, it gives preference to journals in the English language. Furthermore, it is criticized for disregarding differences in citation behavior across research fields: research areas that cite publications shortly after their publication are favored. Malsch *et al.* (2007) call this a modernist citation pattern. In contrast, areas with a classicist pattern in which publications are often cited only several years after their publication are penalized. Characteristics of a journal that are independent of its quality further bias the impact factor. For example, a journal with many review articles will have a higher impact than other journals because review articles are more often cited than typical research articles. A further problem is that the impact factor, although indicated for a journal, is applied to individual articles, assuming that the impact of an article can directly be inferred from the impact of the journal. This would be valid if citations were equally distributed over all articles in a journal. However, this is not case as shown in studies by Seglen (1992), Opthof *et al.* (2004), and by the journal Nature ("Not-so-deep impact", 2005): only a small number of publications attract most of the citations, whereas most articles are only rarely cited. Seglen concludes that the article citation rates determine the impact of a journal, and not vice versa. Moreover, the impact factor gives each citation the same weight. Pinski and Narin (1976) argue that citations from a prestigious journal should have more value than citations from a peripheral journal and propose a recursive evaluation of scientific publications.

Citation-based measures are also applied with great success to the evaluation of the importance of websites. In 1998, Google entered the search engine market with its PageRank and outperformed existing search engines. PageRank (Page *et al.*, 1998) is a visibility measure that assigns a rank to every webpage based on the analysis of the hyperlink network of websites. In contrast to the impact factor, PageRank does not only count the number of hyperlinks pointing to a website. On the web, this would be inappropriate because everyone can easily generate a huge network of linked pages and inflate the rank of a page. In order to deal with the extreme variance in the quality of webpages, the rank of the citing page is taken into account: the recursive evaluation by PageRank counts links of websites with a high rank more than links by lowly ranked websites. Motivated by the success of recursive evaluations for webpages, this method gained attention in the evaluation of scientific publications. The ability to publish documents on preprint servers and on personal homepages changes the publication behavior in academics. So it is reasonable to consider the importance of the citing paper. These publications can easily be accessed via search engines like Google Scholar, a search engine specializing in academic publications. Bollen *et al.* (2006) argue that the perception of the importance of an article will change due to the PageRank-based ranking that is provided by these search engines. They propose to evaluate scientific achievement not only by the impact factor but also by measures in the style of PageRank.

2.1.2 Shortcomings of Citation-Based Recommendations

Despite the immense success of visibility measures, three main problems are inherent to citation-based recommending strategies:

- The link semantics is not considered. A high visibility can result from a large number of links that express trust, from many links expressing distrust or from being controversially discussed.

- The visibility is not affected by additional knowledge about the trustworthiness of a document: a well-known, highly visible publication will not lose its visibility if it is proven to be based, for example, on faked datasets.

- Citation-based measures recommend those papers that everybody cites, i.e., what everybody likes. Small communities with a particular view on a certain topic are systematically discriminated against.

Link Semantics

Visibility measures do not take into account the semantics of the links although references can imply a different semantics. Garfield (1965) presented the following fifteen reasons why a document is cited:

1. Paying homage to pioneers
2. Giving credit for related work (homage to peers)
3. Identifying methodology, equipment, etc.
4. Providing background reading
5. Correcting one's own work
6. Correcting the work of others
7. Criticizing previous work
8. Substantiating claims
9. Alerting to forthcoming work
10. Providing leads to poorly disseminated, poorly indexed, or uncited work
11. Authenticating data and classes of fact-physical constants, etc.
12. Identifying original publications in which an idea or concept was discussed
13. Identifying original publication or other work describing an eponymic concept or term as, e.g., Hodgkin's Disease, Pareto's Law, Friedel-Crafts Reaction, etc.
14. Disclaiming work or ideas of others (negative claims)
15. Disputing priority claims of others (negative homage)

The semantics of links ranges therefore from a strong confirmation of the cited document to a clear expression of distrust. For instance, an author might write that he or she replicated the experiments described in a paper d and obtained the same results. Such citation should clearly increase d's visibility. However, if this author would write that the experiment gave contradictory results, d should not gain in credibility. Apart from such objective reasons, distrust can be based on personal rivalry and adherence to different scientific communities; for example, the citing author has a different opinion or promotes a different approach for solving a certain problem. A document can therefore be untrustworthy from an individual perspective although its general visibility is extremely high. Visibility measures as currently used for document recommendations are not able to consider the link semantics. They can neither select only those documents that are highly visible within a certain community nor indicate that a document is controversially discussed.

"Fakes"

Regularly publications are suspected of being "faked". Investigations examine then whether scientific misconduct such as faking results and using fabricated data can be proven. A publication that is officially declared as forged should be retracted. Nevertheless, a large number of such forged publications is not retracted as, for instance, in the case of scientific misconduct by Eric Poehlman in his research on obesity, menopause and aging (Sox and Rennie, 2006). After the official investigation in March 2005, only half of the articles were retracted until November 2005.

In order to prevent faked papers from being recommended or cited, one might think that it is sufficient to announce the retraction in the journal in which the paper was published and in databases from which the article can be downloaded. In famous cases such as in the case of the stem-cell researcher Woo Suk Hwang which was discussed in 2005/2006 worldwide in the scientific community as well as in newspapers, this might be sufficient. However, many cases of scientific misconduct are not discussed as extensively, and faked articles are often cited several years after the retraction as several studies on scientific misconduct have shown. Kochan and Budd (1992) analyzed the case of John Darsee who forged publications in the domain of biomedical research. They classified the citations which the fraudulent papers received during the nine years after their publication into three categories: firstly, citations in papers dealing with scientific misconduct or retraction, secondly, negative citations which discuss problems with Darsee's methodology or findings, and thirdly, positive citations which accept the methodology and the findings. Darsee's publications received about 300 citations in English language journals of which 85.9% were positive, 8.4% negative and 5.7% in the context of scientific misconduct. Retracted articles were even cited in those journals from which they were retracted. Pfeifer and Snodgrass (1990) came in their study of postretraction citation also to the conclusion that there is a large number of citations to retracted articles. Budd *et al.* (1998) confirmed these findings in a study on MEDLINE, an archive with publications from the medical domain. They examined the articles that were formally retracted between 1966 and 1997.

These cases show that retracted publications are still cited positively several years after their retraction and continue to be considered as valid work (Budd *et al.*, 1998). In terms of visibility measures, these articles still accumulate citations and obtain a high visibility score. This demonstrates that we cannot uniquely rely on citation-based measures when retrieving information. Kochan and Budd (1992, p. 492) acknowledge this: "the fact that it is older and can be traced through the citations of former works is not necessarily evidence of its accuracy, validity, or honesty". They claim that researchers have to select more carefully the literature on which they base their work. As recommendation strategies that are exclusively based on the document network cannot prevent faked articles from being recommended, additional information should be considered. In practice, researchers often discuss such aspects with colleagues whom they deem as trustworthy in the respective research domain. This allows for scientists to consider further information, and also takes into account those cases in which publications are suspected to be forged but have not (yet) been officially investigated. This is to say that people use their personal social network of colleagues in order to form their opinion. The problem, however, is to find those persons who are able to give the best information about the article in question. For this it would be necessary to know which articles they already read. Moreover, a leading researcher might not be able to handle hundreds of requests for evaluating papers personally. Thus, it is complicated to find someone trustworthy who can recommend the article.

Personalized View

Visibility measures do not allow for personalizing recommendations. Measures that are merely based on the citation network recommend those documents that are frequently cited by important documents. Documents that are of a high quality but on a very special topic, hence only cited in a small community, will not have a chance to get a high position in the ranking. Their visibility will be very low. Users who are interested in papers from this particular community will thus not get any papers recommended that correspond to their information need. A personalization strategy is required that is able to modify the visibility of papers from complete subnetworks of the document reference network based on the user's individual perspective.

How to Address the Shortcomings?

In order to address the above discussed shortcomings of mere citation-based measures, this work introduces a trust-based recommender system that integrates information from a trust network between individuals and a document reference network. In addition, information from further networks such as an organization network can be considered. A recommendation system that builds on such a multi-layer architecture can combine citation-based measures with personalized information by trustworthy peers. Such recommendation system would also permit bridging long time spans. Several months after a retraction, most people might no longer remember the details of a retraction. The retraction of a paper can be for different reasons and therefore leads to a different opinion on the author of the retracted paper. In the most extreme case, an article is retracted because it is based on fabricated data. This clearly leads to a distrust in the author. More often, however, a situation has arisen that the author has discovered some irreparable errors in her or his data or the method applied and has asked for the retraction of the paper. This retraction should not lead to distrust in the author as he or she has corrected the error directly. A trust-based recommender system stores this information in a distributed way in the form of trust statements and reviews and uses it for generating recommendations. A simple database of retracted papers would not permit dealing with these differences.

2.1.3 Example for a Multi-Layer Architecture

The multi-layer architecture integrates the different types of information that are available in the context of scientific publications and analyzes them jointly in order to recommend documents. Such architecture is sketched for the recent case of scientific misconduct by Woo Suk Hwang. The events presented in the following are, for instance, described in news@nature.com (2006b). The stem-cell researcher had gained international reputation from his research on cloning human cells. His work has been considered as a real breakthrough. He published two articles in the journal Science in 2004 and 2005, together with Gerald Schatten from the University of Pittsburgh and other researchers. The close collaboration between Hwang and Schatten resulted in two further joint articles. This situation is represented in a multi-layer architecture. The different layers are derived from the above description. Hwang and Schatten are displayed together with their coauthors in a first layer, an author trust network. The second layer is the document network with the four publications that are directly involved in the case of Hwang. Further publications that cite these papers are sketched. The authors are connected with the papers they have written. The third layer is an organization network with organizations to which the persons are affiliated.

Figure 2.1 shows the situation in September 2005, which is still characterized by positive trust relationships between Hwang and Schatten. As the respective universities supported the displayed scientists' research activities, trust from the organizations to the scientists is assumed. The articles by Hwang and Schatten appeared in high impact journals after peer-reviewing. Considered as landmark papers, they attracted much attention, also in the form of citations. A citation-based measure would therefore compute a high visibility for them.

At the end of September 2005, however, the situation changed. Schatten declared that he stopped all collaborations with Hwang due to possible irregularities in the donation of eggs used for Hwang's research (see e.g. news@nature.com, 2005). In the months following this first accusation, the integrity of Hwang's research concerning both Science publications was constantly questioned. The suspicions led to an official investigation by the Seoul National University, which concluded in January 2006 that both papers published in Science were based on fabricated data sets (see e.g. news@nature.com, 2006c). The paper published in Nature, however, was not forged; the dog Snuppy is a clone.

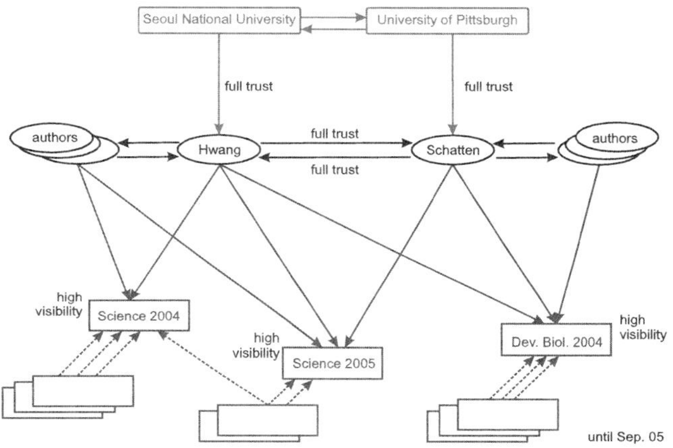

Figure 2.1: Multi-Layer Architecture in the case of Hwang in September 2005

Tracking these events in the multi-layer architecture, the 'full trust'-link from Schatten to Hwang is changed into a distrust relationship. As we have no official declaration by Hwang concerning his collaboration with Schatten, we do not know explicitly how his trust to Schatten was affected. The investigation by the Seoul National University with official results in January 2006 makes clear that its trust shown formerly for Hwang changed to distrust. The University of Pittsburgh finished its investigation in February 2006. Schatten was cleared of the accusations of scientific misconduct, but was rebuked for presenting himself as lead author despite being rarely involved in the research by Hwang (University of Pittsburgh, 2006). The results suggest a 'no trust'-relationship. Figure 2.2 presents the situation in February 2006. The visibility of the publications by Hwang and his coauthors remains high despite their retraction because the citations to these papers in already published articles cannot simply be removed. A visibility-based recommendation strategy would therefore continue to recommend these papers although the content is absolutely untrustworthy.

Investigations were extended to the complete work of Hwang and his colleagues (see e.g. news@nature.com, 2006a). Interpreting this in the terms of visibility measures, we can say that distrust is not restricted to a single publication but propagates throughout the networks. The authors of a forged paper are under general suspicion, i.e., all their publications may be distrusted. Moreover, publications that directly refer to the forged publication and build up on its results have to prove their correctness, too. Suspected work might be considered as valid if the coauthors accept full responsibility

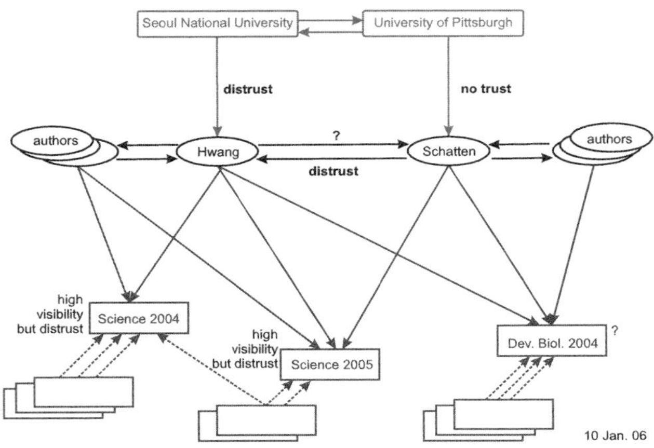

Figure 2.2: Multi-Layer Architecture in the case of Hwang in January 2006

for its integrity (Sox and Rennie, 2006). However, one might question the coauthors' trustworthiness.

Cases of scientific misconduct are regularly detected and come up in various research areas. Further famous examples are the case of scientific misconduct by the physician Jan Hendrik Schön in 2004 (see e.g. Bell Labs, 2002) who was already considered as candidate for the Nobel prize, or the case of Friedhelm Herrmann and Marion Brach, whose fraud in the area of cancer research was revealed in 1997 (see e.g Hagmann, 2000). The suspicions were not restricted to the accused author(s) but in fact all coauthors were suspected and the responsibility of the supervisors was called into question. Schön's supervisor Bertram Batlogg was listed as coauthor on many publications. So he himself should have validated the extraordinary results presented by Schön (Brumfiel, 2002). Furthermore, these cases show that not all publications can unequivocally be proven as forged or valid, but that a quite large number of papers has to be classified as 'gray'. For these papers, no general recommendation can be given. Some users might prefer not to consider such papers at all whereas others use them with caution.

2.1.4 Document Recommendations with Multi-Layer Networks

Generalizing the example of the previous section, a multi-layer network for recommendations consists of two or more networks. The central part is the network between authors or reviewers who express their trust in other users with respect to their role as reviewer or as author. Individuals are connected with the documents they have written or reviewed. The documents are linked via references. The two-layer architecture can be extended to a multi-layer architecture by adding, for instance, an organization network as in the example of Hwang.

A typical request that evaluates the information from the different layers is "Should I cite this article?". Figure 2.3 sketches the query answering in a two-layer network. The users' web of trust and the document reference network are jointly analyzed. Having a reviewer trust network, the recommendation concerning document p_3 for user u_2 is not merely based on the visibilities of the documents citing p_3, namely p_5, p_6, p_7 and p_8, but also on the opinions of users u_1 and u_3 who are trusted by u_2. The recommendation is the higher, the better are the trust-weighted reviews and the reference-based visibility. Alternatively with an author trust network, the trust in the author influences the recommendation. In figure 2.3, u_2 is connected with u_1, who authored document p_3. The trust from u_2 to u_1 modulates the reference-based visibility of p_3. High trust increases the visibility whereas distrust decreases the visibility.

This approach efficiently handles faked articles. An article will be marked as 'not recommended' either if other users or organizations distrust its author(s), or if it received adverse reviews. By declaring an author as untrustworthy, the trust-enhanced visibility of all articles (co)authored by this user can be decreased down to zero, depending on the degree of distrust and on the trustworthiness of the individuals or organizations who expressed the distrust. This corresponds to a general suspicion that the author is providing bad or even faked publications. Organizations assign distrust on the basis of an official investigation such as in the case of Hwang. Users do not have to wait for results of an official investigation but can directly express their suspicions in their personal web of trust. A reviewer trust network with reviews on the documents differentiates between papers by the same author: some papers might be good, others not. In the case of scientific fraud, this would be appropriate, if the articles are already checked for authenticity. Distrust ratings by persons whom the requesting user does not trust should not affect the recommendation.

2.1.5 Uncertainty in the Recommendation Process

Users want to obtain from a document recommender system a recommendation for a particular document or a set of documents. They can choose on the web from many

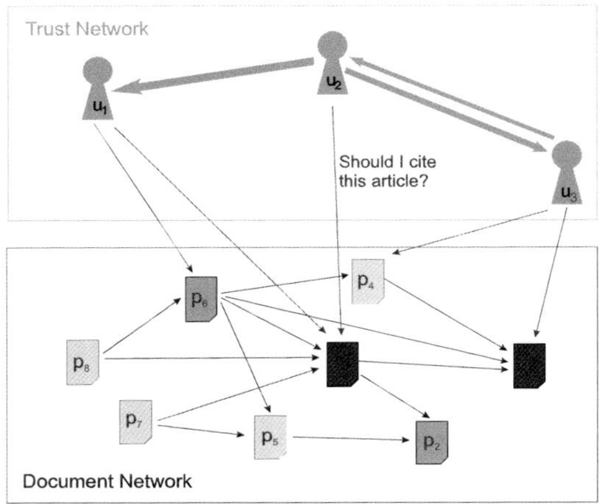

Figure 2.3: Recommendations for Publications

services that generate such recommendations and from various document collections
that grant access to the recommended publications. During the process of obtaining
a document that corresponds to the personal information need, the user has to face
different types of uncertainty. In order to identify the types of uncertainty that affect
the quality of the document recommendation, I look at the distinct steps in the recommendation process. The user may ask for a document recommendation in the style:
"I'm interested in document d. Is it worth reading? If it is, I want to have d from a
reliable source." More generally stated, the user searches for a set of documents in the
style: "I'm interested in documents on topic t (or by author a, etc.). Which ones are
worth reading? Can I obtain them from a reliable source?"

Uncertainty with Respect to the Choice of the Recommendation Service

The user can choose from different types of recommendation services on the web:

- Search engines specialized in scholar publications, such as Google Scholar, index
  documents crawled from document repositories and from researchers' personal
  and departmental webpages. To access the documents, the user is normally referred to the respective source collection or webpage. The access to the document
  may be free or restricted.

- Digital libraries base their document collection on publications in selected journals, conference proceedings etc. Examples are the ACM digital library or Springer Online. Abstracts and bibliographic references are often freely available whereas full documents are restricted to subscribers and pay-per-view access.

- Services such as CiteSeer are a mix of search engine and digital library. The collection is based on a web crawl, as in the case of search engines. Freely accessible documents can directly be downloaded because local copies are cached.

- Metasearch engines provide a unique search interface over several document collections. The answers obtained from different digital libraries or search engines are aggregated and returned to the user.

Users might be uncertain as to which recommendation service to chose. Basically, there are two types of uncertainty related to the choice of the service. Firstly, does the document recommender system provide good recommendations, i.e., do I easily find the papers I want to find, or do I have to reformulate my query several times? Is the search interface too complicated? Are the results presented in a sensible way, or is there some nonsense on the first ranks or is the same document listed several times? The users' confidence in the recommendation service highly depends on their past experiences with this service and with other recommendation systems. The type of search might also influence the choice. Search engines might be preferred for broad searches on a certain topic whereas digital libraries might be a better choice when searching for a specific topic or a particular paper. However, the boundaries between both blur as the example of CiteSeer shows. The second uncertainty refers to the quality of the documents provided. For example, does the document actually correspond to the version in the printed journal? Many users might consider libraries with restricted access to have a higher quality than free services. However, many users cannot afford to pay for a subscription or a pay-per-view article: hence they rely on the free services.

Uncertainty with Respect to the Document Recommendation

Having selected a recommendation service, users formulate the query that represents their information need. They type in keywords, paper titles, fragments of paper titles or author names at the search interface. The service returns a set of documents that is supposed to match the user's query. Reference-based visibility measures and trust-enhanced visibility measures are a way to reduce the users' uncertainty with respect to the quality and the degree of interest of a particular document compared to other documents on the same topic. The quality of the recommendation depends on the quality of the documents. If a document index contains errors, e.g., the references were not correctly extracted, the reference graph would contain errors which affect the quality of the recommendation.

Search engines and federated digital libraries may have crawled the same document from several sources. The document collection and the respective index may thus contain duplicates and near-duplicates. These duplicates have to be filtered or clustered before being presented to the user because a ranking that presents the same document several times is not appealing. Google Scholar, for instance, presents the documents recognized as duplicates in groups. By clicking on a link next to the cluster, the user can decide from which source collection to download the document. The problem of duplicates typically arises in collections with free access which crawl the documents from the web and from document collections of diverging quality. Libraries with restricted access normally have a better quality assurance. For example, Springer Online, which contains the documents published by Springer, ensures that each document is indexed only once.

It is not sufficient to filter duplicates only before presenting the ranking to the user. They have to be identified before generating recommendations because duplicates can distort reference-based rankings. The rank of a paper might be much too low because the paper is available in slightly different versions, and citations refer to these different versions. Consider two versions of a paper, the pre-print and the print. The impact of this paper should be determined based on the links to the pre-print as well as to the print because there might be a number of citations to the pre-print when the print was not yet published. Conversely, reference-based measures should not count the citation by a document and its pre-print twice. Mirrored websites raise the same problem because links may point to the different mirrors. For example, tutorials for programming languages are often mirrored by servers on different continents in order to provide users a near access point. Users in Europe might now more often refer to the European mirror whereas users in the US might prefer the US mirror. The importance of this website, however, should be based on the links to both mirrors.

Duplicates can give a misleading picture not only of the incoming links but also of the outgoing references. A duplicate's citation list might be incomplete because not all references were correctly extracted or because the content of mirrored websites slightly differs. If duplicates originate from sources with a different quality, not all references that are listed might be taken as granted. A reference indicated in a document from a source with a reputation for high quality is more likely to be considered correct than a reference that is only present in a duplicate from a low-quality source. The question is now, based on which graph should the rank of a document be computed. It is therefore important to first consider the question of duplicates when generating the recommendation. In order to address this problem, this thesis develops an approach that is able to deal with duplicates in the document reference network. Moreover, a measure for the quality of the ranking will be given.

Uncertainty with Respect to the Choice of the Document Source

The recommendation does not say anything on whether a certain copy is a correct version of the paper. This uncertainty arises when search engines or federated digital libraries offer several links from which to download the article. In general, users have more confidence in the quality of the documents offered by digital libraries than in those from personal homepages. For example, a paper downloaded from Springer Online corresponds to the version that is printed in the respective Springer publication. The paper from the author's homepage might be some preliminary version, such as a pre-print of the article. Apart from the documents, users might be interested in obtaining correct bibliographic information. The collection from which the document is selected also depends on the user's subscriptions or budget for pay-per-view articles.

In summing up, I can say that – above all for (freely accessible) services that crawl papers from the web and from various document repositories – duplicates introduce much uncertainty with respect to the quality of the recommendations. The uncertainty produced by duplicates is as follows:

- Rankings that list duplicates several times, i.e., which do not filter and cluster duplicates, are not professional. The users are likely to lose their confidence in the ranking.

- If duplicates are not considered when computing reference-based visibilities, the ranks might be distorted because a wrong set of incoming and outgoing links is taken as a basis.

- Different versions of the same document from different collections cause uncertainty because the user might not know which one to take. First-year students, for example, do not yet have sufficient experience with the different document collections.

As this thesis is concerned with the recommendation and ranking aspect, it will address the uncertainty caused by duplicates in the reference-based ranking.

2.2 The Quality of Wikis

The open online encyclopedia Wikipedia[3] made the wiki paradigm known. Web users can easily contribute to this encyclopedia. By clicking on the edit-button that is presented at each wiki page, users can, for instance, add new information or restructure

---

[3]http://www.wikipedia.org/

existing text. The Wikipedia project is a real success, both with respect to the number of contributions and the number of read accesses. The English language Wikipedia[4], for example, encompassed in March 2007 over 1.7 million articles. The internet ranking service Alexa ranks Wikipedia's website in April 2007 number 11 with respect to the traffic received.[5] The idea of a wiki goes back to Ward Cunningham who in 1995 named his invention of the online collaborative authoring environment "WikiWiki-Web". He had developed this concept in order to facilitate the collaboration between programmers. The term "wikiwiki" means "quick" in Hawaiian. Leuf and Cunningham (2001, p. 14) define a wiki as "a freely expandable collection of interlinked Web "pages", a *hypertext system* for storing and modifying information – a *database* where each page is easily editable by any user with a forms-capable Web browser client".

Trust in the authors and the site administrators of a wiki, and consequently in the reliability of articles, is a big issue. Recently, the case of Essjay, a Wikipedia contributor hit the headlines and led to vehement discussions on Wikipedia's credibility. In February 2007, the New Yorker attached an editor's note to an article by Stacy Schiff published in July 2006 in which Essjay was interviewed on his work on Wikipedia (Schiff, 2006). Essjay had contributed to around sixteen thousand articles. He was at that time one of the Wikipedia administrators and member of Wikipedia's mediation committee. This means that he was responsible for the quality control of a set of articles. Administrators have the right to handle disagreements. They can protect articles from future edits, exclude users from Wikipedia, revert text efficiently, and in order to handle extreme cases, they are allowed to delete articles. Essjay had received several Wikipedia barnstars. These are rewards for outstanding contributions and committed work for Wikipedia. In the editor's note, the New Yorker revealed that Essjay acted under a faked identity. He had claimed to be a tenured university professor of religion. In reality, he was 24 years old and did not hold any university degree, let alone a position as professor. Essjay invented his identity as a religion scholar.

The use of a false identity might not be considered a problem as the first reaction by Jimmy Wales, one of the founders of Wikipedia, showed: he considered it to be just a matter of using a pseudonym. Subsequently, however, it emerged that Essjay used his faked credentials when arguing in content disputes in order to impose his opinion. Wikipedia contributors consider such behavior clearly as a violation of their trust in Essjay. Jimmy Wales also stressed in his statement the importance of trust: "Wikipedia is built on (among other things) twin pillars of trust and tolerance. The integrity of the project depends on the core community being passionate about quality and integrity, so that we can trust each other."[6] This shows the need for assessing the

---

[4] http://en.wikipedia.org/

[5] Retrieved on April 19, 2007 from http://www.alexa.com. For the current ranking see http://www.alexa.com/data/details/traffic_details?url=wikipedia.org.

[6] See Jimmy Wales' comment in the Wikipedia mailing list http://lists.wikimedia.org/pipermail/wikien-l/2007-March/064440.html (last access April, 17, 2007).

trustworthiness of the contributors as well as for measuring the credibility of an article. Such measures have to take into account that the way in which articles are published in wikis differs from the scholar publication model. Before developing such measures, we need a better understanding of wikis and the underlying interaction paradigm.

2.2.1 The Wiki Interaction Paradigm

The main advantage of wikis over other types of media is their simple interaction concept: everybody can contribute easily by editing wiki pages in an ordinary web browser. No special software has to be installed. Principally, everybody can make changes to the wiki articles. In many wikis, users don't even need to register. Just by clicking on the edit-link, users can add text, correct or delete erroneous content or restructure the article. The page history keeps track of all these changes. If required, a page can be reverted to a previous version. The wiki interaction paradigm thus sharply contrasts with the classical interaction concept of 'normal' webpages, which can only be modified by a certain group of distinguished authors, and with the peer reviewing process used in scholarly publication. Lih (2004) speaks in this context of participatory journalism which means that the users participate in the content creation, structure, comment and discuss the content.

Wikis collect information on a certain topic at a single page. To this end, they better support users who are looking for information on a certain topic, than discussion forums and blogs where a topic might be discussed in various postings. Users can easily create a new wiki page. Typing a so-called WikiWord, a term that comprises two or more words starting with capital letters and run together, automatically creates a hyperlink. When a user follows this link, a new page is created. In Wikipedia, the encyclopedic terms are interlinked in this way. Apart from the internal links, external links indicate, for instance, the source of information or recommend additional reading on the topic. The hyperlinks set in wiki pages thus give a document reference network just like in the case of 'normal' webpages or of scientific papers.

The collaborative authoring concept leads to a division of the workload in content creation, e.g., between the members of an organization. Wikis have a low entry barrier because sketches and first ideas are welcome. On classical webpages, authors typically do not publish any preliminary versions but well-elaborated texts. In wikis, people don't have to write a whole article but they can start with some introductory remarks or a concrete problem, e.g., an error message produced by some software. These initial comments encourage other people to contribute by extending the already written parts or by reorganizing text fragments. Knowledge is thus described in an incremental process. Clearly, this is often not straightforward; getting a consensus on some topic may require much discussion. Jimmy Wales (2007) used the term "thoughtful disagreement": an objective and well-founded discussion (e.g. on the basis of scientific articles) is likely to increase the quality of an article considerably while monocultures tend to contain more errors. To facilitate discussions, wiki systems offer an additional discussion page to each wiki page. Contributors can use these to explain why they added or removed some part, or say what is in their opinion still missing. Wikis are therefore an efficient and well-accepted tool for letting people produce knowledge in a joint collaborative form. They shift the focus from a mere browsing of webpages to an active participation in authoring articles. By this, they turn the web into a writable media (Buffa, 2006).

This participatory culture in which everybody can contribute to an article directly poses the question of how the quality of wiki articles can be assured. In the introductory remarks in this section on wikis, Jimmy Wales was cited with his statement that trust is an essential factor for the credibility of Wikipedia. This gives a hint on a relation between an article's quality and trust in the contributors. Exploring this relation, we should be aware that Wikipedia, although the best known and most intensively studied wiki, is not the only type of wiki. Besides such public wikis, there are a growing number of corporate wikis which might require a different perspective on the question of quality.

2.2.2 Quality and Trust in Wikis

Quality of Wiki Contributions

The advantages as well as the shortcomings of wikis are in the collaborative approach to knowledge creation and the joint ownership of the contributions. As no-one is personally responsible for the content of a wiki page, the quality of certain articles may be low. There is no continuous quality assurance by experts – analogous to the peer reviewing process in scholar publication – which at least guarantees that the information provided is not obviously false. In wikis, the quality can vary within an article because the quality of contributions by different authors may differ. As public wikis such as Wikipedia allow everyone to edit articles, they can easily become the target of vandalism and malicious users may disseminate false information. This is normally not a problem in corporate wikis which can be accessed only by employees and business partners after registration. Instead of rational discussions that reach a consensus, edits wars may be frequent. That means that users mutually delete their texts and revert to their previous version. This clearly affects the quality of the articles. Users might get every time they access the article a completely different version with a different argumentation. Users who disagree with an article but who do not want to fight an edit war might just create alternative pages on this topic.

This leads to confusion on the side of the reader and the perceived quality of the whole wiki decreases. Although the Wikipedia content policies claim that articles have to be written from a neutral point of view[7], some articles may be biased. Wiki communities often have a strong internal community. Users with a high reputation can heavily influence the quality of an article – in the positive but also in the negative sense. For instance, a high reputation gives a higher authority in edit-wars and can be used to impose one's personal opinion on an article. Trust and reputation mechanisms therefore play an important role.

Despite the problems discussed above, the information provided by Wikipedia is, in general, fairly good. A study comparing the quality of Wikipedia and of the Encyclopedia Britannica showed that Wikipedia articles are at least equal, if not better in their quality (Giles, 2005). However, in the same article, Giles refers to recent discussions on errors and the maliciously inserted false information in Wikipedia. The generally high quality, together with the fact that some erroneous information remains undetected is attributed to the manner in which the community of Wikipedia contributors works.

The Self-Healing Effect of Wikis?

Wikis are often claimed to have a type of self-healing effect because the quality assurance is carried out by the community: users who observe errors correct them immediately. Vandalism and errors are in general detected by the huge number of authors reading and improving articles. In Wikipedia, users can add articles to their personal watch lists. If any change is made to these articles, they are notified and can directly check whether they agree with the changes made or whether a roll back to an earlier version is necessary. Wikipedia's 'featured articles' are also a way to use the community's rating and reviewing capabilities. Wikipedians vote to upgrade articles to featured article status. In this process, the said articles have to meet certain quality criteria.

Braendle (2005) showed in a study on Wikipedia that this control by the community is sufficient for often accessed articles that receive much and constant attention. In other words, the quality of relevant topics that are addressed by a considerable number of different authors tends to be high. Alternatively, a high standard can also be achieved from a small group of authors who take the responsibility for the article (Rateike et al., 2007). But who cares about the non-relevant articles – which outnumber the relevant articles? When no one feels responsible, errors tend to remain quite for a long time. So we can state that the self-healing effect has only a limited power. There is a constant struggle to protect high quality articles against vandalism and to create new high quality articles.

---

[7]See http://en.wikipedia.org/wiki/Wikipedia:Neutral_point_of_view

Administrators, Arbitration Committees... – Can they ensure a high Quality?

Guidelines and policies establish a whole bunch of procedures in order to increase or to preserve the quality of wiki articles. In Wikipedia[8], for instance, users who have the status of an administrator have additional power to implement the Wikipedia policies. Arbitration committees handle disagreements that cannot be resolved between the involved users. However, these arbitration committees do not review the article, i.e., they do not check its correctness but decide on the basis of the users' behavior. Exerting only such social control, they do not preserve truth but protect the community (Kohlenberg, 2006). Members of mediation and arbitration committees are elected by the Wikipedians. Like administrators, they are typically users with a high reputation in the community and who are considered to be highly trustworthy.

Some publicly available wikis try to raise the quality by introducing regulations. For example, only registered users or users with a certain status may be allowed to edit pages. Citizendium[9], a recent approach to a free online encyclopedia, aims at proving more reliable information than Wikipedia. Citizendium contributors have to use their real names. Moreover, Citizendium introduces "gentle expert oversight"[10], i.e., experts take the responsibility for the quality of the articles. Users can register as authors or editors. While everybody can register as author, editors need the qualifications for a tenure track academic position[11]. Credentials such as links to her or his departmental homepage, proceedings or journal articles have to be presented. All registrations are handled semi automatically in order to check the user's identity and credentials. Only a few months after Citizendium went online in November 2006, it is too early to make any predictions on how it will evolve compared to Wikipedia. Citizendium is often criticized for its small number of contributors and it is claimed that articles are rather on topics that are too special and not relevant to the broad public (see e.g. Anderson, 2007). Larry Sanger, the founder of Citizendium, claims in his progress report in March 2007 (Sanger, 2007) that the growing number of contributors and the growth in the number and size of the articles shows that this project can really work.

In wikis, the manual monitoring of edits requires a lot of work on the part of the contributors, while the number of articles steadily increases. As it can be seen in Citizendium, a manual control of all new registrations is very time consuming – it may take up to 24 hours to get an account at Citizendium. The next section therefore discusses how the computer sciences can help to establish measures of quality that support contributors in quality assurance and provide a guideline to readers.

---

[8]For information on the quality of the Wikipedia articles and the established measures to ensure this quality from the side of Wikipedia, see `http://en.wikipedia.org/wiki/Wikipedia:About#Strengths.2C_weaknesses_and_article_quality_in_Wikipedia`.

[9]`http://en.citizendium.org`

[10]`http://www.citizendium.org/about.html`

[11]See `http://www.citizendium.org/cfa.html`, retrieved on April 23, 2007

2.2.3 Measures of Quality for Wikis

In order to make from Wikipedia and other wikis a source of reliable information which can be cited, users must be able to assess the credibility of the information presented in an article. An indicator for the quality of an article and its fragments is clearly of interest to the readers of a wiki article but also for the contributors because it may help them to differentiate between articles that require immediate editing, articles that need only slight improvement and edits which can likely be kept as they are. As Wikipedia is the biggest wiki with respect to the number of articles and contributors, many measures of quality focus on Wikipedia, or use at least the Wikipedia data for the evaluation.

Statistical and Reference-based Measures on Wikis

Several approaches try to assess the quality of an article on the basis of statistical information such as the number of edits or the traffic a page received. The page history, which list the edits on a certain page and the users who made these edits, is used, too. Stvilia et al. (2005) defined seven metrics for information quality, such as the authority of an article, based, for example, on the number of edits by registered and anonymous users, the number of broken links (internal or external links) or the recency of the article. In an experiment on Wikipedia, the information quality metrics discriminated featured articles from the rest of the collection. However, it is not obvious that these metrics really measure the quality of the article or rather the level of interest sustained in the topic. A high recency does not necessarily mean that the information is kept up to date, but can also result from an ongoing edit war. Also the differentiation between the registered "good" users and the "bad", anonymous, users constitutes too much 'black and white' thinking. Viégas et al. (2004) observed in their study on Wikipedia some registered users vandalizing articles, too. Contrariwise, there were anonymous users who showed a great responsibility for the quality of certain articles. Anthony et al. (2005) even attribute the highest quality contributions to the large number of anonymous, infrequent contributors, the "Good Samaritans".

The hyperlinks that are set on the wiki pages give a reference network, analogous to the citation network between scientific publications. Reference-based measures such as PageRank, possibly adapted to specifics of the wiki graph, can be used to measure the importance of a wiki article or of the topic addressed in this article. Using these measures of importance as quality measures provides many problems, some of them similar to the problems discussed in the context of scientific publications. Articles may be well-written but contain faked information; so the wiki contributors who set the hyperlink to the faked wiki article might not have been able to detect the fake. Moreover – which could not happen in the case of published scientific papers – the information on the referenced wiki page could have changed. Users who feel responsible for the referencing article might monitor constantly the changes on this article but not on all referenced articles. Furthermore, a link does not necessarily constitute a vote for the quality of the referenced article because the semantic expressed in the link text can also be disapproving, or, as probably frequent in wikis, the link is completely neutral because a hyperlink constitutes the basis for the creation of a new page. At the time of setting this link, the new article does not yet exist. Such a link is clearly not a vote for the quality of the referenced article. Last but not least, hyperlinks between encyclopedia terms are set by default. An author who uses a term which is explained in a distinct article sets the link to this article, maybe even without reading this article. This leads to the fact that the more special the topic of an article is, the fewer links it will attract, regardless of its quality. Users who are not satisfied with the quality of the referenced article will not remove the link but rather try to improve the quality of this article. Summing up, a reference-based measure on the article network is more likely to measure the importance of the article's topic and the usefulness of the information provided than the quality of the article. For instance, many links may point in a corporate wiki to the company's phone directory. This does not mean that this is a highly qualitative article but that the article provides useful information.

Trust- and Reputation-Based Measures for Wikis

The quality of an article strongly relates to the contributors' trustworthiness to provide credible and well-investigated information. This aspect is neither considered by statistical nor by reference-based measures. User reputation can on the one hand be used to measure the quality of articles, i.e., the higher the reputation and the trust in the contributors, the more likely that an article is of high quality. On the other hand, the degree of trust in the user who edited some text can indicate to other contributors whether they should check immediately the modifications made by this user, i.e., author reputation can be used for alerting and may support the watch-list functionality. Authors with low reputation could be deprived of their edit rights for certain articles. A user's reputation is often assessed on the basis of the number of past contributions (see e.g. Ciffolilli, 2003). Simply counting the number of contributions, however, is inappropriate. An author who just contributed a little bit on many articles, e.g., corrected some typing errors, would get a high reputation, whereas a user who made a high quality contribution on a single article would have a lower reputation.

A step further, but still vulnerable to attacks is to consider not only the number of articles to which the user contributed but their quality. This is done in the scope of the approach by McGuinness *et al.* (2006). They indicate the trustworthiness of a fragment based on the authoritativeness of the author of this fragment. Firstly, the authoritativeness of an article is computed based on PageRank or the link-ratio, a measure that is special for encyclopedias and which takes into account the citations and non-citations of encyclopedia terms. The trust in an author is then given by the authoritativeness of all the articles to which he or she contributed. This author trust is attributed to the different text fragments. In future, Wikipedia pages could then comprise a "trust tab" where for each fragment the trust in its author is shown. Computing an author's trustworthiness in this way is critical to attacks because minor changes on highly authoritative articles give high trust. Future low quality contributions or even vandalism by this author would then be marked as highly trustworthy. There are also problems due to the way the authoritativeness of an article is measured. As discussed in the previous section, reference-based measures such as PageRank only measure the importance of an article. An author has thus a high reputation if he or she contributed to many important, not necessarily high quality articles.

In order to address the problem that malicious users can easily establish a high reputation by "trivial" edits, the quality of the contributions has to be considered. Korfiatis *et al.* (2006) (see also Korfiatis and Naeve, 2005) take the subsequent edits, such as roll-backs or removals, to measure the quality of a contribution. An acceptance factor indicates the percentage of text that is kept by the user who makes the subsequent contribution. Adler and de Alfaro (2007) refine this approach. They call this way of computing an author's reputation as "content-driven" because it considers the evolution of the content of the articles. They differentiate between textual and structural modifications and measure hence the text life and the edit life. The increase or decrease of an author's reputation after he or she has made a contribution is then computed, proportional to the size of the textual and structural contributions, to their life spans and to the subsequent author's reputation. The main problem of such content-driven approach is that subsequent changes are not necessarily improvements or corrections but could also be just alternative formulations which are preferred by this author. In articles that focus on current events, modification can simply be updates. Removing, for example, a flag indicating that an article needs some formatting after having formatted the article, is not related to the quality of other user's contributions.

The content-based approach can be especially useful when complemented with ratings between users as provided in the scope of a trust network. Such social relationship information are implicitly available. In the study by Viégas *et al.* (2004), veteran Wikipedia users explained that they scan the contributors' names in the edit history of the articles they "watch" for unfamiliar names and IP addresses. They recognize the names of regular contributors. This information could be formalized in a trust network. Then, reputation (or authority) could be replaced by a personal trust value between the contributors. In the German Wikipedia, some users started to actively establish a trust network between the contributors.[12] Their goal is to make visible the

---

[12]`http://de.wikipedia.org/wiki/Wikipedia:Vertrauensnetz`, only available in German, retrieved on April 26, 2007

social relationships in the Wikipedia community. A trust relationship is based on past experiences and discussions with the trusted user in Wikipedia as well as on personal contacts. Trust refers only to this user's activities in Wikipedia. Users create pages that list the users they trust and distrust, respectively. The recommendation by the initiators of this project is to deal carefully with distrust as this might seriously harm the community of Wikipedians. The personal page by the user Langec[13] shows how trust relationships are specified.

2.2.4 A Multi-Layer Architecture for Wikis

Various types of information are available in wikis, such as the information on the community of the contributors, the reference structure of the wiki articles and the information derived from the edit history. This information can be integrated in a multi-layer architecture, analogous to the multi-layer architecture for scientific publications. In the case of wikis, the multi-layer architecture encompasses a trust network, too. It formalizes the relationship information implicitly expressed by subsequent edits, i.e. that removing text by someone else means to distrust her or his contribution while keeping the text shows some trust in her or his capabilities as wiki contributor, and by the general authority that users have in the wiki due to their role as editor or administrator, as well as personal ratings, i.e. users make explicit trust statements. In corporate wikis, relationship information external to the wiki, such as organizational hierarchies, can be considered, too. The wiki articles are connected by hyperlinks, forming thereby a document reference network. Webpages external to the wiki can also link to wiki articles. Articles and contributors are related. In wikis, the strength of this relationship can be indicated – which is not feasible for scientific publications – based on the number of contributions to this text and the size of the edits and structural modifications to the article. Figure 2.4 shows this.

This setting allows for combining reference-based measures and trust information. Trust-enhanced measures could also use the structure of the article network to propagate information. A trust-enhanced measure can be used to assess the quality of an article. Moreover, it provides a personalized view on the wiki. In the FAQ pages of a corporate wiki describing, for instance, how to deal with a certain software problem, users might search depending on their personal background for a rather technical or a non-technical description. A personalized recommendation for the appropriate FAQ article should consider the specific personal information need. This can be achieved by using the relationship information that is expressed in the social trust network.

Measures of visibility and quality can be used by contributors not only to monitor articles, i.e., to get alerted when an article on their watch list decreases in quality,

---

[13]http://de.wikipedia.org/wiki/Benutzer:Langec/Vertrauen, only available in German, retrieved on April 26, 2007

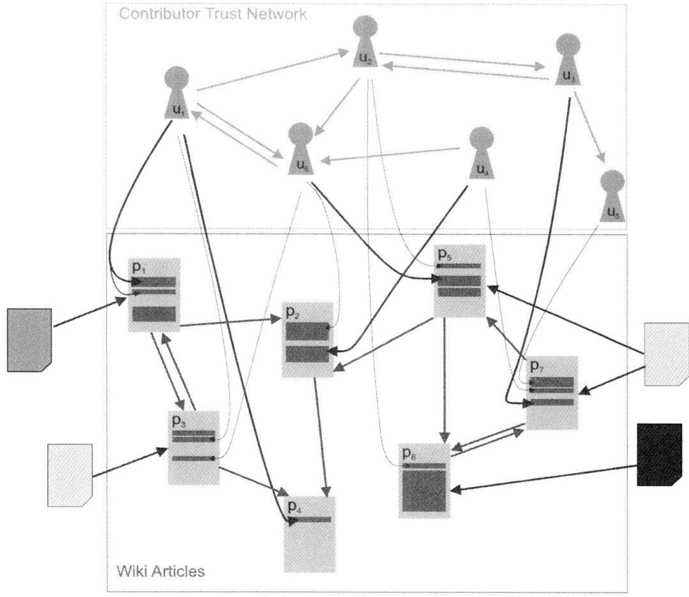

Figure 2.4: Multi-Layer Architecture for Wikis

but they can provide guidance in selecting for the next contribution such articles that increase their personal reputation. This is closely related to the contributor's motivation. As users can contribute to every article and start writing new articles on any topic, there is obviously the question of which topic they should contribute articles. Clearly, users should only contribute to topics of which they have at least a basic understanding. As one's personal reputation is a strong motivation for contributing to public as well as to corporate wikis, users might ask which contributions would increase their personal reputation. An increased reputation often goes along with an increased authority in the wiki. In organizations and companies, a reputation can be used to increase one's personal influence in the organization, which might be of advantage for future promotion. The following list gives some strategies for the selection of the wiki article to contribute and the corresponding measures.

- Contribute to highly visible articles so that everyone notices the contribution. Highly visible articles are basically those articles that are often accessed, often referenced and read by important people. The visibility of wiki articles can be measured by classical reference-based measures adapted to wikigraphs, probably including the access statistics. However, a high visibility does not yet say anything on the quality of the article. Important people in the wiki community are people with a high reputation.

- Contribute to intensively and controversially discussed articles in order to influence the consensus building process and future decisions in the organization. Whether an article is intensively discussed can be seen in the page history and the article's discussion page.

- Contribute to articles to which important people contribute, so that they will remember your name in other situations. Another decision criteria might be to select articles to which people contribute who work in a constructive way because the resulting article should be of a high quality. The question of whether someone considers another user to be someone who discusses differences constructively cannot be answered based on statistical information, but is highly subjective. To answer this question, measures that include the user's personal trust network are required.

2.3 Requirements for Trust-Based Recommendations in a Multi-Layer Architecture

Based on the described application scenarios for recommendations in a multi-layer architecture, the requirements for such an architecture can be determined.

Multi-Layer Architecture: Document reference networks constitute one of the primary sources of information for document recommendations in digital libraries. Reference-based measures compute document visibilities based on these document networks. The scenarios described in the use cases have demonstrated that mere citation-based recommendation strategies are too restricted. Considering in addition social trust information can address the identified drawbacks. A framework for coupling different types of networks, above all, of trust networks and document reference networks is required. This framework has to define how layers can be connected and to state the general conditions for the joint analysis of the information from the different layers.

Trust-Enhanced Visibility Measures: Propagation mechanisms have to be developed that integrate the information from social trust networks with classical reference-based measures on document networks, giving trust-enhanced visibility measures. These new measures should have the following properties:

- Provide for each user a personalized view on the document collection. Documents, whether scientific publications, websites or wiki articles, that are considered by a certain user or by her/his trusted colleagues and friends as low quality should be efficiently decreased in their visibility and their rank; hence, they should no longer be recommended to this user. Papers that are important within the own community, even if it is only a very small community and even though they might have a very low global visibility, should be recommended.

- Compute trust-enhanced visibilities for *all* documents in the document network and not only for those documents that are directly reviewed, or for which the trust in the author is directly known.

- Decrease the rank of faked papers so that they are no longer recommended. In a ranking that are based on a simple reference-based visibility measure, documents that are revealed to be faked keep their visibility and thus their position. By considering trust information, trust-enhanced visibility measures should decrease the visibility and exclude them from being recommended.

- Provide the recommendation in direct response to a user query. Users who are asking for a document recommendation or a ranking should obtain it immediately.

Duplicate Documents: Duplicates in document collections, such as slightly different versions of the same publication or mirrored websites, can distort the recommendations computed by reference-based measures. As trust-enhanced visibility measures build on classical reference-based measures or use the reference structure to propagate information, they are affected by the duplicates, too. An approach is therefore required that handles duplicates in the computation of trust-enhanced visibility measures.

3 Types of Networks

This chapter presents the basic types of networks integrated in the multi-layer architecture: trust networks and document reference networks.

3.1 Trust Networks

3.1.1 A Survey of Trust Networks

In the last few years, many social networking websites went online. Millions of users are registered in communities such as Friendster[1]. Contact lists itemize the users' acquaintances; often they include the type of acquaintance and where they met. Apart from free text descriptions, users may specify some degree of friendship. Social networking sites offer simple services such as querying your friends' contacts by navigating through the social web. Applications in which users specify trust relationships currently gain attention and communities are constantly growing. Implicit trust relationships can be expressed, for example, in del.icio.us[2] and CiteULike[3]. In del.icio.us, adding someone to one's personal network represents a trust statement because it implies that one considers another user's bookmarks as useful. The idea of CiteULike is similar; bookmarks are to online available academic publications. Formalized trust statements, in the simplest case binary trust values, offer the possibility of generating personalized trust-based recommendations, such as showing potential new friends, a likely interesting movie, or the best reviews to read about a certain product. This kind of online social networking where one may interact with either direct or indirect acquaintances reflects the word of mouth that we are apt to use on a day-to-day basis.

FOAF Networks

A general approach to formalizing and publishing social relationships is the FOAF vocabulary. The Friend-of-a-Friend (FOAF) project (`http://www.foaf-project.org`)

---

[1] `http://www.friendster.com`

[2] `http://del.icio.us`

[3] `http://www.citeulike.org`

aims at supporting the creation and the use of machine-readable homepages. The FOAF vocabulary (see the FOAF Vocabulary Specification by Brickely and Miller, 2005) defines a basic set of tags for representing personal information, such as name, email, homepage, and tags for describing friends (e.g. Dumbill, 2002). In a FOAF file, users describe themselves and link to friends. Users are identified by their email addresses, assuming that an email address belongs to a distinct person. Email addresses may be disguised for reasons of maintaining privacy and to avoid spam by encrypting it with the SHA1 mathematical function. Table 3.1 lists basic FOAF tags.

FOAF Tag	Description
foaf:Person	represents people
foaf:name	the name of something
foaf:mbox	a personal internet mailbox
foaf:mbox_sha1sum	the sha1sum of the URI of a mailbox
foaf:knows	indicates some interaction between the connected users but does not imply friendship

Table 3.1: Basic FOAF Tags

The following FOAF code shows the use of the tags. The FOAF vocabulary is based on RDF, the Resource Description Framework, a language that was developed by the World Wide Web Consortium (W3C) in order to represent information about web resources. The RDF statements contain a subject, a predicate and an object. For instance, the subject "me" has the name (predicate) "Claudia Hess" (object).

```
<rdf:RDF
    xmlns:rdf="http://www.w3.org/1999/02/22-rdf-syntax-ns#"
    xmlns:rdfs="http://www.w3.org/2000/01/rdf-schema#"
    xmlns:foaf="http://xmlns.com/foaf/0.1/">
  <foaf:Person rdf:ID="me">
      <foaf:name>Claudia Hess</foaf:name>
      <foaf:mbox_sha1sum>
          5305e6b40a400f85b7dbaebf61993d8f55b072ea
      </foaf:mbox_sha1sum>
      <foaf:knows rdf:nodeID="Klaus"/>
  </foaf:Person>
  <foaf:Person rdf:nodeID="Klaus">
      <foaf:name>Klaus Stein</foaf:name>
      <foaf:mbox_sha1sum>
          677a62cacc0132e8575c55662f05b582cf2a0663
      </foaf:mbox_sha1sum>
  </foaf:Person>
</rdf:RDF>
```

FOAF files are stored and maintained in a distributed way. Files published by users on their homepages can be crawled and used by social networking applications. On joining a new social networking community, users can incorporate these external FOAF files by simply linking to them. This has the advantage that they do not need to start from scratch indicating their personal data and their social relationships, but can extend their already existing FOAF file. Social networking software often generates FOAF files for the users, too.

Trust Module for FOAF

In order to give users the possibility to specify not only whom they know but also whom they trust – which is far more expressive than the simple knows-statement, Golbeck defined an extension to the basic FOAF vocabulary[4]. Users assign trust values to the persons they "know", ranging from 1 (no trust) to 10 (very high trust). The following example shows the use of the trust module.

```
<foaf:Person rdf:ID="me">
    <trust:trustsRegarding>
        <trust:TopicalTrust>
            <trust:trustSubject rdf:resource="#ScientificPapers"/>
            <trust:trustedPerson rdf:resource="#Klaus"/>
            <trust:trustValue>9</trust:trustValue>
        </trust:TopicalTrust>
    </trust:trustsRegarding>
</foaf:Person>
```

The trust module is used in the Trust and Reputation Project[5], a research project at the University of Maryland, USA. Two applications collect FOAF files with trust statements. For the first network[6], people are asked to create a FOAF file and to indicate relationships as well as trust values. Users can invoke some small applications and view network statistics. The second network is the basis for the trust-based recommender system FilmTrust[7] which generates personalized movie recommendations.

---

[4]For the trust ontology see: `http://trust.mindswap.org/ont/trust.owl` (retrieved on May 8, 2007)

[5]`http://trust.mindswap.org`

[6]`http://trust.mindswap.org/trustProject.shtml`

[7]`http://trust.mindswap.org/FilmTrust`

Online Communities with Trust Networks

In online communities, social trust networks constitute the basis for finding new friends, for dating or for getting in contact with new business partners. To establish new contacts, the user's web of trust is explored, assuming that users will like the friends of their friends, too. An example for an online community website is Orkut[8]. Orkut users search for new friends based on the user profiles that give information on hobbies and interests. They can also get to know other people or search for mutual acquaintances by following the connections that their friends have indicated. PeopleAggregator[9] is based on the idea of a friendship network, too. Users control the access to their personal data and to the content they publish, such as photos, MP3s or bookmarks, based on the social relationship information. Users specify how close the relationship is such as: haven't met – acquaintance – friend – good friend – best friend. This can be considered as a sort of trust. RepCheck[10] is a web application that uses the community's trust network to give users more accurate information on other users, for example, on a potential new babysitter. Users post information on other users' reputations, resulting in a reputation score. A personalized reputation score is computed by giving more weight to the opinions of users that the searching user considers as trustworthy. The trust score differentiates social trust and business trust. Both are indicated on a scale from 0 to 5.

Overstock.com Auctions[11] is an online auctions platform. In contrast to ebay.com where users are rather anonymous, Overstock.com Auctions puts emphasis on the personal relationships between buyers and sellers. It aims to facilitate the selection of the appropriate trading partner and to enhance the level of trust in the transaction. Users describe themselves on their personal homepages within Overstock.com and maintain a personal network as well as a business network. In the personal network, the degree of friendship – a sort of trust – is given by a star rating of 0-5 stars. A user's personal rating is based on the ratings given by direct acquaintances. Based on the business network, a second rating, the business rating, is generated. Ratings in the business network are provided by the buyer and seller after each completed auction as a numeric rating from -2 to $+2$.

Trust Networks with Web Mining Approaches

Creating trust networks manually requires much effort from the users' side. Users must decide on whom they should make a trust statement, and in order to establish a

---

[8]http://www.orkut.com

[9]http://www.peopleaggregator.net

[10]http://www.repcheck.com

[11]http://auctions.overstock.com

network, some of the rated users must participate, too. One alternative is the use of semi-automatically extracted networks. Matsuo *et al.* (2004) and Mika (2005) build social networks by analyzing publicly available data on the web with web mining techniques. Matsuo *et al.* demonstrated their approach by extracting a social network of the Japanese Society of Artificial Intelligence (JSAI). Mika built a social network of Semantic Web researchers. An early approach in this direction is the Referral Web by Kautz *et al.* (1997), a social network which can be explored to find human experts.

In the approach presented by Matsuo *et al.*, the users are the contributors from the last few annual JSAI conferences. Co-occurrences of two users' names in webpages give a hint that these users should be interlinked. The relevance $rel(x, y)$ of an edge between two persons x and y is calculated with the Jaccard coefficient on the number of documents obtained by querying a search engine with the terms X and Y representing the names of x and y:

$$rel(x, y) = \frac{|X \cap Y|}{|X \cup Y|}$$

The search engine queries can be refined by including the persons' affiliations. An edge is set if the Jaccard coefficient is above a threshold. In the next step, labels are assigned to the edges. Based on a content analysis of query results containing the user pair at issue and on a set of classification rules, four labels are attributed, namely coauthors, members of the same institute, colleagues in a project, participants of the same workshop or conference. Edges can have several labels. This gives a social network generated by a web mining approach. In their evaluation, Matsuo *et al.* could show that they achieved a considerable precision, i.e., the identified relationships were mostly correct. The recall, however, was quite low, i.e., many edges were missing. This is probably because older authors do not have all their papers on the web. In the next step, Matsuo *et al.* transformed the social network into a trust network. They calculated a global trust value, a sort of authoritativeness, for each node with a kind of weighted PageRank. Based on this global trust, individual trust between pairs of users was inferred.

It is also possible that a first version of a user's web of trust is automatically extracted from a person's email folder or postings in newsgroups. Users could then enhance the suggested values and add distrust. Boykin and Roychowdhury (2004) constructed a user's web of trust on the basis of the emails received. Then they classified subnetworks in the ones containing trusted email addresses and the ones related to spam. Although such an approach is not able to cope with the possibility that a user might consider someone from a 'trustworthy subnetwork' as untrustworthy (e.g. a colleague or a project partner), it can support users establishing their personal web of trust.

3.1.2 Trust-Based Recommendations

Recommender Systems

Recommender systems (Resnick and Varian, 1997) generate recommendations for users about various types of objects such as products[12] or movies[13]. They are an essential part of e-commerce sites where they support users in navigating through the range of products and in purchasing items that are likely to be interesting to them (Schafer *et al.*, 1999).

Recommender systems differ in the information they use as a basis for the recommendations. *Content-based filtering* makes use of the features of the items. It recommends items that have similar features to the items of known interest (Burke, 2002). A book, for example, will be recommended if it is described by the same attributes, such as fiction/non-fiction, as a book that the user marked previously as interesting. This approach requires that features are known or that they can be extracted. The main drawback is that a feature-based similarity says neither anything about the quality of the recommended item, nor whether it is in general liked or disliked. *Demographic recommender systems* take a similar approach. Instead of grouping items based on their features, similar users are identified on the basis of their personal attributes, such as their place of residence (Burke, 2002). The main problem of demographic recommender is that of obtaining the required data because users tend to dislike providing detailed profiles. *Collaborative filtering* is one of the most popular techniques applied in recommender systems (Herlocker *et al.*, 2004). It predicts preferences on the basis of ratings given by users or on the basis of the purchase history. In contrast to content-based recommender systems, collaborative filtering does not need any information on the properties or the internal structure of the items to be recommended. Collaborative filtering techniques are therefore not restricted to a certain type of object, e.g. text, but can be applied to various types of items. Two main techniques are distinguished: user-based and item-to-item collaborative filtering.

The idea of *user-based collaborative filtering* is that people who liked the same items in the past will now like the same items, too (Resnick *et al.*, 1994). An item will thus be recommended to a user if it is liked by users who provided identical, or at least similar, ratings. GroupLens by Resnick *et al.* was one of the first approaches to user-based collaborative filtering and was originally designed for the purpose of recommending news on the web. It requires the following information: a set of items (objects) O and a set of users U who provide ratings on items (e.g. on a scale from 1 to 5). GroupLens generates recommendations for a user u_i in two steps. In the first step, the similarity

---

[12]See, for instance, `http://www.amazon.com` for books.
[13]See, for instance, MovieLens, `http://movielens.umn.edu`.

40

between users is computed. On an intuitive level, two users have a high similarity if they provided mostly identical ratings. More precisely, the correlation coefficient indicates how much two users u_i and u_j tend to agree with respect to their ratings on those objects that both u_i and u_j have rated. In the second step, the recommendation for an object o_i is computed based on the ratings given by similar users: the weighted average of all ratings on o_i is used. Thereby, the rating by a certain user is weighted with the user similarity. Generating recommendations with user-based collaborative filtering has several problems as already mentioned in the GroupLens article. As it requires user ratings, it has to face the ramp-up problem (also known as the cold start problem): an item has to be rated at least once in order to be recommended. So it may take quite a long time until sensible recommendations can be made for a large proportion of the objects. Moreover, comparing user profiles is time consuming and no longer feasible when the number of users is large.

Item-to-item collaborative filtering was developed as a possible solution to the problem of the enormous computation load of user-based collaborative filtering in mind. It is particularly applied when the number of users is considerably higher than the number of items. Examples are the recommendations by Amazon for books (Linden et al., 2003) and by TiVo for television shows (Ali and van Stam, 2004). Item-to-item collaborative filtering differs from user-based collaborative filtering in the sense that the similarity is computed between items, and not between users. In the setting described by Linden et al., there is a set of users U and set of objects O. An entry s_{ij} in the matrix $S = O \times U$ gives the number of purchases (selections) of item o_i by user u_j; user ratings are not required. Recommendations are generated in two steps. In the first step, a 'similar items table' is built. The similarity score between two items o_i and o_j is the number of users who are interested in both o_i and o_j, relative to the number of users interested in o_i or o_j. So the similarity score is based on correlations between the purchases of items. A high score between two objects indicates that many users have purchased both objects. An important aspect of this step is that the calculation of the similar items table is performed offline. This reduces the computation load at query time, i.e., when a recommendation is generated in direct response to a user's action. The similar items table is re-computed periodically to reflect the community's current interests. In the second step, a user's personal recommendation list is generated. Firstly, the items of known interest are selected from the total list of items. These can be, for example, items that the user has already purchased, either items that the user rated positively, or items that the user has placed in the electronic shopping cart. Next items, that correspond to the items of known interest, are retrieved from the similar item table i.e., those that have a high similarity score. This similar item list is sorted on the basis of the similarity scores; the similarity scores can be modulated by weights, for example, derived from the user's personal item ratings. Finally, items can be filtered out and further items can be added. This gives the personalized recommendation list.

In practice, recommender systems often do not use one single recommendation technique but instead combine different approaches. Such recommender systems are called hybrid recommender systems (Burke, 2002). They merge, for example, the results obtained by different recommendation techniques or apply a second recommendation technique to filter and refine the results provided by the first one. Using a different technique has the effect of compensating for the shortcomings of the technique previously used, and addresses, for example, the ramp-up problem that is faced by (user-based) collaborative filtering.

Trust-Based Recommender Systems

Due to its poor scalability, collaborative filtering is not suited for large decentralized recommender systems, such as peer-to-peer systems, or for the evaluation of statements on the Semantic Web (Ziegler and Golbeck, 2006). Trust-based recommender systems are discussed as an alternative. Ziegler and Golbeck (2006) demonstrated on the basis of data from current trust-based recommender systems that a positive relation of trust and user similarity holds: the difference in the ratings of movies decreases as the trust in the reviewing user increases. The findings by Sinha and Swearingen (2001) show that it is a good idea to take into consideration recommendations by friends. They asked users to evaluate the quality of recommendations generated by recommender systems and those provided by friends. Users preferred their friends' recommendations. Moreover, trust-based recommender systems are particularly appropriate when the trust in the quality of someone's reviews takes precedence over past preferences. Avesani *et al.* (2005) show this in the example of ski tours. Ski tour recommendations must be absolutely trustworthy because they contain information that is strongly related to personal safety such as snow conditions and the associated avalanche risk. The recommending system Moleskiing therefore asks users to make statements about other users' trustworthiness, i.e. whether they evaluate ski tours carefully with respect to such criteria as the level of difficulty or the snow conditions etc. Ski tour reviews will only be displayed to a user if written by someone he or she trusts. This trustworthiness is more important than whether users liked the same ski tours in the past.

Classification Scheme for Trust-Based Recommender Systems   In recent years years, much research has been done on trust-based recommending, see for example, Montaner *et al.* (2002), Kinateder and Rothermel (2003), Ziegler and Lausen (2004a), Avesani *et al.* (2005), Golbeck and Hendler (2006), Bedi and Kaur (2006). I propose the following classification scheme in order to structure and to characterize approaches to trust-based recommending. I define the classification axes recommendation approach and recommendation type.

By the *recommendation approach*, I distinguish between *trust-only* recommender systems in which the recommendation is exclusively computed by trust-based recommending techniques, and *hybrid* approaches in which trust-based recommending is used complementary to other recommendation techniques, and *integrated* approaches in which the trust information is integrated in other recommendation techniques, for example, collaborative filtering. Most approaches proposed are pure trust-based recommender systems such as Avesani *et al.* (2005), Golbeck and Hendler (2006) and Bedi and Kaur (2006). Hybrid approaches are only feasible if the information required by the respective recommendation technique is available, such as the attributes of the items to be recommended. Montaner *et al.* (2002), for example, use trust-based recommending in combination with content-based filtering. By content-based filtering, the similarity between the item to be recommended and the items that were previously used or bought is computed based on the features of the items. If content-based filtering does not provide a clear vote for or against the item at issue, the recommendation will be then based on the experiences of trusted users. O'Donovan and Smyth (2005) developed an integrated approach. They enhanced collaborative filtering by using trust information directly in the standard prediction formula of GroupLens. When generating a recommendation for a user u_i for an item o_k, the weight that is given to the rating provided by u_j is based on the similarity between u_i and u_j and on u_i's trust in u_j. Alternatively, the users whose ratings are taken into account can be filtered on the basis of the trust in them. O'Donovan and Smyth derive the trust information from the past predictions. Although they call it 'trust', this value represents rather a user's reputation than personal trust in this user. Instead, values taken from a trust network can be used, too.

With the *recommendation type*, I distinguish between *trust-based filtering* and *trust-weighted reviews*. Filtering information means that reviews, information or statements are filtered based on the trustworthiness of the users who provided them. Epinions[14] is likely to be the most prominent example of a recommender system that uses social trust information in order to select the information to be presented. It is an online consumer review platform offering users the possibility of sharing their experiences with products ranging from software and books to household appliances. Users add other users to their 'Web of Trust' or their 'Block List', their personal lists of trusted and distrusted Epinions members. A user's web of trust is visible on the Epinions platform whereas the block list is not displayed. Reviews provided by trusted users and by users trusted by friends are shown in a prominent way. Reviews by users on the block list are hidden. Avesani *et al.* (2005) take a similar approach in Moleskiing in which only those ski tour descriptions that were provided by trustworthy peers are shown to a user The exchange of bibliographic data, spam filtering or the exchange of bookmarks can be supported by trust-based information filtering, too. An application

---

[14]http://www.epinions.com

supporting users in exchanging bibliographic entries is Bibserv[15]. Users specify their trust in other users with respect to the quality of their bibliography entries. The trust network is used to distinguish trustworthy bibliographic entries, i.e., entries that can directly be used without verifying all information, and entries which should be used only partially or even not at all. The approaches by Golbeck and Hendler (2004), Boykin and Roychowdhury (2004) and Chirita et al. (2005) use trust networks or social networks, respectively, for spam filtering. The social trust network can be based on explicitly indicated trust relationships (Golbeck and Hendler) or be established on the basis of the email communications of participating users (Chirita et al.). Golbeck and Hendler rank in their email client TrustMail the incoming emails according to the degree of trust in the sender of the email. They give the example of a student who emails a professor whom he or she does not know personally. The email might get a higher visibility if the student's supervisor and this professor trust each other.

Trust-weighting of reviews means computing a recommendation for an item based on reviews on this item which are then weighted with the trust in the users providing the reviews. These trust-weighted reviews are then aggregated. The FilmTrust website for trust-based movie recommendations (Golbeck and Hendler, 2006; Golbeck, 2006) generates recommendations in this way. FilmTrust users build up a list of friends and indicate the degree of trust with respect to movie recommendations. The FilmTrust website advises users to assign trust ratings based on the following consideration: "Think of this as if the person were to have rented a movie to watch, how likely is it that you would want to see that film". Apart from the social networking component, users rate movies on a scale of a half star to four stars and write free-text reviews. A personalized rating is now provided, the so-called "recommended rating". The recommendation r_{m_d,u_n} for a movie m_d is computed from the perspective of a user u_n. In order to compute it, the users u_p in whom u_n has the highest personal trust $t_{u_n \rightarrow u_p}$ are selected from all users who have reviewed the film. This gives the set U of users. The weighted average of the ratings provided by these trusted users gives the recommended rating:

$$r_{m_d,u_n} = \frac{\displaystyle\sum_{u_p \in U} t_{u_n \rightarrow u_p} \, r_{m_d,u_p}}{\displaystyle\sum_{u_p \in U} t_{u_n \rightarrow u_p}}$$

Montaner et al. (2002) also include in their trust-based recommending component the weighted average over the trust-weighted reviews. Bedi and Kaur (2006) proceed in a similar way. They have, however, fuzzy sets as reviews (instead of single values). Consequently, a fuzzy set is weighted with the trust in the one who provided it.

---

[15]http://www.bibserv.org

Recommendation Quality   The question is now on whether the quality of trust-based recommendations is higher than that of classical recommendation strategies such as collaborative filtering. In FilmTrust, Golbeck analyzed the accuracy of the recommendations by comparing the average rating (i.e. the average of all ratings given to a film), the recommended rating (i.e. the trust-based recommendation) and a recommendation based on collaborative filtering with the user's actual rating. A high difference between the average rating and the recommended rating shows that the user differs from the average, i.e., that he or she does not correspond to the mainstream. Over all FilmTrust users, trust-based recommendations do not provide better results than the average rating. However, if the focus is on non-mainstream users, trust-based recommending outperforms collaborative filtering and clearly also the average rating. This shows that trust-based recommender systems are in general very useful. Especially for users who do not correspond to the average, trust-based recommendations are significantly better than standard collaborative filtering.

O'Donovan and Smyth conducted a similar experiment as Golbeck in which they compared the results by the trust-based approach with the actual user ratings. They used the dataset from MovieLens. The prediction error is calculated for the different approaches that incorporate trust in collaborative filtering with respect to the recommendation with the GoupLens formula. The experiments showed that all trust-based approaches improve the accuracy of the recommendations. For the combined filtering and weighting by trust information, the average prediction error is reduced by 22% compared to mere collaborative filtering. Based on the findings of these experiments, I can summarize that trust-based recommendations are a promising alternative to classical recommending techniques. They provide a mean to address the scalability problems of traditional approaches and can be used in decentralized settings when the number of both items and users exceeds the millions.

3.1.3 Definition and Properties of Trust

Trust

In computer science, the term 'trust' is used in various contexts. Probably the oldest notion of trust is in the context of IT security. Here, a trusted system is a component in a security architecture that is considered as reliable regarding security issues (for a survey see e.g. Abrams and Joyce, 1995). The term trust is also used in the area of authentication. Digital signatures ensure that a particular email, website or document has actually been written by the person who is indicated as sender or author. The so-called trust centers issue such certificates. The term 'web of trust' has its origins in authentication, too (Stallings, 1995). Instead of having a central authority which issues certificates, users mutually sign their certificates (Abdul-Rahman, 1997). This is widespread for PGP (Pretty Good Privacy Encryption). Although authentication can ensure the authenticity of the sender, it cannot make any statement on the quality of the information, e.g., whether some text is carefully worded.

Only recently, computer scientists became interested in the concept of "social trust" and its use in information systems, above all, in the context of the (semantic) web (see e.g. Swartz and Hendler, 2001), in multi-agent systems (see e.g. Castelfranchi and Falcone, 1998), and, as discussed above, in recommender systems. Social trust is discussed in various research disciplines ranging from sociology, psychology, philosophy to economics with each of them providing a number of definitions of trust. Marsh (1994b, chapter 3) gives a thorough overview of trust definitions across different research domains. He discusses in detail the work by Morton Deutsch (based on Deutsch (1962)), Niklas Luhmann (based on Luhmann (1979)), Bernard Barber (based on Barber (1983)) and Diego Gambetta (based on Gambetta (1990b), above all the chapter by Gambetta (Gambetta, 1990a)). Trust definitions differ in the level of trust being studied: trust is considered at a personal (individual) level or on a social level. Marsh and Dibben summarize (social) trust definitions from various disciplines as follows: "trust, in general, is taken as the belief (or a measure of it) that a person (the trustee) will act in the best interests of another person (the truster) in a given situation, even when controls are unavailable and it may not be in the trustee's best interests to do so" (Marsh and Dibben, 2005, p. 19). Definitions for trust from the computer science perspective aim to map the complex notion of social trust into a machine-processable concept. In contrast to the rather general trust definitions in other disciplines, social trust is related to a particular application domain, for instance, the trust in someone's movie recommendations.

Trust Values

In most social networking applications that formalize trust relationships, trust is expressed in a single numerical value or label. We call the formalized trust relationship *trust value*. Applications differ with respect to the range of the trust value. Binary statements only distinguish whether or not a user trusts another user. Although they can easily be assigned by users, it is generally acknowledged that we trust other people to different degrees (e.g. Gambetta, 1990a; Marsh, 1994b). The range between distrust (or no trust) and full trust is expressed by continuous or discrete values. While trust metrics are designed for continuous values (e.g. Richardson *et al.*, 2003; Ziegler and Lausen, 2004b), most trust-based applications use discrete values. Golbeck (2005, p. 74) argues that discrete values are more user-friendly than continuous ones because it is easier for the user to provide ratings and to interpret results inferred from the trust network. She proposes discrete values from 1 to 10 in order to approximate continuous values. Marsh (1994b) argues that only continuous values reflect the continuous nature of trust: we can always trust someone a little bit more than another one and these differences should be represented. This high sensitivity and accuracy also has disadvantages. Is there any real difference between a trust value of 0.78 provided by a user Alice and a trust value of 0.79 provided by a user Bob, or is the difference artificially created? Griffiths (2005) describes this as the risk of overfitting because irrelevant differences in the trust values influence the computations made on the basis of the trust values. The measures that I develop in the course of the following chapters work well with continuous values. On the user interface, however, I prefer discrete values because I think that these are easier for the user.

There may be interindividual differences in the interpretation of values, e.g. someone considers '7' as rather high, and someone else as just above the medium. In order to clarify the meaning of a trust value, labels can be added to discrete values, e.g. $9 =$ very high trust. Continuous values can be stratified as described in Marsh (1994), e.g. $+1 =$ blind trust; $> 0.9 =$ very high trust. Instead of numerical values, Abdul-Rahman and Hailes (2000) propose four different degrees of trust, namely, very untrustworthy, untrustworthy, trustworthy and very trustworthy. There is no mapping to numerical values. They argue that these strata provide a clear semantics. However, trust degrees are less suited for computations than trust values. Abdul-Rahman and Hailes make only rather simple computations with the trust degrees. For example, they adjust recommendations on the basis of the differences in the evaluation of past experiences. Summing up the current approaches for modeling interpersonal trust, I can say that most approaches work with numerical values. The most important reason – and also the reason why I chose to use numerical values – is that computations such as trust propagation can more easily be realized in this way.

No Trust, Untrust, Distrust and Mistrust

Marsh and Dibben (2005) claim that most research in the area of trust-based recommender systems, trust management and online trust has focused on trust as a positive relationship between persons, whereas the 'darker' side of trust has been ignored or only mentioned as something to be discussed in future work. The scale used in FilmTrust with 1 for low trust and 10 for high trust is such an example: negative relationships are completely ignored, trust is only expressed in the case of a – at least slightly – positive relationship. While in general the upper bound of the scale is absolute trust[16], trust-based applications often fail to clarify the meaning of the lower bound used. *Untrust, no trust,* and *distrust* are often mixed up. Should 'no trust' be set if no information is available, or if the evaluating user is neutral with respect

---

[16]Sometimes the term 'blind trust' is used, even though this term might suggest that the user did not really think about the value but assigns trust in a naive way. In order to avoid this, Marsh (1994a) only allows trust values in [-1, 1).

to the other user? Or does it mean that I have bad experiences with this user and therefore consider her or him as untrustworthy (e.g. Kinateder and Rothermel, 2003)? In Richardson *et al.* (2003), for example, 0 may denote no information, indifferent and no trust due to negative experiences. Marsh (1994a, 1994b) subsumes 'unknown' and 'impartial' by the concept 'no trust' (also called 'zero trust'). I propose the following clarification:

- Ignorance / unknown: the user does not have any (or not enough) information about the other user. In the case of a trust-based recommender "unknown" means not knowing whether to consider the information and reviews provided as accurate.

- Impartial / neutral / indifferent: the user has neither positive trust nor distrust, e.g. because positive and negative experiences are balanced, or because the quality of the reviews varies greatly. As in the case of "unknown", a user is not sure as to whether some information by this person is correct or false.

- Distrust: the user is sure that the reviews by a distrusted person are of low quality. Distrust is in general based on some previous experiences or past events. Depending on how strong the definition of distrust is, it is assumed that the distrusted person intends the information to be false, i.e., there is a willingness to betray others (see Marsh and Dibben, 2005) or that the distrusted person might also do this unintentionally because they do not know any better.

Trust in Trust-Based Recommender Systems

In the cases described in chapter 2, there must exist the possibility to express distrust, for example, in the author of faked publications. Distrust is also set if the evaluating user considers the evaluated user's reviews as false and misleading. Neutral trust is set if the evaluating user adopts a neutral position with respect to the evaluated user, or if the evaluating user does not have enough information in order to decide on the degree of trustworthiness (but too much information for saying that this person is completely unknown). Trust statements should therefore represent trust ranging from absolute distrust to absolute trust with some value representing neutrality. A scale from -1 to 1 is appropriate with -1 for distrust, 0 for a neutral position, and 1 for full trust.

Having distinguished the basic types of trust, we are now interested in how the trust in a user affects the impact that is given to this user's reviews. Certainly, reviews by trustworthy persons have a higher impact on the overall recommendation than reviews by less trustworthy persons. Reviews by distrusted persons are not considered at all. However, it is not obvious how to deal with the reviews by unknown people. In general, they are not taken into account – unknown persons are hence handled as if they were explicitly distrusted. Kinateder and Rothermel (2003) argue that users can easily create a new pseudonym when their old pseudonym is deemed as untrustworthy. In this case, a distinction between impartial (neutral) and distrust becomes obsolete. I claim, however, that users should decide themselves how much they are willing to trust unknown people, and consequently the degree of impact that these persons' reviews have, because in the physical world as well as in the online world, we often have, by default at least a little trust in unknown people. For example, we ask complete strangers for directions. This shows that reviews from unknown people can be a valuable source of recommendations. In fact completely ignoring these reviews would automatically discard huge amounts of information. Section 5.1.3 addresses this topic.

Direct Trust and Recommendation Trust

Trust definitions differ with respect to the question on whether or not to distinguish *direct trust* from *recommendation trust*. The terms direct trust and recommendation trust (also recommender trust) were already introduced by Beth *et al.* in 1994 and they are widely used. There are also the terms "domain expert trust" and "recommendation expert trust" (e.g. Ding *et al.*, 2004), and the terms "referral trust" and "functional trust" (e.g. Josang and Pope, 2005). Beth *et al.* (1994, p. 5) distinguish both concepts as follows: "To trust an entity directly means to believe in its capabilities with respect to the given trust class. Recommendation trust expresses the belief in the capability of an entity to decide whether another entity is reliable in the given trust class and in its honesty when recommending third entities." However, why should just two concepts be sufficient? Why not define a third trust type for evaluating the "recommender recommender", and a fourth, and so on? An example illustrates this: in a three step recommendation chain with users Alice $\rightarrow$ Bob $\rightarrow$ William, Alice would trust Bob to recommend someone who is good at doing x, namely William. Adding another user Carol so that the chain is Alice $\rightarrow$ Bob $\rightarrow$ Carol $\rightarrow$ William, the trust purpose would be different. Now, Alice trusts Bob to recommend someone who can recommend someone (Carol) who is good at doing x (William). The trust purpose becomes more complicated with each step in the recommendation chain. Jøsang *et al.* (2003) argue that a single type of recommendation trust can be defined due to the recursive structure shown in the trust expression, namely the trust in someone's ability to give recommendations. Following this argumentation, only recommendation trust is propagated between the users in the network. Trust is separated in a transitive component, the recommendation trust, and into an intransitive component, the direct trust, which cannot be passed between users.[17] (Abdul-Rahman and Hailes, 1997) therefore consider trust to be "conditionally transitive".

---

[17]For the metrics calculating the trust propagation in the trust network see section 3.1.5. These metrics also consider that trust is not transitive in the strict mathematical sense but decays with longer trust chains.

In contrast to this differentiation, Golbeck argues that a single definition captures both direct trust and recommender trust: *"Alice must trust Bob if she commits to an action based on a belief that Bob's future actions will lead to a good outcome."* (Golbeck, 2005, p. 47), which is in accordance with the definition by Marsh and Dibben given above. Adopting the definition by Golbeck to the trust-based document recommendation system described in chapter 2.1 (with a reviewer trust network), the semantics of trust is as follows. Alice determines the degree of trust that she assigns to Bob by comparing the criteria that she applies when writing reviews with the criteria used by Bob. Given that Alice considers her own criteria as reference[18], high trust means that she trusts Bob to apply in his reviews the same criteria as herself. So a review by a highly trusted user should be of the same quality as her own reviews. This applies to direct trust, i.e. Alice trusts Bob with respect to Bob's reviews, as well as to recommender trust, i.e. Alice trusts Bob to recommend other reviewers because, as Alice trusts Bob to apply the same criteria in the evaluation, Alice can trust the persons trusted by Bob. In my opinion, this definition is appropriate for trust-based recommender systems as it should be easy for the users to make trust statements. I think that this is also the main reason why current trust-based recommender systems on the web use a single trust value. In my thesis, I also take this approach.

3.1.4 Trust Networks – A Special Type of Social Network

Newman defines a social network as "a set of people or groups of people with some pattern of contacts or interactions between them" (Newman, 2003, p. 5). A social network is thus a graph.

Definition 1 *A social network is a graph $\mathcal{G} = (V, E)$ with a set V of persons (the vertices) and a set $E \subseteq V \times V$ of (directed or undirected) edges connecting persons via the social relationship studied.*

Social network analysis focuses on relationships between people (Wasserman and Faust, 1994). Various types of relationships can hold, such as friendship or business contacts. A trust network is a social network in which persons are connected via explicit trust relationships. Social network analysis views persons as embedded in a complex structure formed by interpersonal relationships which again influences the individuals' actions; persons are hence not regarded as independent but as interdependent entities (Wasserman and Faust, 1994, p. 4). As networks range from social networks to information networks, technical networks and biological networks (Newman, 2003), methods and tools in social network analysis are influenced by research

---

[18]However, a user could also give another user a higher trust than herself, for example, because she knows that he or she has better knowledge in this domain than her.

in the social sciences, mathematics, physics and computer science. Apart from *user* or *person*, the term *actor* is often used in social network analysis denoting any social entity such as a person, a company or a computer agent. The term *agent* is frequently used in the context of multi-agent systems.

Trust relationships are a special type of social relationship. They are in contrast to relationships such as 'colleague-of' directed and do not imply a symmetric relationship from the trusted to the trusting user. Trust edges are weighted with numeric values. Figure 3.1 shows a small trust network both in graphical form and in matrix representation. *Person*1, for example, trusts *Person*3 with 0.7 ($t_{13} = 0.7$).

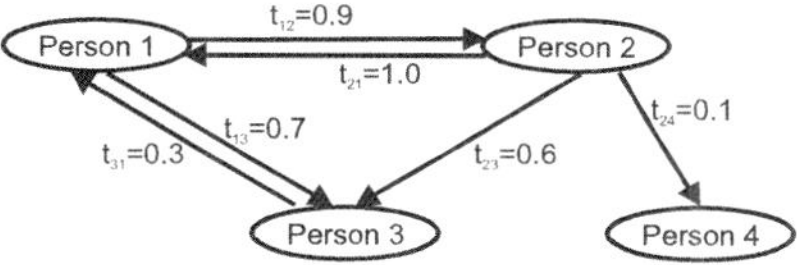

	1	2	3	4
1	0	0.9	0.7	0
2	1.0	0	0.6	0.1
3	0.3	0	0	0
4	0	0	0	0

Figure 3.1: Trust Network as Graph and as Matrix

I thus define a trust network as used for trust-based recommendations as follows:

Definition 2 *A social trust network is a graph $\mathcal{T} = (U, T)$ with a set U of users and a set $T \subseteq U \times U \times [-1, \ 1]$ of directed and weighted edges between users. The edge $(u_m, u_n, t_{u_m \to u_n})$ gives the degree of trust that user u_m has in user u_n.*

Degree Distribution

The degree of a node indicates the number of nodes to which a node is connected. In the case of directed edges, the in-degree of a node gives the number of incoming links and the out-degree the number of links set by a node. The degree distribution of a network thus corresponds to the histogram of the degrees of its nodes (Newman, 2003). The degree distribution of many real-world networks, such as the Internet or the World Wide Web, follows a power-law (Barabási and Albert, 1999). This also holds true for trust networks, as Guha (2003) showed for the Epinions trust network[19]. In a network following a power-law distribution, the probability $P(k)$ that a node is connected to k other nodes decays as a power-law with $P(k) \sim k^{-\gamma}$. Few nodes have a huge number of links pointing to them whereas most nodes only have a very small in-degree. These networks are called *scale-free* because the number of connections with other nodes is not limited.

---

[19]The 'winner takes all phenomenon', however, is damped because Epinions has introduced mechanisms that make it possible for newcomers who are writing reviews to attract links on themselves.

Barabási and Albert (see Barabási and Albert (1999) and Barabási (2001)) explained why many real networks are scale-free. In their model simulating the growth of networks, each newly generated node is connected to existing nodes according to *preferential attachment*: nodes are selected which already have a large number of links pointing to them. A new node is connected to an existing node i with a probability Π depending on the connectivity k_i of this node so that $\Pi(k_i) = k_i / \sum_j k_j$. Networks constructed according to this model have a degree distribution that follows a power-law with an exponent $\gamma_{model} = 2.9 \pm 0.1$. This evokes a "rich-gets-richer" phenomenon, i.e., nodes that already have a large in-degree will attract more and more links. In random graphs according to the graph model of Erdös and Rényi, however, each link is present or absent with equal probability. The degree distribution is therefore binomial or Poisson.

By adding nodes continually, the growth model by Barabási and Albert differs clearly from the models that focus on the static structure of networks like the random graph model of Erdös and Rényi (1959) and the small world model by Watts and Strogatz (1998). The small world effect is a characteristic property of social networks. It has already been described by Milgram in the the 1960's and says that social networks are sparse graphs with a small diameter, i.e., although each node has only a few connections to other nodes, the maximum distance – with the (geodesic) distance being the shortest path between two nodes – between any pair of nodes is small. Watts (1999) explains the presence of the short paths in highly clustered networks (i.e. networks in which people form groups and all nodes within a group are connected but there are only few connections to outsiders) by the fact that the long distances between the clusters are shortened by a very small proportion of long-range shortcuts. The expression *six degrees of separation* claims that any two people on the world are connected via maximum six steps, which is based on Milgram's experiments. This shows that in the case of trust networks, propagating trust over six persons does not make much sense because any two persons are linked.

Measures on Social Networks

Methods developed in social network analysis offer different levels of analysis from the individual actor embedded in the network to groups of actors. On the individual level, methods for measuring an actor's importance – or power – are of particular interest. Other methods are applied to pairs of actors, so-called dyads, and to triads. Analysis on the network level are, for example, concerned with the identification of cohesive subgroups such as cliques. As we are interested in recommender systems that assess the reliability of information (or reviews) provided by a certain user, methods of importance could be useful. Measures for the importance of an actor (or a group of actors) are based on the idea that an actor's location in the network determines her or his importance, i.e., actors in strategic locations are considered as important. Classical measures for an actor's importance are the degree centrality, the closeness centrality and the betweenness centrality. They can be applied to directed as well as to undirected graphs. The measures for an actor's importance can be extended to measures for the importance of a group of actors. Note that all measures can be standardized by the number of actors.

Degree Centrality: The degree centrality considers the actor who has the most ties (relationships) to other actors to be the most important one. The degree centrality $C_D(n_i)$ of a node n_i is defined by Wasserman and Faust (1994) as

$$C_D(n_i) = d(n_i) = \sum_j x_{i \to j} = \sum_j x_{j \to i}$$

with $d(n_i)$ being the degree of a node and $xn \to m$ being an edge from node n to m. As the degree centrality does not consider the direction of an edge, the number of edges $x_{i \to j}$ equals the number of edges $x_{j \to i}$.

Closeness Centrality: The closeness centrality $C_C(n_i)$ takes those actors as central who have the shortest paths so that they can interact easily with the other actors. So the distances $d(n_i, n_j)$ between node n_i to all other nodes n_j, i.e. the length of the shortest path, are considered. With g being the total number of nodes, Wasserman and Faust define the closeness centrality of n_i as

$$C_C(n_i) = \frac{1}{\sum_{j=1}^{g} d(n_i, n_j)}$$

The closeness centrality decreases with an increasing length of the shortest paths to the other nodes.

Betweenness Centrality: A high betweenness centrality $C_B(n_i)$ means that an actor is between many others and has so some type of control over these paths. While g_{jk} is the total number of shortest paths between j and k (with i being distinct from j and k), $g_{jk}(n_i)$ is the number of shortest paths via node n_i. It is defined by Wasserman and Faust as

$$C_C(n_i) = \sum_{j<k} \frac{g_{jk}(n_i)}{g_{jk}}$$

Applying these measures from social network analysis to trust networks ignores the essential information in trust networks: the edges weights. Measures specific for trust networks are therefore discussed in the next section.

3.1.5 Trusting a Friend of a Friend

A personalized trust-based recommendation is based on the experiences made by trusted users. Here, not only the direct friends are considered but the friends of the friends, too. Trust between indirectly connected users can be inferred by analyzing the paths between the users: if Alice trusts Bob and Bob trusts Carol, it will be inferred that Alice trusts Carol to a certain degree. The trust chain can be extended to Dave, who is a friend of Carol. This trust inference mechanism reflects that trust is considered to be transitive, although not in the strict mathematical sense. If trust is passed between people, trust may decay. This is to say that Alice is likely to trust Dave to a lesser degree than Carol trusts her direct friend Dave, just because Alice is some steps away from Dave. In computer applications, we need a concrete value for Alice's trust in Carol and Dave, respectively. We have to define exactly how to compute this trust value. Apart from inferring trust relationships by analyzing chains of trust statements, trust can be measured on the basis of similarities in trust statements. Ding *et al.* (2004), for instance, define such similarity-based trust relationships. Guha *et al.* (2004) whose trust metric is presented later on, use similarity-based trust, too.

Classification Scheme for Trust Metrics

The methods that infer trust and reputation on the basis of explicitly stated trust value are called *trust metrics*. Trust metrics have been developed in different domains such as authentication (e.g., Levien and Aiken (1998), Beth *et al.* (1994), Reiter and Stubblebine (1997), Gray *et al.* (2003)) and recommender systems for online communities (e.g. Guha (2003), Kinateder and Rothermel (2003), Montaner *et al.* (2002)).

Ziegler and Lausen (2004b) classify trust metrics according to three dimensions: the network perspective, the computation locus and the link evaluation. The *network perspective* distinguishes *global* and *local* trust metrics. This is an important differentiation. Global trust metrics compute a universal trust value for each actor, the actor's reputation. It is based on all trust statements in the network and is independent of the requesting user. Global trust metrics are often influenced by Google's PageRank. In contrast, local trust metrics compute trust values individually from each actor's point of view. Levien and Aiken (1998) and, Golbeck and Hendler (2004) are such local trust metrics. Massa and Avesani (2005) compared local and global trust metrics with respect to their accuracy in predicting trust values and their coverage. Based on their experiments on Epinions data, they conclude that local trust metrics should be preferred when many users are controversially evaluated, i.e., both highly appreciated and heavily distrusted. Local trust metrics can infer trust values only for actors that are connected via some path with the requesting actor; they may not cover the whole network. As personalized trust-based recommendations have to be based on subjective trust values between users, and not on global reputation scores, I focus in the following on local trust metrics.

The *computation locus* distinguished *centralized* and *distributed* computations. Centralized metrics (also called local metrics in the sense of the place of computation) compute all trust values on a single machine which is granted access to all trust information (either centrally stored or distributed in the network). Distributed approaches split up the computation between all nodes; consequently, the computation load is distributed, too. Each node makes some computations which are passed on to other nodes which merge the received information with their own computations. Nodes can thus keep their trust values secret. Results can differ highly, depending on which users are currently online and are participating in the trust calculation. While most trust metrics are centralized, the metric by Richardson *et al.* (2003) is an example for a distributed trust metric.

The classification criteria *link evaluation* differentiates *scalar* and *group* metrics. This differentiation was proposed originally by Levien (2003). Scalar metrics calculate trust ratings independently for each node, whereas group metrics compute trust ratings for all nodes at once. Most trust metrics are scalar metrics. Examples for group metrics are the Advogato trust metric by Levien (2003) and the Appleseed trust metric by Ziegler and Lausen (2004b).

Designing Local Trust Metrics

I want to point out several design criteria that need to be considered when defining metrics for inferring trust values. In the following, the term 'source' denotes the user from whose perspective the indirect trust is computed, and 'target' refers to the indirectly connected user. In my opinion, there are two central questions from a path algebraic point of view:

- Trust values are inferred for users who are connected via a chain of trust statements. How should the trust values be concatenated on any one path from the source to the target? And how should one deal with distrust?

- There might be several paths from the source to the target. How should the values, which are calculated for the different paths, be aggregated?

Distrust is an important topic in trust metrics. Currently, most trust metrics are not able to cope with negative values, and distrust is often represented by -1. Metrics based on a random surfer model (Markov chains), for example, will compute negative values for the probabilities, if negative trust values are allowed. Shifting all trust ratings so that they are equal to or greater than zero would destroy the semantics of the neutral trust value which is in general set to zero. Guha *et al.* (2004) discuss a number of research issues on distrust and the development of a metric for distrust. In path algebraic metrics, distrust has to be dealt with when trust values are concatenated.

Regardless of how values are concatenated and paths are aggregated, cycles in a trust graph should not influence a trust metric in a way that users can increase the trust that is set in them by modifying the trust values they assign to other users.

Concatenation of Trust Values In the example network in figure 3.2, u_1's trust $t_{u_1 \rightarrow u_3}$ in u_3 is calculated on the basis of u_1's trust $t_{u_1 \rightarrow u_2}$ in u_2 and u_2's trust $t_{u_2 \rightarrow u_3}$ in u_3. The values can be concatenated by multiplication, i.e. $t_{u_1 \rightarrow u_3} = 0.27$. It is also conceivable to take the minimum value on the path, i.e. $t_{u_1 \rightarrow u_3} = 0.3$. According to the standard rules of network capacity, the maximum trust that can "flow" from the source to the target is limited by the smallest trust weight on that path. A trust metric should thus not assign the target a higher trust than any node on the path. Both multiplication and minimum value satisfy this rule.

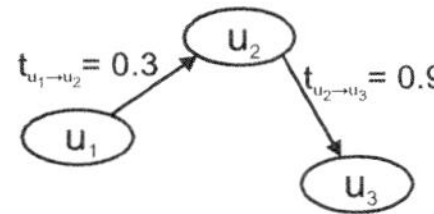

Figure 3.2: Trust Values on a Path

In this example, trust is propagated from u_1 to u_3 via one intermediary, namely u_2. This propagation can be extended to longer paths. As discussed before, trust is not transitive in the mathematical sense but decays. Should the paths thus be restricted to a certain length? Intuitively, one might say yes. However, there are cases in which long paths are not an issue. For instance, customers do not think about how many people are working on their order at a e-commerce website. It only matters that the order is filled correctly. Long paths can also be accepted if all actors in the chain are responsible for their actions. Trust metrics should thus be parameterizable with respect to the path length considered.

A metric that copes with distrust has to combine successive distrust values. The question is on whether two distrust statements cancel or intensify each other? Guha *et al.* (2004) distinguish the multiplicative and the additive trust propagation. Multiplicative distrust propagation means that two successive distrust statements result in trust, i.e., if $t_{u_1 \rightarrow u_2} = -1$ and $t_{u_2 \rightarrow u_3} = -1$, then $t_{u_1 \rightarrow u_3} = (-1) \cdot (-1) = 1$, so u_1 trusts u_3. The enemies of my enemies are thus my friends. In contrast, additive trust propagation implements in the same setting that u_1 distrusts u_3:

$t_{u_1 \to u_3} = (-1) + (-1) = -2$, and with some normalization, the result is -1. None of these approaches are really appealing. Moreover, a multiplicative trust propagation in several iterations has undesirable side effects in networks containing directed cycles with trust and distrust values: concatenating the values, users may end up distrusting themselves and their original trust ratings may be negated. A better approach to integrate distrust propagation in trust metrics is to stop trust propagation when reaching a distrusted person (e.g. Ziegler and Lausen, 2005; Guha, 2003). Persons rated only by distrusted persons are attributed the same trust as unknown persons.

Aggregation of paths Aggregating distinct paths from the source to the target raises two main questions. Firstly, should all paths be considered, only the shortest ones, or just the n most trustworthy ones? Alternatively, only the paths through those neighbors whose trust value is above a certain threshold could be taken. Secondly, it has to be decided how to aggregate the values computed for each of the paths. Taking average seems the most obvious suggestion. The average can be a simple average of the number of paths considered, or a weighted average where the trust into the path (e.g., the trust in the source's neighbors) is taken as weight. Alternatively, the maximum of all paths could be taken as trust rating for the target. An aggregation, however, is problematic if the trust values computed via the different paths are contradictory, for instance, a full trust rating and a distrust rating, both by persons whom the source highly trusts. In this case, it might be more appropriate to give a degree of controversy.

Examples for Local Trust Metrics

Over the last few years, a number of trust propagation mechanisms have been developed. They have a different mathematical or physical background, ranging from graph theory with its path algebraic approaches (e.g. the work by Golbeck summarized below, Beth et al. (1994)), matrix operations (e.g. the metric by Guha et al. (2004) presented in the following) to probabilistic interpretations such as random surfer models (e.g. Richardson et al., 2003) and spreading activation strategies (e.g. Ziegler and Lausen, 2004b). I present two metrics. Firstly, a path algebraic trust metric is discussed because path-based approaches are intuitive and widely used. Secondly, a metric for distrust is presented. It operates directly on the matrices.

Trust metrics should be validated in a cross-validation using data from real trust networks (or at least generated trust networks). That means that some of the actual trust statements are removed in the data set which serves as input for the trust metric. These missing links are then predicted by the trust metric and compared with the original values. It is difficult to directly compare trust metrics because they differ in the allowed input, and hence in the data sets used: some of them only permit binary values, others only positive trust values and again others include distrust. Moreover, the output is often different: some metrics infer trust between users, other metrics only rank users according to their trustworthiness.

A Path Algebraic Trust Metric: TidalTrust Golbeck developed a set of path algebraic trust metrics. A trust value $t_{i \to s}$ is computed for the source i to an indirectly connected sink s by analyzing the paths from i via its direct neighbors j to s. In Golbeck *et al.* (2003), $t_{i \to s}$ is defined for positive values as:

$$t_{i \to s} = \frac{\sum_{j=0}^{n} \left\{ \begin{array}{ll} (t_{j \to s} t_{i \to j}) & \text{if } t_{i \to j} \geq t_{j \to s} \\ (t_{i \to j}^2) & \text{if } t_{i \to j} < t_{j \to s} \end{array} \right\}}{\sum_{j=0}^{n} t_{i \to j}}$$

The trust value t_{is} is computed by a recursive algorithm which considers the maximum capacity of each path to the target: it thus corresponds at most to the smallest trust value (i.e. the smallest edge weight) along the path between i and s. The function takes the weighted average of all paths from i to s, regardless of their length. The weighted average gives more weight to the trust values provided by nodes that the source highly trusts. Golbeck and Hendler (2004) take the simple average of all considered paths. This, however, is problematic because a lowly trusted node can significantly influence the trust values that are inferred for other nodes. Figure 3.3 illustrates this. To an existing network with the nodes u_1, u_2, u_3 and u_4, a new path is added between u_1 and u_3 via u_5. Although u_5 is not trusted by u_1, its trust in u_3 significantly decreases $t_{u_1 \to u_3}$: from 1 to 0.7.

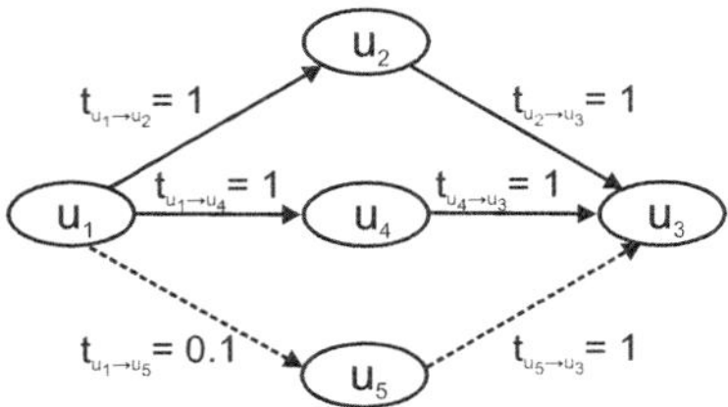

Figure 3.3: New Link with Low Trust

TidalTrust (Golbeck, 2005) differs from the weighted average function in the sense that only the shortest path(s) (there could be several paths with the same shortest length) are considered. The shortest paths are taken because some nodes might not be reachable at the fixed length. An alternative is to use only those trust ratings that are provided by the most trusted neighbors, i.e., those neighbors $j \in adj(i)$ of source i. Here, a threshold is calculated in each trust computation, and only paths with trust above this threshold influence the final trust value. TidalTrust is defined as:

$$t_{i \to s} = \frac{\displaystyle\sum_{j \in adj(i)} t_{i \to j} t_{j \to s}}{\displaystyle\sum_{j \in adj(i)} t_{i \to j}}$$

From these three functions, TidalTrust provides the best results on trust data from the TrustProject and FilmTrust, and this also applies in comparison with the trust metric by Beth *et al.* (1994). Interestingly, the weighted average does not outperform the simple average. According to Golbeck, this result could be due to the small size of the network, or because the weighting is too weak. Golbeck suggests adapting and fine-tuning TidalTrust depending on the characteristics of the particular network.

Limiting the trust propagation to users at a certain distance seems to be very successful. Avesani *et al.* (2005) take with MoleTrust a similar approach as TidalTrust. They identify in a first step all users who are reachable from the source in the maximum of n steps. This destroys cycles in the network and provides an efficient computation of trust predictions because each node is walked on only once (instead of several times until convergence). The trust propagation horizon n defines the distance to which trust values are propagated. Avesani *et al.* set $n = 3$. In the second step, the indirect trust is computed for all users identified in the first step. They also use the weighted average such as TidalTrust. However, only the trust statements by users to whom the source has a rating greater than 0.6 (with trust in [0,1]) are taken.

Trust and Distrust Metrics The trust metric proposed by Guha *et al.* (2004) combines a basis set of atomic trust propagations. There are the matrices T for the trust ratings and D for the distrust ratings ratings in $[0, 1]$. All atomic propagations are operations on a matrix B containing the 'beliefs' of the users, represented by T and/or D. The atomic trust propagations are:

- Direct Propagation: trust is propagated along an edge. If a user i trusts a user j who trusts a user k, then i also trusts k. The direct propagation means as matrix operation that the new matrix contains all paths with the length 2 of the initial belief graph, i.e., B^2.

- Co-Citation: a user trusts those users who are trusted by users providing similar trust ratings as him- or herself. If user i_1 trusts users j_1 and j_2, and user i_2 trusts user j_1, too, then user i_2 will also trust j_2. The matrix operation is $B^T B$.

- Transpose Trust: if a user i trusts a user j, then j will start to trust i to some extent, represented in the belief matrix by B^T.

- Trust Coupling: user i's trust of j propagates to user k when j and k trust the same people. The matrix operation is BB^T.

These four atomic propagations are combined. The weight of each element is set in a vector $\alpha = (\alpha_1, \alpha_2, \alpha_3, \alpha_4)$. The resulting matrix $C_{B,\alpha}$ contains the trust values between all users:

$$C_{B,\alpha} = \alpha_1 B + \alpha_2 B^T B + \alpha_3 B^T + \alpha_4 BB^T$$

Distrust can be handled in different ways. Firstly, only positive trust values are considered and distrust is not taken into account at all. Secondly, trust ratings by someone who is distrusted are not considered in the computations. Thirdly, trust and distrust are propagated together. The trust metric was cross-validated with data from Epinions. The atomic propagations were combined with varying weights. Best results were obtained by the one-step distrust propagation with direct propagation and co-citation having the most, and transpose trust and trust coupling having only little influence on the result. The path length was limited to a few iterations.

3.1.6 Interorganizational Trust Networks

In the last few years, much research has dealt with interorganizational trust as a specific type of relationship that holds between organizations (e.g. Lane and Bachmann, 1998; McEvily *et al.*, 2003; Bachmann *et al.*, 2001). Trust is considered to be an important means of coordinating business behavior. Bachmann (2003) considers economic theory as economic exchanges between social actors and aims at integrating sociological concepts into economic theory. He claims that trust and power play an essential role in interorganizational relationships. Interorganizational networks, in the following *organization networks*, are intensively studied due to their important role in economy and society. Castells (1996) demonstrates in his book on the network society that networks have been dominant within recent decades and continue to be so in our present era.

Definition 3 *An interorganizational trust network is a graph $\mathcal{O} = (O, I)$ with a set O of organizations and a set $I \subseteq O \times O$ of directed and weighted edges between organizations. Edge weights $t_{o_i \to o_j}$ on the interorganizational edges represent the degree of trust that an organization o_i has in an organization o_j.*

An Organization Network for the Multi-Layer Architecture

We can add to a multi-layer network an organization trust network. The nodes of this network may be companies, universities, institutions, departments or project teams. In a concrete setting for a certain recommendation task, we have to agree upon the specific level of abstraction, i.e., whether whole companies (or universities and research institutions) are considered or whether a finer granular level is better suited, i.e., to have departments, project teams or research groups as nodes in the network. This depends on the type analysis aimed at. If, for instance, a researcher's credibility should be derived from the granting organizations that funded the research and the university in which he or she conducted the research, it will be more appropriate to have universities and funding organizations as nodes than project teams.

Interorganizational Trust

The trust values $t_{o_i \to o_j}$ between organizations are in $[-1, 1]$, ranging from distrust to full trust. If no trust information is available, relationships of the type "cooperates-with" and "competes-with" can be modeled between organizations. The edges between the organizations would be again directed and weighted. Consider, for instance, two organizations o_1 and o_2 with o_1 being a small company and o_2 being a big company. While o_1 might consider o_2 as a very important interaction partner and give much weight to the cooperates-with relationship with such a big company (which is quite fair from o_1's perspective), the inverse will likely not hold. From o_2's perspective, o_1 might be just one of many small cooperation partners who can easily be replaced. So the organization network has weighted cooperates-with edges $c_{o_i \to o_j}$ between the organizations o_i and o_j. A competes-with relationship is then a cooperates-with relationship with a negative weight. We have thus $c_{o_i \to o_j} \in [-1, 1]$ with -1 characterizing a highly competitive relationship and +1 a highly cooperative relationship.

Trusting another organization clearly differs from cooperating with it. A cooperation can take place without trust. Its good outcome can be ensured by contracts such as service level agreements. Trust is a much stronger relationship between organizations. Some forms of cooperation between organizations are not even possible without trust because they involve tasks which cannot simply be regulated in contracts, but rather demand alternative control mechanisms (Sydow, 1998). Trust particularly facilitates those tasks that require the sharing of highly sensitive information (e.g. Lane, 1998).

Interorganizational trust differs from interpersonal trust as it is not only a matter of individual personality (Lane, 1998). A trust relationship between organizations is often the result of hard work on the part of those members of the organizations who are responsible for the contact and the relationship between both organizations

(Sydow, 1998). This might lead to an enhanced trust between these persons, which in turn might stabilize the business relationship. However, this does not mean that trust relationships between the members of organizations can be derived from the interorganizational trust relationships or vice versa. (Bachmann, 2003, p.9) notes that "familiarity at the level of personal contacts cannot be expected to be the sole basis of building trust among economic actors" and claims that institutional-based trust plays an important role in interorganizational trust relationships. This means that the trust relationships are based on a set of institutionalized social rules and behavior to which the actors in the organizations tend to comply. The more regulated the present institutionalized framework (e.g. by governmental policies and contract law), the more the trust relationships will be institutional-based. In contrast, in weakly regulated settings, the interpersonal aspect will be more dominant (Bachmann, 2003).

Measures of Trust and Reputation for Organizations

Based on the cooperates-with or the trust relationships between the organizations, the global authority of an organization can be measured. In social network analysis, a number of measures exist for authority – also known as centrality – that can be applied to organization networks (for a more detailed overview on these measures see section 3.1.4). A well-known measure is the degree centrality. Measuring the degree centrality of organizations means to consider as central such organizations that have many incoming and/or outgoing links. The findings by Powell *et al.* (1996) support the idea that an organization's integration in an organizational network is related to its success and hence to its authority: they claim that the number and the intensity of the alliances in a certain sector influence the intensity of research and development activities and hence the technological know-how. Centrality measures from social network analysis do not normally consider edge weights. Therefore, it is more appropriate to compute them on a subset of the organization network with either positive cooperates-with edges or positive trust edges. Taking into account only competes-with edges (i.e. $c_{o_i \to o_j} \leq 0$) would give a different type of centrality.

Apart from the measures used in social network analysis, measures in the style of PageRank can also be applied to organization networks in order to determine an organization's authority. This would mean that any one organization that cooperates with many other important organizations would have a high authority or reputation. An example taken from the academic world illustrates this: a research institute that has many collaboration partners with a high reputation typically has a fairly high reputation, too, because these collaborations demonstrate that it is well embedded in the research community. Technically, PageRank should be computed only on the basis of the positive interorganizational relationships (i.e. $c_{o_i \to o_j} > 0$, or $t_{o_i \to o_j} > 0$, respectively). An extension of PageRank that uses weighted edges could be used, too.

Regardless of which measure is used to derive the importance of an organization from the network structure, we assume in the following chapters to be able to compute for each organization o_i its organization authority (reputation) $rep^o_{o_i}$.

As the edges in the organization network are weighted, the question arises on whether a propagation of these values is possible, analogous to the propagation in the trust network. A propagation is only sensible when the relationship at issue is transitive. This is not the case for the cooperates-with relationship: given the information that only organization o_1 cooperates with organization o_2, and o_2 cooperates with o_3, it cannot be inferred that o_1 cooperates with o_3. Interorganizational trust can be propagated to a limited extent by metrics in the style of trust metrics (see section 3.1.5). In triadic relationships, this might still work. For instance, in a business project in which some new software application is developed, an enterprise may recommend its cooperation partner as a company that is capable of fulfilling some specific task within this project, e.g. to provide the design of the application. This corresponds to a recommendation via two steps: organizations o_1 and o_2 have direct, positive trust relationships $t_{o_1 \rightarrow o_2}$ and $t_{o_2 \rightarrow o_1}$ and organization o_2 is connected with o_3 by $t_{o_2 \rightarrow o_3}$. A new trust relationship might be $t_{o_1 \rightarrow o_3} = t_{o_1 \rightarrow o_2} \circ t_{o_2 \rightarrow o_3}$.

3.2 Document Reference Networks

3.2.1 A Survey of Document Reference Networks

Many documents are publicly available such as webpages, wikis, blogs, newsgroup discussions and scientific publications. The corresponding document reference networks can easily be established because references such as hyperlinks or citations are directly embedded in the documents.

Definition 4 *A document reference network is a directed graph* $\mathcal{D} = (D, C)$ *with a set D of documents and a set of directed, unweighted citations $C \subseteq D \times D$ between documents.*

The references between documents represent a rich source of information because their analysis does not require looking at the textual content. They can be analyzed regardless of the language in which the document is written. With the web, a large dataset became available for data mining. Applying data mining methods to webpages and developing new approaches that are especially suited for web data has led to a new research area called *web mining* (Etzioni, 1996). Web mining is often categorized in three areas: web content mining, web usage mining and web structure mining (see e.g. Kosala and Blockeel, 2000). *Web structure mining* deals with the analysis of the link structure of the web and is hence also known as link analysis or link mining. Structure mining also applies and further develops methods from social network analysis and citation analysis. Getoor and Diehl (2005) give an overview on link mining tasks. A major task is link-based object ranking, which uses the link structure in order to rank a set of objects. Besides other tasks, they mention link-based classification, which aims at predicting the category of an object based on its incoming and outgoing links and the properties of the linked objects. *Web content mining*, on its part, is interested in the content of webpages, for example, the textual content. *Usage mining* focuses on the users' behavior, for instance, by analyzing click histories.

3.2.2 Properties of Document Reference Networks

Reference Structure Analysis

Document reference networks such as the web show the small world effect (see e.g. Barabási, 2001) which has already been discussed in the context of the properties of trust networks. The distribution of the references in document networks follows a power law, too, such as the link distribution in social networks. So old documents that are already frequently cited attract more and more citations from new documents. Barabási and Albert (1999) demonstrated the scale free distribution of hypertext degree. This distribution arises due to the growth of the network. In the web, new webpages are linked to existing ones by preferential attachment. Menczer (2002) developed a web growth model which describes how authors link their webpages to pages that are both textually similar and popular. According to this generative model, in each step t, a new page p_t is added and m links are set from this page. A page p_i is selected as target for a link with probability $Prob(p_i, t)$. Depending on the lexical distance $r(p_i, p_t)$ between p_i and p_t, this probability is calculated in a different way. With $k(i)$ being the in-degree of p_i, $\rho*$ being a lexical distance threshold and α and c_1 being constants, the probability is defined as:

$$Prob(p_i, t) = \begin{cases} \frac{k(i)}{m} & \text{if } r(p_i, p_t) < \rho*, \\ c_1 r^{-\alpha}(p_i, p_t) & \text{otherwise.} \end{cases}$$

If p_i and p_t are highly similar, the probability is thus independent from the lexical distance. If the similarity is below a fixed threshold, the probability is calculated on the basis of the similarity of p_i and p_t. The probability of a link decreases with decreasing similarity of the pages.

Börner *et al.* (2004) analyzed the simultaneous growth of coauthor and paper citation networks. Their growth model, called TARL model, considers in the growth process the aspects of topics, aging and recursive linking. The basic architecture encompasses a coauthor network and a network of scientific papers. Persons are linked via coauthor relationships; the number of coauthored paper defines the strength of the relationship. Authors are connected with the papers they have written and with the papers they have read. Papers are coauthored by authors working on the same topic and are, consequently, about the topic in which their authors are experts. Börner *et al.* simulate the simultaneous growth of both networks with the TARL model. In each iteration, new authors are generated who produce papers. Papers are coauthored by a randomly selected set of authors. Authors read a number of randomly selected papers (no visibility function is used to select these papers) and cite some of them. Authors may also cite such papers that are cited in the papers that they have read. References are thus followed a limited number of steps – here, the recursive linking comes into play. The aging factor further restricts the set of papers that can be cited, e.g. in the sense that recently published papers are favored. As the citations in the papers read by the authors are followed up, a paper that is often cited has a higher probability of being further cited by a newly generated paper. The TARL model was validated against a set of articles published in PNAS in a 20-year period.

Cyclic or Acyclic Structure

Reference structures are cyclic or acyclic. This is closely related to the temporal ordering of the documents. Citation networks and discussion groups are mostly acyclic – papers are published at a distinct date and citations go back in time. There are only few cyclic references between scientific papers, e.g., when two papers are published at the same conference or in the same journal. Newsgroups are not in the strictest sense true document networks because each message thread is a tree: each thread consists of one initial posting and replies. Webpages, wikis and blogs have a cyclic reference structure. In contrast to scientific publications, they can be updated at any time with new hyperlinks. Although the individual postings in blogs are presented in chronological order, references between entire blogs can clearly be acyclic.

3.2.3 Reference-based Visibility Measures

The reference structure of the document reference network gives a hint on the prominence of the documents, i.e., on their (social) visibility (Malsch and Schlieder, 2002). Visibility refers to the accessibility of a document and how likely it will attract new links, citations or reply messages. The intuition behind reference-based visibility measures, in the following visibility measures, is that the importance of a document can be determined by looking at the documents that cite it: a document that is cited by many other documents must be somehow important, otherwise it would not be cited so often. The analysis of citation networks is one of the major research areas in bibliometry and scientometry. Citation analysis is made on the level of papers or of whole journals. Osareh (1996a and 1996b) gives a detailed overview on citation and co-citation analysis. In the following, I present well-known reference-based measures for the visibility of a document.

Impact Factor

One of the first and still widely used referenced based visibility measures on scientific publications is the *impact factor* (Garfield, 1972). The impact factor IF (for a two-year time span) of a journal j is for a certain year y:

$$ \mathrm{IF}_j = \frac{\text{number of citation in } y \text{ to articles in } j \text{ during } (y-1) + (y-2)}{\text{number of articles in } j \text{ during } (y-1) + (y-2)} $$

PageRank and its Extensions

As most visibility measures have been developed for ranking search engine results, it is useful to look at how document rankings are generated on the basis of user queries. There are two tasks: (i) selecting those documents that match the search terms given in the user query with regard to their content and (ii) ranking the documents according to their importance. The selection of the documents is made using methods from information retrieval. The ranking is very important because users mostly look only at the highest ranked documents. The order in which both tasks are executed may differ. On the one hand, there are approaches that compute all document visibilities offline. Answering a user query, the documents matching the search terms are presented in the order of their precomputed rank. PageRank by Page *et al.* (1998) is the best known representative of these query-independent measures. On the other hand, there are approaches that select the matching documents at query time and compute then the ranking on this subset of the document network. The best-known query-dependent ranking measure is HITS by Kleinberg (1999). We discuss in the following both PageRank and HITS as well as some more specialized visibility measures.

PageRank   PageRank is based on a visibility measure developed by Pinski and Narin (1976) already in 1976. Pinski and Narin proposed a recursive evaluation of the importance of journals: a paper (or a journal, respectively) is the more visible the more it is cited by significant papers (or journals). The visibility of a document depends not only on the number of incoming links, but also on the importance of the citing papers. Pinski and Narin calculate the visibility (rank) vis_{j_d} of a scientific journal j_d by using the weighted sum of the ranks vis_{j_k} of the journals j_k with papers citing papers in j_d. PageRank slightly adapts this approach to the visibility calculation of webpages. It was originally incorporated in the search engine Google. PageRank defines the visibility vis_{p_d} of a webpage p_d as:

$$\text{vis}_{p_d}^{\text{PR}} = (1 - \alpha) + \alpha \sum_{p_k \in P_{p_d}} \frac{\text{vis}_{p_k}^{\text{PR}}}{|C_{p_k}|}$$

with P_{p_d} being the set of pages citing p_d, and C_{p_k} being the set of pages cited by p_k. The visibility $\text{vis}_{p_d}^{\text{PR}}$ of any document p_d is the combination of a basic visibility $(1 - \alpha)$ given to each page[20] and of a variable part which depends on the visibility of the documents citing it and which contributes with α.

The PageRank definition is based on the idea of a random surfer: a user starts on an arbitrary webpage, follows some link to another page, follows a link from this page to a third one, and so on. The probability that the random surfer gets to a certain page depends on the number of links going to this page and on the visibilities of the referencing pages. PageRank can be formulated as a random walk on graphs: the random surfer starts at some webpage p_a. With probability α, the random surfer clicks on one of C_{p_a} outgoing links of p_a, while with probability $(1 - \alpha)$ he or she stops following links and jumps randomly to some other page. A page p_d can thus be reached by a direct jump with probability $(1 - \alpha)$ or by coming from one of the pages $p_k \in P_{p_d}$, where the probability to be on p_k is $\text{vis}_{p_k}^{\text{PR}}$.

Measuring document visibilities with PageRank gives for n pages a linear system of n equations. As solving this equation system is (for large n) expensive, an iterative approach is used: in a first step all $\text{vis}_{p_i}^{\text{PR}}$ are set to some default value and then the new values are computed repeatedly until all $\text{vis}_{p_i}^{\text{PR}}$ converge[21]. Several approaches have been developed in order to make efficient PageRank computations on large document reference networks (see e.g. Haveliwala, 1999; Kamvar *et al.*, 2003).

Age PageRank PageRank is designed for the cyclic link structure of the web. Document networks which exhibit a mainly acyclic reference structure need other visibility measures such as those discussed in Malsch *et al.* (2007). In these measures, the creation time of a document is much more important because scientific papers or postings are in general not modified after publishing. Such visibility measures therefore consider the aging of documents, i.e., documents will lose visibility the older they are. In

---

[20]With $\alpha \in [0, 1]$. Page *et al.* (1998) set α in general to 0.85. With this, the minimal visibility given to each pages would be $(1 - \alpha) = 0.15$.

[21]For a discussion of convergence problems in leaves see Page *et al.* (1998).

Comte, the simulation environment used for the evaluation in chapter 8, Age PageRank $\mathrm{vis}_{p_d}^{\mathrm{APR}}$ of a document p_d is defined as:

$$\mathrm{vis}_{p_d}^{\mathrm{APR}} = \frac{(1-\alpha) + \alpha \cdot \sum_{p_k \in P_{p_d}} \frac{\mathrm{vis}_{p_k}^{\mathrm{APR}}}{|C_{p_k}|}}{a_{p_d}^n}$$

with α, P_{p_d} and C_{p_k} as above and a_{p_d} being the age of document p_d and n being an aging factor. With an aging factor $n = 1$, for instance, recent documents have a higher visibility than old ones. The aging is speeded up by using an aging factor $n \geq 1$.

TrustRank TrustRank (Gyöngyi *et al.*, 2004) extends the original PageRank. It identifies spam pages semi-automatically by using a small seed set of pages rated by experts. TrustRank is a type of biased PageRank as it uses instead of a static score for the basic visibility that is given to each page (the $1 - \alpha$ in the above PageRank definition) a non-zero static score for those pages that were rated by the experts as non-spam. In the first step, a small seed set of webpages is selected. In a second step, human experts classify these seed pages as good pages (no spam) or bad pages (spam). Gyöngyi *et al.* call this indicator for the spam-status "trust score". It should not be confused with social trust, it only refers to the review that human experts give to a page and has nothing to do with trust in the expert's capabilities to make an appropriate classification into good and bad pages. TrustRank determines in the third step further webpages that are likely to be good. Moreover all pages that can be reached from good seed pages in at maximum m steps are also good. The trust score that is propagated with the biased PageRank along the links is reduced with increasing path length because it is not certain that all pages reachable from the good seed pages are indeed good. This is achieved either by dampening the propagated value or by splitting the amount of trust that is distributed among the outgoing links. This results in a score for all[22] pages. The resulting rank is not personalized although the term "trust" in the name 'TrustRank' might suggest this.

Wu *et al.* (2006) extended the TrustRank approach by a distrust propagation for identifying spam pages. This means that a trust and a distrust score is computed for each webpage which are combined for the final ranking. The distrust score determines potential spam pages based on the set of seed pages classified as bad. Distrust is propagated from the bad seed pages back to its predecessors in order to penalize pages that link to spam. For the back-propagation, a measure in the style of TrustRank is applied to the reverse transition matrix of the pages and their hyperlinks.

---

[22]Unreferenced good pages which are not in the seed set, however, obtain a score of 0.

HITS: Hubs & Authorities

Kleinberg (1999) introduced an alternative approach for measuring the authority of a document based on the reference structure. He separates documents (in his case webpages) into hubs and authorities. Hubs are pages linking to many relevant authoritative pages (e.g. link lists for certain topics). Authorities are pages that are referenced by many hubs. This approach is also known as HITS, the hypertext induced topic selection (Gibson *et al.*, 1998). The hub value h_{p_d} and the authority value a_{p_d} of a page p_d are computed as follows:

$$ h_{p_d} = \delta \sum_{p_k \in C_{p_d}} a_{p_k}, \qquad a_{p_d} = \gamma \sum_{p_l \in P_{p_d}} h_{p_l} $$

with P_{p_d} and C_{p_d} defined as for PageRank. The computation of the hub and authority values starts with default values for all documents p_i, namely $a_{p_i} = 1$ and $h_{p_i} = 1$. In an alternating way, the hub and authority values are updated in several iterations. A page p_d has a high hub value h_{p_d} if it points to many pages with a high authority value a_{p_d}. In other words: a good hub knows the important pages. The other way round, p_{p_d} has a high authority value a_{p_d}, if it is pointed to by many good hubs; i.e., it is listed in the important link lists. While the authority a_{p_d} provides the visibility of the document p_d, the hub value h_{p_d} is only an auxiliary value.

As HITS is query-dependent, it differs from PageRank not only in the equations used, but also in the set of pages used. PageRank computes the visibility offline on all pages in the document reference network and selects at query time from the matching pages the pages with the highest rank. In contrast, HITS determines in the first step a subset of all documents from which the most authoritative pages are selected by applying the above described formula. This subset is composed by pages that contain the query term (e.g. the highest ranked pages for this query term identified by some text-based search engine), the so called root set, and by all pages referenced by at least one page out of the root set or referencing a page in the root set. As the subset depends on the search query, hub and authority values have to be computed at query time. Calculating these values may be quite time consuming as a single search term can have up to some million matching webpages, even if there are strategies for pre-calculation.

Despite the enormous computation load at query time, query-dependent measures have the advantage over query-independent approaches in that they are able to highly rank webpages that are not necessarily authoritative in general but authoritative on the specific query topic. Different ranking approaches have been developed to adapt the ranking on the search terms given by the user. An example is *Hilltop* by Bharat and Mihaila (2001) which identifies the most authoritative pages for popular topics. When answering a query, so-called "expert documents" are identified in a first step. These are webpages that provide many links to non-affiliated pages on the query topic.

Non-affiliated pages are written by authors from non-affiliated organizations. This is determined, for example, by comparing URLs and IP-addresses. Expert pages are thus in a way directories of links. In the second step, relevant links within the set of expert pages are followed. The ranks of the referenced pages are then computed based on the number and the relevance of the expert pages that link to them. The ranking is done at query time and is specific for the query topics. However, if no experts are found for the query topics, Hilltop provides no results. Bharat and Mihaila argue that Hilltop focuses on result accuracy instead of coverage.

Visibility measures can take into account further criteria as discussed in Malsch *et al.*. For instance, the number of outgoing references that are set within a paper can be considered (instead of the number of citations, the visibility of each of the cited papers can be used, too). Although this criterion is not obvious, it has a certain importance because digital libraries (e.g. Citeseer) often display all the papers citing the paper at issue. The more important a cited paper is, the more often the paper citing it will be presented. Furthermore, the number of readers of a document influences its visibility.

3.2.4 Personalization of Document Rankings

The above presented visibility measures do not personalize the document ranking. Personalization may range from simply allowing the user to select the language in which the documents have to be written to more sophisticated approaches which consider information that is additional to the query terms. External information on the user encompasses the user's profile and preferences (query-independent or specified at query time) and the user's browsing history, bookmarks or email archive. The context of a query provides additional information, too. For example, the terms that the user used in previous queries might give a hint on the user's current information need. This information can be used for selecting matching documents as well as for the ranking of the selected documents. The personalized PageRank and the topic-sensitive PageRank, which both extend PageRank, are two approaches to personalizing reference-based visibilities.

Personalized PageRank

PageRank can be personalized based on a set of pages that a user initially declares as interesting. The uniform distribution used for the basic, minimal visibility of a page $(1 - \alpha)$ is replaced with a user-specific value. A high weight could be given to a user's personal homepage and to bookmarks. This is in line with the intuition that the random surfer sometimes gets bored by just following the links and jumps to a random page chosen based on its basic visibility: a user is more likely to jump to the pages listed in her or his bookmarks than to any other page on the web. This approach to personalizing PageRank was proposed by Page *et al.* (1998) (who developed PageRank) even though they did not describe its computation. The difficulty when implementing this personalization is that it is not feasible to pre-compute and store all personalized page ranks offline. Vice versa, it would require too much time to compute them at query time because the ranks are calculated for all webpages in an iterative approach. Jeh and Widom (2003) discuss an efficient computation of personalized views with this biased PageRank.

Compared with PageRank, the personalized PageRank increases the rank of pages that are referenced by the initially interesting pages. However, as they can be directly reached from the pages the user knows, the user might get stuck in already known pages. We therefore propose in chapter 4 a personalization strategy that avoids this drawback by considering within the recommendation process the preferences of friends, or indeed the friends of friends.

Topic-sensitive PageRank

The topic-sensitive PageRank by Haveliwala (2002) performs a query-dependent, personalized ranking. It considers information such as the query context or the user context. To reduce the computation load at query time, the reference-based computations are made offline, and at query-time, precalculated ranks are combined depending on the query terms and the context. Concretely, 16 topic-sensitive PageRank vectors (i.e. vectors with a rank computed for each page) are calculated offline, based on the 16 main topics of the Open Directory Project[23]. At query time, the similarity of the query (encompassing the terms typed in by the user, the query context and the user context) to each of the 16 topics is measured. The documents matching the query are then ranked by combining the 16 topic-sensitive vectors, weighted according to the similarity between its topic and the query. Thus the personalization does not take place when computing the PageRank vectors, as the personalized PageRank does it, but is achieved by a query-specific combination of topic-sensitive PageRank vectors. In contrast to Hilltop, the topic-sensitive PageRank is not restricted to popular topics.

3.2.5 Link Semantics

Hyperlinks and citations are explicitly set by authors. The authors' intentions for setting a reference are typically encoded in the link text and its context. For instance,

---

[23]`http://dmoz.org/`

the author of a scientific paper might cite another paper because he or she considers it as useful and supports the work. However, the author might also disagree with the cited paper and might want to give an opposite point of view. A link can hence be confirming, criticizing or referential. Human readers can distinguish this based on the text surrounding the reference. For computers, in contrast, it is hard to differentiate the semantics of the link. Although considerable progress has been made in the area of Natural Language Processing (NLP) on identifying expressions of opinion and the strength of the opinion (see e.g. Wilson *et al.*, 2006), these systems have to deal with the enormous creativity that users show in expressing their opinions (Breck *et al.*, 2007). This makes assessing the semantics of a link difficult. Reference-based visibility measures therefore ignore the authors' expressed intentions: each reference contributes in the same way to the visibility of the referenced page regardless of why it is set. So each reference is considered as a positive endorsement of the content of the referenced document even though in reality, this might not be true. Therefore web authors rarely set links of disagreement; they know that this link would increase the rank of the disliked page which is clearly not their intention. However, as Massa and Hayes (2005) showed in some experiments comparing PageRank on a network with weighted and non-weighted edges, it would be beneficial to consider the link semantics.

For HTML, several approaches were proposed that assign semantics to the links in a machine-readable form directly in the link tag. Based on this explicit link semantics, references between documents can be weighted. Google proposed using the attribute rel="nofollow" in hyperlinks[24] in order to specify that this link should be ignored by reference-based measures. This approach is supported, for example, by Google, MSN Search and Yahoo!. In blogs, "nofollow" is often automatically added to a link by the blog software in order to prevent spammers from abusing the blog by setting a huge number of links to their spam pages. This certainly applies to other webpages where users can add links such as guestbooks or wikis, too. VoteLinks[25] is a more sophisticated approach to incorporate link semantics. It defines three values for the *rev* attribute of the HTML link tag: vote-for, vote-abstain and vote-against. Another example is XFN (Xhtml friends network)[26] which aims at representing the relationships to other people on the Web such as friend, colleague or neighbor. They are again indicated in the *rel* attribute of a hyperlink. Apart from "nofollow", which is officially supported by the most influential search engines, these other refinements in the hyperlink tag are neither really adopted by webauthors nor exploited by search engines. Modified link tags offer a new possibility to inflate rankings: someone having a high rank could misuse this influence and set "vote-against"-links to competitors and

---

[24]See on `http://googleblog.blogspot.com/2005/01/preventing-comment-spam.html` the information provided by Google and the specification on `http://microformats.org/wiki/rel-nofollow`.

[25]For the specification see `http://microformats.org/wiki/vote-links.`, retrieved on May 14, 2007.

[26]For the Xhtml Friends Network see `http://www.gmpg.org/xfn/`, retrieved on May 14, 2007.

decrease intentionally their rank (this problem has also been remarked by Massa and Hayes (2005)). We therefore look at whether external information can be used to enhance the link semantics. In chapter 4, we propose an approach to give link semantics based on a social network between the authors of documents.

3.2.6 Duplicates in Document Networks

Duplicates and Near Duplicates

Document repositories may contain duplicates and near-duplicates, i.e., documents that are completely or almost identical. Repositories of scholarly publications often encompass different versions of a paper, for example, a pre-print and print, or a conference paper and its journal version (e.g. as selected paper of the conference track). There can also be erroneous copies of a document. Such errors happen if the check on the identity fails for identical documents, for instance, when a new document is inserted in the repository or when two heterogeneous document collections are merged. Erroneous copies only slightly differ. For example, in the title of a scientific publication, ':' may be replaced by '-', or the first names of the authors are abbreviated in one duplicate and complete in the other duplicate.

The problem of duplicates can be seen at the search interface of CiteSeer (Giles et al., 1998), (Lawrence et al., 1999a) although there is some duplicate detection mechanism applied (Lawrence et al., 1999b). Lee et al. (2006) looked at the results obtained by querying CiteSeer via its search interface for the book "Artificial Intelligence: A Modern Approach" by S. Russell and P. Norvig with the query "Russell and Norvig". The result set contained 23 distinct references of the book, all of them slightly different. When using the publicly available metadata by CiteSeer[27] the problem of duplicates becomes even more evident. The metadata encompasses the bibliographic data of around 700,000 documents. A simple database query that filters out documents with an identical title decreases the number of documents by almost 30%. By using a more comprehensive duplicate detection mechanism, not only the exact correspondences could be filtered but also documents that are almost identical.

The web also contains a huge number of duplicated pages. The fraction of duplicates was estimated by Broder et al. (1997) and Shivakumar and Garcia-Molina (1998) at 30 to 45 %. Duplicates may be legitimate, such as mirrors, but also be malicious copies by spammers, or crawling errors. User manuals, software documentation, or tutorials such as Java or C++ tutorials are often provided by different mirrors. These legitimate copies of websites are often not completely identical. Mirrored websites differ with

---

[27]The CiteSeer metadata is publicly available at `http://citeseer.ist.psu.edu/oai.html`.

respect to their content, the links structure or images included because updates of the original website are often not directly propagated to the mirrors but the mirrors are updated on a regular basis, e.g., daily, weekly or even only monthly (Cho *et al.*, 2000). Moreover, there can be differences in the format between the pages of the original website and the mirrors because documents can be provided, for example, as html, pdf or postscript.

Duplicates produce additional costs for crawling, storing and indexing. They negatively affect the usability of a document recommender system because users do not want to get the same documents over and over again in the result list to a query . Moreover, duplicates negatively affect the ranking by reference-based visibility measures as discussed in section 2.1.5. This is to say that the reference-based visibilities computed on a document collection that contains unrecognized duplicates may be too high or too low. Duplicates also represent a problem for other measures of importance. For example, an author's impact, which is computed on the basis of the papers written by her or him, would be erroneous if the different names under which he or she published the papers – full first and last name, or first name abbreviated etc. – were not consolidated. The author's impact would be split among the duplicates because each of them would have some papers attributed. Lee *et al.* (2006) gives an example from the ACM digital library where the entry for the author "Jeffrey D. Ullman" with the papers written by him, is split into 10 different author entries because of the different spellings, e.g. "Ullman" and "Ullmann". When measuring such author's impact, the citations in which the name is misspelled should clearly be considered, too. It is therefore necessary to apply duplicate detection mechanisms before working with documents crawled from the web or from heterogeneous digital document repositories.

Duplicate Detection

Duplicate detection mechanisms use the different components of digital documents in order to identify duplicates. Often, the textual parts are compared, i.e., the metadata of documents, such as titles or author names, and the text bodies. The edit distance measures the distance between two strings, i.e., it indicates the number of operations necessary to transform a string into another one (depending on the concrete measure, operations are insert, delete and move).

A more efficient approach than the edit distance is to compare the fingerprints of documents. Fingerprints are computed based on the content or the features. Broder (2000) approximates the resemblance of documents by comparing fixed size "sketches". The sketch of a document consists basically of a set of fingerprints of shingles. Shingles are continuous subsequences of n tokens contained in a document p_d. Tokens may be letters, words, lines or even complete sentences. These shingles may omit punctuation or neglect upper and lower case. Shingles on words are also called q-grams. These shingles are then fingerprinted. So the fingerprints are short tags for the shingles. Broder computes the fingerprints with the method by Rabin (1981). Such fingerprints have the properties that, firstly, if the fingerprints of two objects are different, then the objects are actually different, and secondly, the probability that identical objects have the same fingerprint decreases exponentially with the length of the fingerprint. The resemblance $r(p_a, p_b)$ of two documents p_a and p_b is then computed by intersecting their sets of fingerprints S_{p_a} and S_{p_b}.

$$r(p_a, p_b) = \frac{|S_{p_a} \cap S_{p_b}|}{|S_{p_a} \cup S_{p_b}|}$$

Two documents will be associated in a cluster if their resemblance is above a certain threshold. In order to further reduce the computation load, a sketch can be computed for each document on the basis of the fingerprints. The similarity of two documents is thus computed on the basis of statistical information on the content.

Apart from comparing the textual content of documents, identity between objects can be defined on the basis of the link structure in which the objects are embedded (including the attributes of the neighboring objects). If a document is structured, e.g. an XML document, the clustering technique can make use of this structure. The approach presented by de Rougemont and Vieilleribière (2007) for measuring the distance between the schema of a document and a target schema can also be applied to clustering. The distance between two (XML-) trees is computed on the basis of statistical information on the trees, similar to the fingerprints of the text shingles.

Merging or Clustering?

Completely identical objects can obviously be merged into a single version. When documents are highly, but not maximally similar, a merge might be inappropriate. For example, two documents are identical with respect to the content, but the reference lists differ. Merging them, it has to be decided how to proceed with the references that are listed only in one reference list. Should this reference be added to the reference list of the merged object even though it is not certain? Having more than two duplicates to be merged, a majority vote can be applied in some cases. A reference will thus be added to the merged object, if present in the majority of the duplicates. However, what if no such majority exists? Instead of merging, such duplicates can be grouped into clusters. Working with groups of duplicates is also more appropriate when the document's source has to be directly indicated, for example, because certain data providers restrict the access to the documents.

Duplicates within a cluster can differ with respect to their quality. We could, for instance, consider a document as correct for which metadata was carefully determined by a librarian or a merge of duplicates from digital libraries with a high reputation. A duplicate with automatically extracted metadata might be more likely to contain errors. Here, the general quality that is attributed to the source collection of the document plays an important role. For instance, one will probably consider the metadata from the ACM digital library as more accurate than the automatically extracted metadata from CiteSeer. Therefore, each document gets an associated value that indicates its quality, for instance, based on its provenance.

As long as a document collection does not contain any duplicates – as you might assume for Springer Online or the ACM digital library – reference-based visibility measures can directly be computed on the reference network of this collection. However, if duplicates are contained in the collection, some actions must be taken in order to avoid the decrease in the quality of the recommendations caused by the duplicates. Having applied duplicate detection mechanisms, document collections comprise on the one hand unique documents, i.e., documents from which only a single version was crawled or that result from a merge of several identical versions. On the other hand, they include duplicates that are grouped into clusters. In chapter 6, a model of uncertainty is developed for document networks that are built up from a document collection that contains such unique documents as well as clustered duplicates. Visibility measures are then computed on this modified document reference network.

4 Multi-Layer Architecture

4.1 Connecting Different Types of Networks

Trust-based recommender systems have proven to be very useful as they avoid certain problems associated with traditional recommending mechanisms[1]. Especially for some types of "outliers", their accuracy significantly outperforms techniques such as collaborative filtering. Current trust-based recommender systems use the information from a trust network to recommend items. Relations between these items are not taken into account. The central idea of the approach described in this thesis consists in exploiting information from document networks to improve trust-based recommendations. For example, documents authored by untrustworthy sources can be filtered efficiently. In addition, rankings of search engine results can be personalized by considering trust relationship information in structure-based visibility measures. As this means having two networks which are jointly analyzed, namely the trust network and the document reference network, the approach developed can also be described as follows: information from social trust networks is used to enhance document recommendations and document rankings.

This chapter introduces the framework for generating recommendations based on different types of networks. A *multi-layer network* is thus composed of two or more distinct layers, each of them including nodes of a certain type which are connected via a particular relationship. Layers are either directly connected or indirectly via another layer. Information can be propagated between the distinct layers. I consider in my thesis a certain extension of such multi-layer networks, namely those that have as their basis a document reference network and a trust network. These two-layer networks can be extended by further networks. Figure 4.1 shows an example. Authors in a social network are connected via the "author-of" relationship to documents written by them, and via the "member-of" relationship to the organizations in which they work. Documents are linked via citations. Organizations are related, for instance, via cooperation relationships. The direction of the relationship is indicated by the arrows, and in this figure, the strength of the relationship is shown for purposes of clarity by the strength of the edge. Certainly, other types of networks could be combined to a multi-layer network, too.

---

[1] For the details see section 3.1.2.

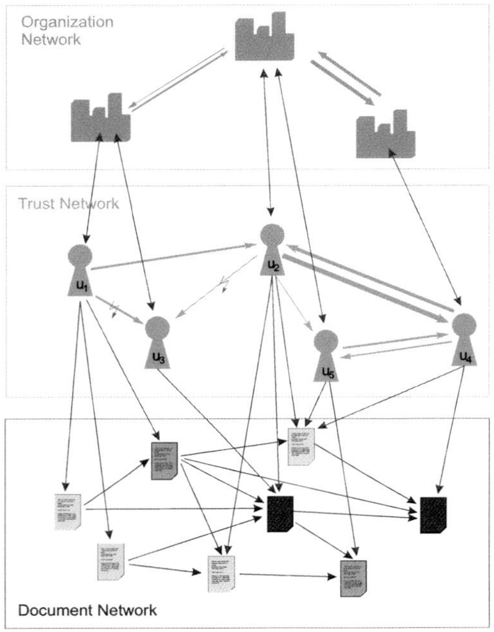

Figure 4.1: Example for a Multi-Layer Architecture

Recently, trust networks have been studied in connection with document networks but never in the context of recommender systems. Börner *et al.* (2004) consider the simultaneous growth of paper citation networks and coauthor networks (see section 3.2.2). This is a completely different question to using such two-layer architecture for making recommendations as this work does. Korfiatis and Naeve (2005) speak in their study on the credibility of Wikipedia articles having two layers of networks (see section 3.1.4 for the approach). Although they have two connected networks, namely the network of users who contribute to Wikipedia articles and the network of references between Wikipedia articles, they do not use the reference structure of the document network. A set of articles without any references specified would be sufficient in order to make all the computations they propose. As they do not analyze the structure of the document network at all, they do not introduce any propagation mechanism on the joint networks. The approach closest to the multi-layer architecture developed in this dissertation project is by García-Barriocanal and Sicilia (2005) who combine the information from a social network and a document reference network. They measure the social relevance of authors by a modified PageRank based on extended FOAF data (no trust information is used). They call this approach PeopleRank. They claim to propagate this measure of social relevance to the documents in order to compute a socially weighted PageRank. The paper by García-Barriocanal and Sicilia, however, does not give any details on the propagation mechanism, let alone an architecture for combining different types of networks. As of the time of writing, this approach has not been clarified or further developed. An overview of the approaches by Korfiatis and Naeve (2005) and García-Barriocanal and Sicilia (2005) and the multi-layer approach Hess (2005) – which were presented fairly at the same time – is given in our joint paper Korfiatis *et al.* (print).

4.2 Multi-Layer Networks

I define a multi-layer network with n layers as follows.

Definition 5 *An n-layer network consisting of n distinct networks $\mathcal{G}_1, \mathcal{G}_2, ..., \mathcal{G}_n$ is a graph*

$$\mathcal{ML}_{\mathcal{G}_1 \to \mathcal{G}_2 \to ... \to \mathcal{G}_n} = \left(\bigcup_{i=1}^{n} V_i, \bigcup_{i=1}^{n} E_i \cup \bigcup_{i=1}^{n-1} R_{i,i+1} \right)$$

with $i = 1, ..., n$ subgraphs $\mathcal{G}_i = (V_i, E_i)$ with V_i being the set of nodes and $E_i \subseteq V_i \times V_i$ being the set of optionally weighted edges. $R_{m-1,m} \subseteq V_{m-1} \times V_m$ is the set of edges connecting nodes of graphs $\mathcal{G}_{m-1}$ and $\mathcal{G}_m$. Edges $R_{m-1,m}$ can be attributed with edge weights.

Multi-layer networks $\mathcal{ML}$ are thus graphs composed by subgraphs $\mathcal{G}_i$. Each subgraph groups the nodes V_i of a specific type, such as authors or documents. The subgraphs correspond to the distinct layers in the multi-layer architecture. Nodes within a subgraph are linked via directed or undirected, weighted or non-weighted edges which represent a particular relationship that holds between the nodes. The users in a trust network, for instance, are connected by directed and weighted edges. So there is one node type per layer.

Subgraphs $\mathcal{G}_i$ and $\mathcal{G}_{i+1}$ are connected by edges $R_{i,i+1}$. The multi-layer architecture does not allow arbitrary connections between the distinct layers but only between subsequent layers. In figure 4.1, the document network is directly connected only with the author network. There are no direct edges between organizations and documents. The edges $R_{i,i+1}$ are weighted or non-weighted. The author-of relationship, for example, is not weighted, whereas a review provided on some document gives a weighted edge. The direction of the links between the layers can normally be turned around; for example, the inverse relationship of "author-of" is "written-by". When connecting two layers, it might be claimed in some settings that each node of some first layer has to be connected with at least one node of a second layer. For example, there might be no documents allowed without at least one author attributed. In the other way round, a user might only be considered as author if he or she has written at least one paper.

The layers in the multi-layer architecture are irreducible, i.e., it is impossible to completely infer the relationships between the nodes in a particular layer from the relationships between nodes in another layer, or from the relationships holding between the nodes of distinct layers. For instance, a reference from a document p_1, written by a user u_1, to a document p_2, written by user u_2, does not permit inferring a trust relationship between users u_1 and u_2, because the link structure does not indicate whether the link is affirmative or deprecatory. Such distinction requires additional information, such as analyzing the text in which the link is embedded.

In social network analysis, networks in which two kinds of (social) entities are connected are called *two-mode networks*. The term *mode* refers to the number of different types of social entities (Wasserman and Faust, 1994). Social network analysis distinguishes two-mode networks with two sets of actors, and two-mode networks with a first set of actors and a second set of events, the so-called affiliation networks. Three- (or higher) mode networks are only rarely considered in social network analysis. The main difference between the multi-layer architecture and the two-mode networks, as studied in social network analysis, is that the multi-layer architecture connects distinct networks. That means that the layers are both internally connected and interconnected. In the two-mode networks: in contrast, there are in most cases no connections between entities of the same type. Two-mode networks are thus bipartite and the analyses focus on the ties between the distinct kinds of entities. Frequently studied affiliation networks are, for example, people and their membership in clubs, such as the data set by Galaskiewicz (1985) which records club and board memberships of a sample of CEOs. In two-mode networks, connections among the entities of the same type can be established on the basis of the ties that link the different types of entities. Coauthorship networks establish ties among authors based on the is-author-relationship which connects authors and documents. A link between two authors indicates that they have coauthored at least one paper (for coauthorship networks see e.g. Newman, 2004). In the multi-layer architecture, we would not do this. The coauthorship ties between the authors do not provide any additional information, because the is-author-edges are already used when generating the recommendations.

4.3 Propagation Mechanisms

4.3.1 Propagation Within A Layer

Before propagating information between the distinct layers of a multi-layer network, information is typically propagated within a certain layer. In a multi-layer network with a trust network and a document reference network, this would mean, for instance, predicting trust values between indirectly connected users with a trust metric before propagating this information to the document layer. Typically, there is a set of measures that is explicitly defined for a certain type of network, such as the reference-based visibility measures on document networks or the trust metrics on trust networks. The presented framework is general and allows for applying on each network the measure that is suited for the type of network, the particular application context and network-specific characteristics.

4.3.2 Propagation Between Layers

By propagating information between the distinct layers of the multi-layer network, the information provided in the different layers can be jointly analyzed. There are two basic propagation mechanisms for propagation information from a first layer $\mathcal{G}_1$ to a second layer $\mathcal{G}_2$. I explain them in the example of a concrete extension of a multi-layer network: trust information is propagated from an author trust network to a document reference network.

Propagating author reputation to documents: An author's reputation, which is measured on the basis of the author trust network, and which is thus a property of this author node, can be propagated to all documents written by this author. This is shown in the left part of figure 4.2.

Propagating trust values to document references: A trust rating from an author a_1 about an author a_2 is mapped to the references from documents written by author a_1 to the documents written by author a_2. The trust values that are propagated to the document references are either directly provided by users or are predicted by some trust metric. The right part of figure 4.2 shows this propagation.

Generalizing from this concrete example, I call the first type of propagation mechanism the *node-to-node propagation*. It propagates properties of the nodes in $\mathcal{G}_1$ to nodes in $\mathcal{G}_2$ along the edges $R_{1,2}$ that connect $\mathcal{G}_1$ and $\mathcal{G}_2$. The second propagation mechanism is the *edge-to-edge propagation*. It propagates edge weights from the edges E_1 of layer $\mathcal{G}_1$ to the edges E_2 in layer $\mathcal{G}_2$. These two basic propagation mechanisms work regardless of whether the edges connecting the layers are weighted or non-weighted.

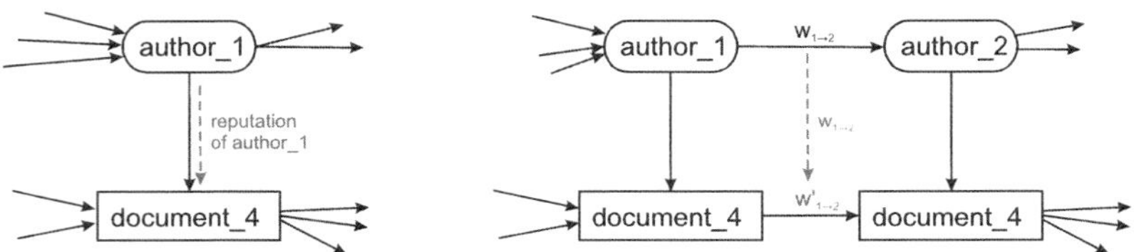

Figure 4.2: Propagation Mechanisms in Multi-Layer Networks

In the multi-layer networks, information is propagated between connected layers in a feed-forward way. For example, the information from an organization network with organizations of which the authors are members can be used to enhance the trust information. This information is, in turn, forwarded to a document network. Reference-based document rankings are then personalized on the basis of the information received from the preceding layers. Input can be used from several layers. In the example, the information from a "journal network", i.e., the journals, books etc. in which the documents were published, might additionally be used.

4.4 Multi-Layer Networks for Recommendations

In the previous sections, I have defined what multi-layer networks are and I have shown how information is propagated with a certain layer and then to subsequent layers. What type of recommendation can now be computed in such an architecture? I consider in the following those two-layer networks that comprise a trust network and a document reference network and that can be extended to multi-layer networks, for example, by an organization network. Such multi-layer networks permit personalizing document recommendations as motivated by the application scenarios discussed in chapter 2. A visibility measure is enriched with information from a trust network and potentially from an organization network, too. This gives *trust-enhanced visibility measures*. In the next chapter, I define such trust-enhanced visibility measures. It is also a possibility of propagating information in the other sense, i.e. from the document reference network to the trust network between users. Trust or reputation values could be enhanced with information from the other layers, for example, in order to recommend experts.

5 Generating Multi-Layer-Based Recommendations

In this chapter, I will define a set of measures for making recommendations on the basis of a multi-layer architecture, starting with two concrete extensions of a two-layer architecture. Firstly, I'll develop trust-enhanced visibility measures for a two-layer architecture with a reviewer trust network connected with a document reference network. Secondly, I'll define the appropriate trust-enhanced visibility measures for a two-layer network that encompasses an author trust network connected again with a document network. Then, I'll extend these two-layer architectures with an organization network and describe how to generate recommendations in this particular three-layer architecture.

5.1 Reviewer Trust Networks & Document Networks

Reference-based visibility measures can be personalized by considering a second type of information on the documents: reviews. Reviewers may be readers or editors. They rate documents on a numerical scale, using criteria similar to those applied in the reviews for scientific conferences or journals. Referring to the quality of the document, they ask, for example, whether it is correct, complete and understandable and whether it is up-to-date in its discipline. The reviews connect users and documents: i.e. there are directed and weighted edges between reviewers and documents. Apart from the document ratings, reviewers assign a trust value to reviewers whose work is known to them. A high trust implies that the evaluating user appreciates the evaluated user's reviews, for example, because he or she applies similar criteria when evaluating documents. This particular two-layer architecture is defined as follows.

Definition 6 *A two-layer network with a reviewer trust network $\mathcal{T}$ and a document reference network $\mathcal{D}$ is a graph*

$$\mathcal{ML}_{\mathcal{T} \to \mathcal{D}} = (U \cup D, T \cup C \cup R)$$

with two subgraphs $\mathcal{T} = (U, T)$ and $\mathcal{D} = (D, C)$ and a set of reviews $R \subseteq U \times D \times [0, 1]$ connecting reviewers and documents. The edge (u_m, p_d, r_i) gives the rating that user u_m has provided on document p_d.

A joint analysis of both layers permits the generation of personalized recommendations: a recommendation for a document (page) p_d is made from the perspective of a user u_m. The personalized recommendation integrates the structure-based visibility of p_d, e.g. its PageRank or its authority computed with HITS, and the reviews, in which the impact of a review depends on the trust that u_m has in the reviewer. The *trust-review-enhanced visibility*, called the TRE-visibility ($\mathrm{vis}^{\mathrm{TRE}}_{p_d,u_m}$), provides a recommendation for p_d from u_m's point of view. I define in the following a set of TRE-visibility measures. Table 5.1 gives an overview of them.

TRE-Visibility Measure	Description
trust-weighted review visibility	The visibility of a document is exclusively based on its direct reviews.
simple TRE-visibility	A basic approach for integrating the reference-based visibility of a document (e.g. its PageRank) and its direct reviews.
integrated TRE-visibility	A measure that jointly propagates reference-based visibilities and reviews.
review-propagating TRE-visibility	An efficient alternative to the integrated TRE-visibility. Two review-propagating TRE-visibility measures will be defined.

Table 5.1: Overview on the TRE-Visibility Measures

5.1.1 Interpolations

Starting from the unpersonalized base case with document recommendations made by simply analyzing the structure of the document reference network, the TRE-visiblity is computed by interpolation on the connected layers. Interpolation means here, as in the case of interpolations of functions, to estimate personalized document visibilities on the basis of the reviews given for those documents that have no direct reviews, or little or no reviews by trustworthy persons. These interpolations have firstly been proposed in Hess *et al.* (2006). Specifically, there are two possibilities for interpolation which are then combined:

- Interpolation on the trust layer

- Interpolation on the document layer

With interpolation on the trust layer, the reviews provided by the other users in the trust network can be considered. The visibilities of reviewed documents are obtained by combining the direct trust values and the trust values predicted by a trust metric with the reviews on the documents. The degree of trust in a reviewer indicates the influence of her or his reviews on the recommendation $\mathrm{vis}^{\mathrm{TRE}}_{p_d,u_m}$: the reviews made by users whom user u_m considers as trustworthy should have most impact. Figure 5.1 shows how document recommendations are personalized based on the user's view on the trust network. Applying this first interpolation, personalized recommendations can be generated for user u_1 for documents p_2, p_4, p_5, p_6 and p_7. Review r_2, which has directly been provided by u_1, influences the visibility of p_5. Depending on u_1's trust in users u_2 and u_4 (who are directly connected with u_1), their reviews r_1, r_3, r_5 and r_6, respectively, influence the TRE-visibilities of documents p_6, p_2, p_5 and p_7. Trust propagation also allows for considering the reviews by indirectly connected users, such as u_3 and u_5: a trust metric infers the degree of trust in these indirectly linked users. Review r_4 by u_3 personalizes the recommendation for document p_4.

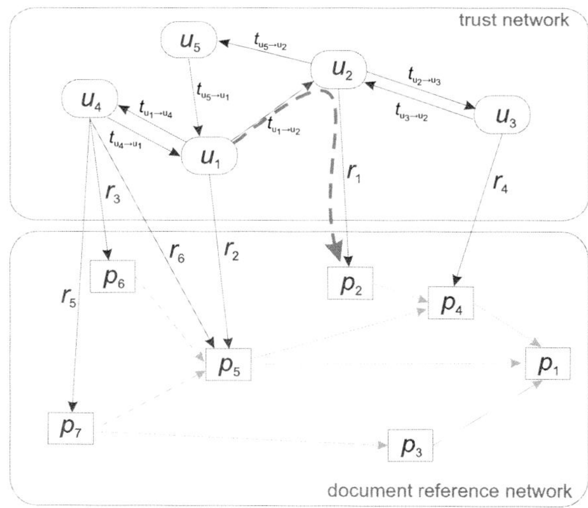

Figure 5.1: Interpolation on the Trust Network

The interpolation on the document reference network propagates the TRE-visibility of a document, which is modified by the requesting user's reviews, with some reference-based visibility measure in the document network. Therefore, reviews influence not only the visibilities of the reviewed documents but also the visibilities of the documents referenced by the reviewed documents, and – certainly to a smaller degree – the visibilities of the documents cited by the cited documents and so on. This interpolation is illustrated in figure 5.2.[1] User u_1's review on document p_5 directly modifies p_5's TRE-visibility. Document p_5's new TRE-visibility is then propagated along its outgoing edges, thereby personalizing the visibilities of p_1 and p_4 for u_1.

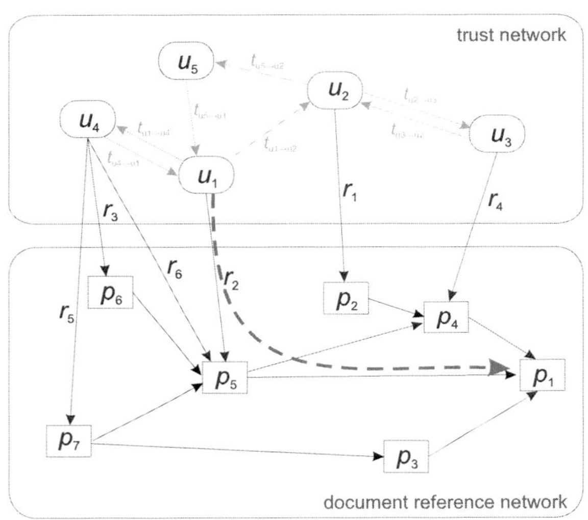

Figure 5.2: Interpolation on the Document Network

The combination of both interpolations provides personalized recommendations for all remaining documents, i.e., for those documents for which recommendations could not be personalized by applying either the first or the second interpolation. The example in figure 5.3 illustrates the combined interpolation steps: assumed that u_1 trusts u_4, the visibility of document p_3 is personalized for u_1 based on the review r_5 given by u_4. This review modifies directly the visibility of p_7, and indirectly the visibility of p_3 by propagation on the document network. The visibility of p_1 is personalized in the same way. Therefore, personalized TRE-visibilities are computed for all documents.

---

[1]For the algorithms developed in the following, it does not matter whether the networks are cyclic or acyclic. The figure shows an acyclic document network because the explanation is easier to follow.

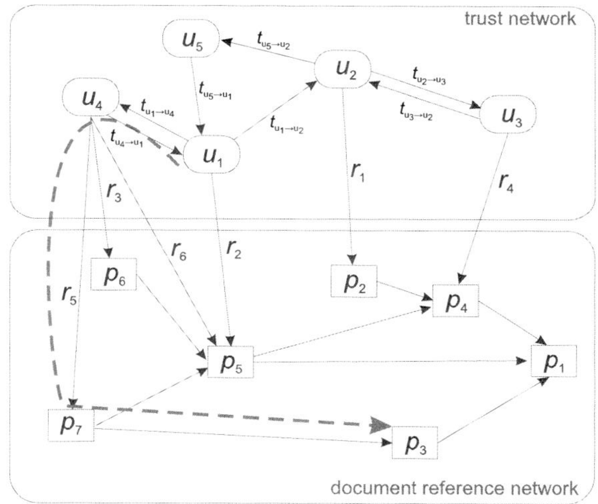

Figure 5.3: Combined Interpolation

5.1.2 TRE-Visibility

TRE-visibilities are used for personalized document rankings: the documents that are identified as results to a user's search engine query are ranked in descending order of their TRE-visibility. As document repositories can contain millions of documents and the TRE-visibility has to be calculated for all of them, the TRE-visibility must be efficiently computable. The users should not have to wait for their query to be answered. A low computation load at query time can be achieved by precomputing as much as possible offline, as for example Google does with the PageRank. However, generating and saving personalized rankings of all documents for all users is not feasible. This problem has to be kept in mind when designing the TRE-visibility.

Measuring the TRE-visibility $\mathrm{vis}^{\mathrm{TRE}}_{p_d, u_m}$ of a document p_d from u_m's perspective, we have to perform the following tasks:

1. Compute the trust in all reviews from u_m's point of view (section 5.1.3).

2. Compute the impact that a review has on u_m's personalized document recommendation, i.e., weight reviews with the trust in the user providing the reviews (section 5.1.4).

3. Combine trust-weighted reviews and structure-based document visibilities (section 5.1.5).

The subsequent sections discuss these three steps in detail. The definitions used in the following are given in table 5.2.

Identifier	Description
p_d	document to be recommended
u_m	user for which the recommendation is generated
r_i	review i on a document p_d
R_{p_d}	set of direct reviews on p_d
$t_{u_m \rightarrow u_n}$	u_m's (subjective) trust in user u_n
t_i	u_m's trust in the review r_i, which is derived from u_m's trust in the user providing this review
$\mathrm{vis}^{\circ}_{p_d}$	document base visibility; it is calculated with some reference-based visibility measure such as PageRank on the document reference network
vc	visibility contribution; the weight that is given to the document base visibility $\mathrm{vis}^{\circ}_{p_d}$ within a TRE-visibility
c_{r_i, p_d}	the contribution of a review r_i on the TRE-visibility of p_d
k_{r_i, p_d}	the distance of a direct review $r_i \in R_{p_i}$ to p_d: the length of the shortest path from p_i to p_d (if p_i and p_d are not connected: $k_{r_i, p_d} := \infty$)

Table 5.2: Definitions for the TRE-Visibility

5.1.3 Trust in Reviews (Task 1)

A user's trust in the reviews is measured on the basis of the explicitly declared trust relationships in three steps:

1. Predict a user's trust in all reviewers that are reachable within the maximum distance allowed by the trust metric applied.

2. Set the trust in all unknown reviewers. Step 1 and 2 result in a fully propagated trust network with a degree of trust between all users.

3. Derive the trust in a review from the trust in the reviewer.

Step 1: Propagating Trust

The first step involves computing a user u_m's trust to all other users reachable from her or him. Applying some trust metric gives for each user u_m the trust $t_{u_m \to u_n}$ to all users u_n to whom a path from u_m exists and which does not exceed the maximum length allowed by the trust metric (this length is typically around 3 steps). The explicitly declared trust values as well as the inferred trust values are in [-1, 1], ranging from distrust to full trust. As defined in section 3.1.3,0 represents neutral trust where the evaluating user has an impartial opinion. So any trust metric that is able to deal with distrust can be used.

Trust-based recommendations require up-to-date trust values because trust relationships might change suddenly from complete trust to absolute distrust. An example is the case of scientific misconduct by the stem-cell researcher Hwang. His colleague and coauthor Schatten decided to stop all cooperation within one day (see e.g news@nature.com, 2006b). Such modification should certainly have an immediate impact on the final document recommendation. Using up-to-date trust values is not contradictory to an efficient computation of personalized visibilities. Trust propagation can be made offline as long as it is ensured that the inferred trust values are re-calculated when some trust value is modified or a new one is inserted. This is feasible unless changes are made in an extremely high frequency.

Step 2: Trust in Unknown Reviewers

As we have seen in step 1, depending on the structure of the trust network and on the applied trust metric, there might be users u_i for which no trust value can be inferred from the trust values explicitly given. In this case, I assign an "unknown-trust" $t_{u_m \to u_i} = t_{\text{unknown}}$ to the unknown user u_i in order to be able to also consider u_i's reviews. This unknown-trust is set after trust propagation and is used only during the calculation of the impact of the reviews. It does not influence any trust propagations on the trust network.

Setting $t_{\text{unknown}} = 0$ offers a clear semantics for trust-based recommendations. Consider a chain of trust statements as given in figure 5.4. Calculating u_1's trust for u_3 by multiplying the values on the path from u_1 via u_2 to u_3, we obtain a trust value close to 0 for u_3. This is close to the unknown-trust assigned to unknown users. This is fairly intuitive: as u_1 has a low trust in u_2, u_2's opinion on u_3 does not provide much information on u_3. So it is appropriate that u_1 trusts u_3 to the same degree as someone unknown, such as u_4. Computing recommendations for u_1, u_3's reviews would thus have the same impact as u_4's reviews. With a scale $[0, 1]$ (with 0 for distrust and 1 for trust) and additionally $\bot$ for unknown users, this would not work (at least not without modifying the trust metrics): with longer trust chains and a propagation function as outlined above, the trust to the indirectly connected user would tend to 0, i.e., to distrust, although $\bot$ would be appropriate.

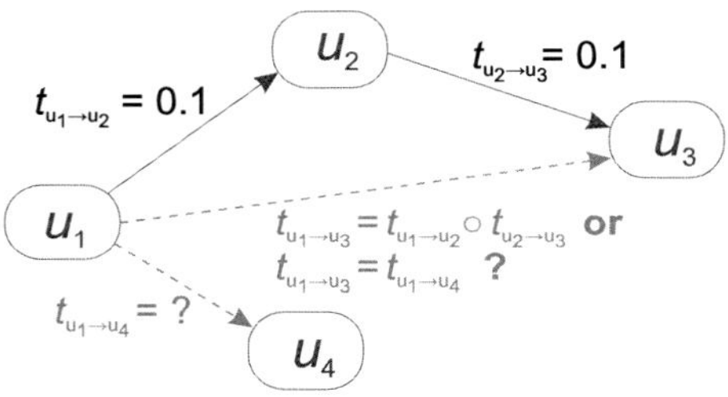

Figure 5.4: Unknown vs. Low Trust

Alternatively, the results of global trust metrics can be used to estimate the trust in an unknown user u_i, i.e., the global reputation value $rep^t_{u_i}$ that is computed by evaluating all trust statements in the trust network. This gives $t_{u_m \to u_i} = rep^t_{u_i}$. The reputation, however, is not personalized and might be based on the trust values by users whom u_m highly distrusts. We therefore use in the following $t_{\text{unknown}} = 0$.

▶ **Results of Step 1 and 2:** We now have for each user u_m her or his trust $t_{u_m \to u_n}$ in *all* users u_n, either directly given or predicted by a trust metric or given as default trust when u_n is unknown. This gives the trust network $\mathcal{T}_{\text{prop}}$, the fully propagated version of $\mathcal{T}$. It can be precomputed offline. The multi-layer network that combines the original document network $\mathcal{D}$ with the fully propagated reviewer trust network $\mathcal{T}_{\text{prop}}$ is denoted as $\mathcal{ML}_{\mathcal{T}_{\text{prop}} \bullet \mathcal{D}}$, which will be used in the further process of generating recommendations. ◀

Step 3: Trust in a Review

At this point, I will specify the trust t_j in reviews r_j made by reviewer u_n. The trust in the review is derived from u_m's trust $t_{u_m \to u_n}$ in u_n, because our trust in someone indicates how much we should consider this user's opinion in our decision. As the trust in a review will give the impact of a review on the recommendation, we need $t_j \geq 0$. A mapping function I regulates the mapping of the interpersonal trust values $t_{u_m \to u_n} \in [-1, 1]$ to the trust in the reviews $t_j \in [0, 1]$ made by u_n.

$$t_j = I(t_{u_m \to u_n}) \quad \text{with } I : [-1, 1] \to [0, 1]$$

The mapping function has to guarantee that the reviews made by someone whom u_m highly trusts influence the recommendation for u_m considerably, whereas the reviews by distrusted persons have no impact. This is achieved by mapping absolute distrust (-1) to 0 and full trust (+1) to 1. A special case is the trust value 0. It occurs either when a user u_m sets $t_{u_m \to u_n} = 0$ in order to express an impartial position towards u_n, or as unknown-trust in the case that no trust value could be inferred. In the simplest case, this zero-trust is mapped to 0. This means that these reviews are not considered at all. However, in some situations it might be appropriate to give them some weight, i.e., to map interpersonal trust of 0 to a default trust greater than zero. The mapping functions will thus vary with the application context. In some highly critical application domains, it might be better to apply caution and to neglect reviews by not explicitly trusted persons (i.e., the default impact would be zero), whereas in other domains where the involved risk is low (e.g. movie recommendations), the default trust might be clearly above zero. Considering the rather low risk involved, I suggest to use for the document recommendations a mapping function that gives $t_j > 0$ for interpersonal trust of 0. Figure 5.5 shows this mapping.

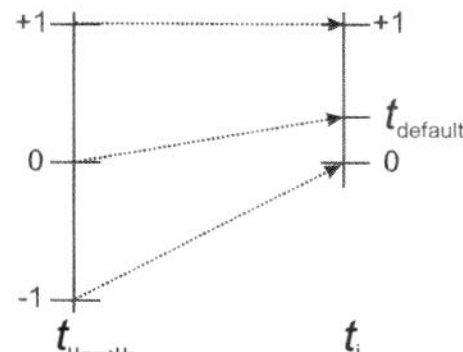

Figure 5.5: Mapping Interpersonal Trust to Trust in Reviews

A mapping function can now be defined which gives $0 \leq t_j \leq 1$ for all reviews r_j. For a concrete example see section 7.3.2 where I define the mapping function used in the trust-based document recommendation system SPRec. Users will likely want to adjust the mapping function according to their personal disposition to trust (also called 'propensity to trust'), i.e., their *"general willingness to trust others"* (Mayer *et al.*, 1995, p. 715). A person's disposition to trust unknown people depends, for example, on past experiences in general, the personality type and the cultural background (Mayer *et al.*).

Note that neither inserting new reviews nor modifying existing reviews requires a recalculation of the interpersonal trust values $t_{u_m \to u_n}$. The impact of a review can simply be derived from applying the mapping function to the precalculated trust values.

▶ **Result of Task 1:** The first task required for generating the personalized TRE-visibility $\mathrm{vis}^{\mathrm{TRE}}_{p_d,u_m}$ is now complete: we have computed for user u_m her or his personal trust t_j in *all* reviews r_j on document p_d. ◀

5.1.4 Trust-Weighted Reviews (Task 2)

The next task is to compute the influence of a review on the recommendation. The previous step provided the trust t_j in each review r_j. The trust in the review t_j can directly be considered as a weight of r_j, giving *trust-weighted reviews*: $t_j \cdot r_j$. Now that the mapping function has been applied, reviews by distrusted persons have no impact on the recommendation because in this case $t_j = 0$. Reviews by completely trusted persons have full impact because $t_j = 1$.

Taking the weighted average of all trust-weighted reviews of a document achieves a first personalized visibility. The visibility of a document p_d depends solely on its direct reviews $r_i \in R_{p_d}$. This *trust-weighted-review-visibility* trv is defined for any document p_d with at least one review (i.e. R_{p_d} is not empty) as:

$$
\mathrm{trv}_{p_d,u_m} \quad = \quad \frac{\sum\limits_{i=1}^{n} t_i r_i}{\sum\limits_{i=1}^{n} t_i}
$$

The trv-visibility, however, has several drawbacks. Firstly, it fails to provide a recommendation if p_d was not reviewed. Depending on the overall number of reviews, a recommendation might not be computable for a large proportion of documents. Secondly, the results are rather unintuitive if all reviews on p_d are provided by reviewers who are considered as untrustworthy by u_n. Consider the following small example (with trust in [-1, 1] and reviews in [0, 1]): there is a single review $r_1 = 1$ on document p_1 by a user u_2 who is not trusted by u_1, e.g., $t_{u_1 \to u_2} = -0.7$. When applying a mapping function, this might give the trust in the review $t_1 = 0.05$. The resulting visibility $\mathrm{trv}_{p_1,u_1} = \frac{0.05 \cdot 1}{0.05} = 1$ is appropriate insofar this review is the only information available on p_d, and this information is used instead of having no information at all on p_d. However, this result is certainly not intuitive. The following section discusses how to extend the trv-visibility.

5.1.5 Integrating Trust-Weighted Reviews and Document Visibilities (Task 3)

The trv-visibility will not provide satisfying results if the requested document has not been reviewed at all or only by distrusted users. A personalized visibility function that considers both trust-weighted reviews on a document and the document's structure-based visibility addresses this problem. Thereby, the trv-function is extended to the *simple TRE-visibility* $\text{vis}^{\text{TRE}_s}_{p_d,u_m}$. Therefore, document base visibilities $\text{vis}^{\circ}_{p_d}$ are computed for all documents p_d with a visibility measure such as PageRank, any of its derivations such as Age PageRank or by a measure in the style of HITS. The personalized TRE-visibility is obtained by combining the user-independent document base visibility $\text{vis}^{\circ}_{p_d}$ with the direct, trust-weighted reviews $t_i \cdot r_i$ (with $r_i \in R_{p_d}$). High reviews from users trusted by u_m give a TRE-visibility higher than the document base visibility. Low reviews decrease the base visibility. If reviews and document base visibilities are not in the same range, at least one of them has to be scaled. The visibility contribution vc indicates the portion of the simple TRE-visibility $\text{vis}^{\text{TRE}_s}_{p_d,u_m}$ that is determined by the document base visibility, e. g., $\text{vc} := 0.5$. The simple TRE-visibility is now defined as:

$$
\begin{aligned}
\text{vis}^{\text{TRE}'_s}_{p_d,u_m} \;&=\; \text{vc} \cdot \text{vis}^{\circ}_{p_d} + (1 - \text{vc}) \cdot \text{trv}_{p_d,u_m} \\[2ex]
&=\; \text{vc} \cdot \text{vis}^{\circ}_{p_d} + (1 - \text{vc}) \, \frac{\displaystyle\sum_{i=1}^{n} t_i r_i}{\displaystyle\sum_{i=1}^{n} t_i}
\end{aligned}
$$

The disadvantage of $\text{vis}^{\text{TRE}'_s}_{p_d,u_m}$ is that the influence of the document base visibility is fixed (by the vc). It would, however, be more appropriate to neglect the document base visibility if trustworthy reviews were available or otherwise, to give more weight to it if no or only untrustworthy reviews were provided. This is realized by a modified version, the $\text{vis}^{\text{TRE}''_s}_{p_d,u_m}$ which was firstly presented in Hess and Stein (2007a).

$$
\text{vis}^{\text{TRE}''_s}_{p_d,u_m} \;=\; \frac{\displaystyle\sum_{i=0}^{n} t_i r_i}{\displaystyle\sum_{i=0}^{n} t_i} \;=\; \frac{\text{vc} \cdot \text{vis}^{\circ}_{p_d} + \displaystyle\sum_{i=1}^{n} t_i r_i}{\text{vc} + \displaystyle\sum_{i=1}^{n} t_i}
$$

This alternative TRE-visibility takes the document base visibility as an additional review with $r_0 := \text{vis}^{\circ}_{p_d}$. The visibility contribution vc indicates the impact of $\text{vis}^{\circ}_{p_d}$.

So $t_0 := \text{vc}$. With $\text{vc} = 0.5$, there is a positive trust in the visibility received via the incoming links. In $\text{vis}_{p_d,u_m}^{\text{TRE}''_s}$, the influence of the document base visibility on the recommendation depends now on the trustworthiness of the reviews. Algorithm 1 gives the computation of the simple TRE-visibility.

Algorithm 1 Simple TRE-Visibility

1: **function** S-TRE-VIS(User u, Document p, BaseVisibility vis_p, $[0,1]$ vc, Graph $\mathcal{ML}_{\mathcal{T}_{\text{prop}} \overset{\bullet}{\to} \mathcal{D}}) \to \text{vis}_{p,u}^{\text{TRE}_s}$

2:      reviews $\leftarrow \emptyset$

3:      review-edges $\leftarrow \bigcup\limits_{u_m \in U} \{(u_m, p, r) \in R\}$ $\triangleright$ Get all reviews on p

4:      **for all** rev $= (u_m, p, r)$ in review-edges **do**

5:          trust $\leftarrow (u, u_m, t_{u \to u_m})$ $\triangleright$ Get the trust in the reviewer

6:          t $\leftarrow I(t_{u \to u_m})$ $\triangleright$ Get the trust in the review

7:          reviews $\leftarrow$ reviews $\cup \{(r, t)\}$

8:      **end for**

9:      $\text{vis}_{p,u}^{\text{TRE}_s} \leftarrow \dfrac{\text{vc} \cdot \text{vis}_p + \sum\limits_{(r,t) \in \text{reviews}} t \cdot r}{\text{vc} + \sum\limits_{(r,t) \in \text{reviews}} t}$

10:      **return** $\text{vis}_{p,u}^{\text{TRE}_s}$

11: **end function**

> ▶ **Result of Tasks 1 – 3** The result of tasks $1 - 3$ is a TRE-visibility measure that generates personalized document recommendations for all documents by considering trust-weighted reviews and the reference-based visibility. The influence of the reference-based visibility depends on the number and on the trustworthiness of the reviews. The simple TRE-visibility $\text{vis}_{p_d,u_m}^{\text{TRE}_s}$ easily modifies the document base visibility of p_d by the direct reviews on p_d. ◀

The simple TRE-visibility can be computed efficiently because it combines precalculated values. The document base visibilities can be precalculated because references seldom change. For example, references in a published scientific paper cannot be removed. Although links between webpages are modified more frequently, these changes do not require a visibility calculated at query time. Using the precalculated document base visibilities reduces the computation load at query time considerably. As already discussed in section 5.1.3, the trust network is fully propagated offline, too. At query time, only the direct reviews of the document have to be looked up and the respective trust in them is derived from the fully propagated trust network by simply mapping interpersonal trust to trust in reviews.

The drawback of the simple TRE-visibility is, however, that it considers only the direct reviews. This means that a large number of reviews are not taken into account although they might provide insightful information on the documents to be ranked. A review on p_i should affect the TRE-visibility of p_i as well as – to some minor extent – the visibilities of all documents p_d referenced by p_i, and the visibilities of the documents referenced by these documents and so on. Computing the TRE-visibility for p_d, it is not obvious how to include indirect reviews, i.e. the reviews on documents that reference p_d, into the simple TRE-visibility. This problem is addressed in the following two chapters in which the simple TRE-visibility is extended.

5.1.6 Integrating Trust-Weighted Reviews in Visibility Measures

If reviews are propagated as part of a structure-based visibility in the document network, they will exert an indirect influence. The *integrated TRE-visibility* $\text{vis}^{\text{TRE}_i}_{p_d,u_m}$ extends a visibility measure so that it forwards via p_d's outgoing edges a value that is based on both the visibilities of the documents citing p_d (i.e., the documents $p_k \in P_{p_d}$) and the reviews $r_i \in R_{p_d}$, weighted with the trust t_i in them. Extending PageRank to an integrated TRE-visibility function as presented in Hess and Stein (2007a) gives:

$$
\text{vis}'_{p_d,u_m} \;=\; 1 - \alpha + \alpha \sum_{p_k \in P_{p_d}} \frac{\text{vis}^{\text{TRE}_i}_{p_k,u_m}}{|C_{p_k}|}
$$

$$
\text{vis}^{\text{TRE}_i}_{p_d,u_m} \;=\; \frac{\text{vc} \cdot \text{vis}'_{p_d,u_m} + \sum_{i=1}^{n} t_i r_i}{\text{vc} + \sum_{i=1}^{n} t_i}
$$

Figure 5.6 shows how integrated visibilities are computed and forwarded. The integrated TRE-visibility $\text{vis}^{\text{TRE}_i}_{p_5,u_m}$ of document p_5 has two parts: vis'_{p_5,u_m} computed on the basis of the TRE-visibilities received via the edges $p_6 \to p_5$ and $p_7 \to p_5$, and the trust-weighted reviews on p_5, i.e., $t_2 r_2 + t_6 r_6$. The integrated TRE-visibility $\text{vis}^{\text{TRE}_i}_{p_5,u_m}$ is forwarded from p_5 to p_1 and p_4. It is split among p_5's outgoing edges: $\frac{1}{2}$ of the integrated visibility is propagated to each p_1 and p_4. The reviews r_2 and r_6 have an indirect impact on $\text{vis}^{\text{TRE}_i}_{p_1,u_m}$ and $\text{vis}^{\text{TRE}_i}_{p_4,u_m}$ because they directly modulated $\text{vis}^{\text{TRE}_i}_{p_5,u_m}$. The reviews r_3 and r_5, which are one step further away from p_1 and p_4, also exert an indirect influence via vis'_{p_5}, which is a part of $\text{vis}^{\text{TRE}_i}_{p_5,u_m}$.

Instead of extending PageRank, the integrated TRE-visibility measure can be defined on the basis of nearly any other reference-based visibility measure. As an example, I show how to use the basic mechanisms of HITS for computing an integrated TRE-visibility. The hub and the authority value are now defined as:

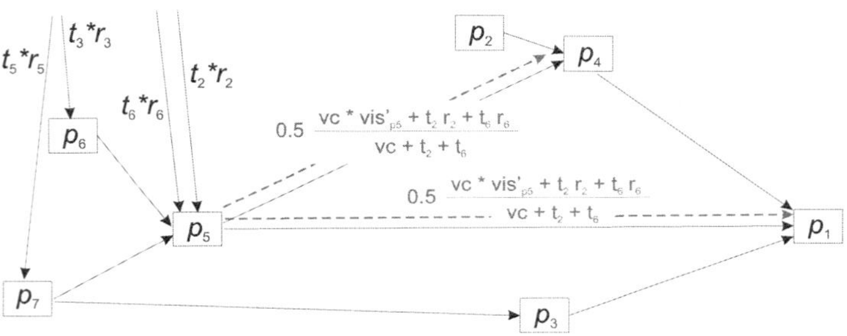

Figure 5.6: Trust-weighted reviews integrated in the visibility propagation

$$a^{\mathrm{TRE}_i}_{p_d,u_m} = \frac{vc \sum\limits_{p_l \in P_{p_d}} h^{\mathrm{TRE}_i}_{p_l,u_m} + \sum\limits_{i=1}^{n} t_i r_i}{vc + \sum\limits_{i=1}^{n} t_i}$$

$$h^{\mathrm{TRE}_i}_{p_d,u_m} = \frac{vc \sum\limits_{p_k \in C_{p_d}} a^{\mathrm{TRE}_i}_{p_k,u_m} + \sum\limits_{i=1}^{n} t_i r_i}{vc + \sum\limits_{i=1}^{n} t_i}$$

The decision whether the reviews are used within the computation of both hub and authority values depends on the meaning of the reviews, i.e. whether a high rating means that a document is a good link list to other webpages or as a review paper to the current state of the art in the respective scientific area, i.e. the rated paper is a good hub, or whether it denotes a document that provides excellent information on a certain topic, i.e. the rated paper is a good authority. So it would be more appropriate to have two types of review values. However, as there will rarely be these two types of ratings on a single document, we can assume that the review refers to the authority of a document as this is the more intuitive way. The authority value would thus be computed as $a^{\mathrm{TRE}_i}_{p_d,u_m}$ while the hub value would be computed as originally proposed, i.e., without considering any reviews.

Extending reference-based visibility measures in this way has the drawback that the entire TRE-visibility depends on the user's perspective because reviews and the user-specific trust in these reviews are propagated with the visibility on the document network. Therefore, the personalized TRE-visibilities have to be computed for all documents at query time. This is only possible for small document sets. It is clearly not applicable to real world document networks such as publication networks or even the web. Precomputing personalized rankings for all users, on the other hand, will be feasible only if the trust network has a small number of users.

5.1.7 The Review-Propagating TRE-Visibility

As $\mathrm{vis}_{p_d,u_m}^{\mathrm{TRE}_i}$ is not efficiently computable, I aim to integrate indirect reviews into the efficient (because based on precalculated document visibilities) simple TRE-visibility $\mathrm{vis}_{p_d,u_m}^{\mathrm{TRE}_s}$. The idea is to add direct and indirect reviews. The review contribution $c_{r_i:p_d}$ modulates the impact of the review r_i on the visibility of p_d:

$$c_{r_i:p_d} = 1 \quad \text{if } r_i \in R_{p_d}, \text{ i.e. } r_i \text{ is a review on } p_d,$$
$$0 < c_{r_i:p_d} < 1 \quad \text{if } r_i \text{ is a review on } p_j \text{ which cites directly or indirectly } p_d.$$

It should be possible to precompute the review contribution offline. Integrating the review contribution into the simple TRE-visibility gives the *review-propagating TRE-visibility* $\mathrm{vis}_{p_d,u_m}^{\mathrm{TRE}_{rp}}$:

$$\mathrm{vis}_{p_d,u_m}^{\mathrm{TRE}_{rp}} = \frac{\mathrm{vc} \cdot \mathrm{vis}_{p_d}^{\circ} + \sum_{i=1}^{n} t_i \cdot c_{r_i:p_d} \cdot r_i}{\mathrm{vc} + \sum_{i=1}^{n} t_i \cdot c_{r_i:p_d}}$$

The Path-Based TRE-Visibility

In order to determine $c_{r_i:p_d}$ for indirect reviews, I look at how trust-enhanced reviews are propagated by visibility measures on the document network. Figure 5.7 illustrates how the review r_2 on document p_{42} influences the TRE-visibility of p_{42}. The trust-weighted review $t_2 \cdot r_2$ is propagated along the three outgoing edges of document p_{42}. It contributes with $\frac{1}{3}$ to the TRE-visibility of the documents p_{31}, p_{38} and p_{44}, respectively. Propagating one step further, $t_2 \cdot r_2$ is forwarded from p_{31} to p_{23}. As p_{31} has four outgoing edges, the contribution of $t_2 \cdot r_2$ to the visibility of p_{23} is $c_{r_2:p_{23}} = \frac{1}{4} \cdot \frac{1}{3}$. Considering all paths, the trust-weighted review $t_2 \cdot r_2$ influences the TRE-visibility of p_{22} via two paths; firstly via $\pi_1 = [\ p_{42} \xrightarrow{\frac{1}{3}} p_{38} \xrightarrow{\frac{1}{2}} p_{22}\ ]$ with $c_{r_2:p_{22}}^{\pi_1} = \frac{1}{6}$, secondly via $\pi_2 = [\ p_{42} \xrightarrow{\frac{1}{3}} p_{31} \xrightarrow{\frac{1}{4}} p_{23} \xrightarrow{\frac{1}{2}} p_{22}\ ]$ with $c_{r_2:p_{22}}^{\pi_2} = \frac{1}{24}$. The total contribution of review

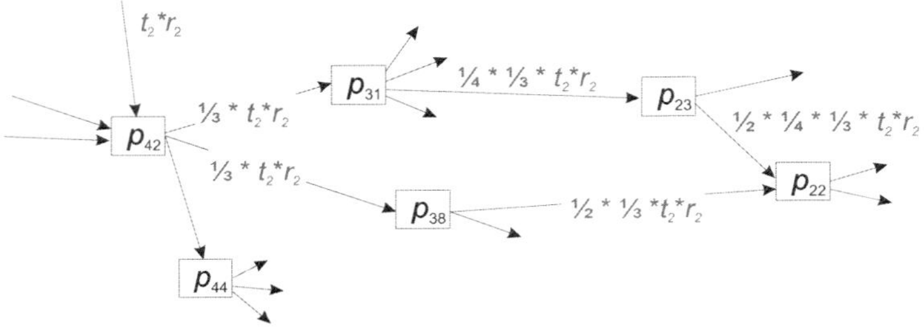

Figure 5.7: Propagation of trust-weighted reviews

$t_2 \cdot r_2$ to the TRE-visibility of p_{22} is the sum of the contributions of all paths, hence
$c^{\pi}_{r_2:p_{22}} = c^{\pi_1}_{r_2:p_{22}} + c^{\pi_2}_{r_2:p_{22}} = \frac{1}{6} + \frac{1}{24} = \frac{5}{24}$.

The contribution of a direct review r_i on p_d is $c_{r_i:p_d} = 1$. The contribution $c^{\pi_l}_{r_i:p_d}$ of a review r_i of a document p_j to p_d's TRE-visibility along a path

$$\pi_l = [\, p_j \rightarrow q_1 \rightarrow q_2 \rightarrow \ldots \rightarrow q_m \rightarrow p_d \,]$$

is defined as:

$$c^{\pi_l}_{r_i:p_d} = \frac{1}{|C_{p_j}|} + \sum_{i=1}^{m} \frac{1}{|C_{q_i}|} = \frac{1}{|C_{p_j}|} + \frac{1}{|C_{q_1}|} + \frac{1}{|C_{q_2}|} + \ldots + \frac{1}{|C_{q_m}|}$$

If a review contributes to the TRE-visibility of p_d via several paths $\pi_1, ..., \pi_n$:

$$c^{\pi}_{r_i:p_d} = \sum_{l=1}^{n} c^{\pi_l}_{r_i:p_d}$$

As the contribution $c^{\pi_l}_{r_i:p_d}$ strongly decreases with increasing length of path π_l [2], it is sensible to restrict the indirect influence of reviews to documents at a maximum distance $k_{\max}$. The version of the review-propagating TRE-visibility that uses the contribution $c_{r_i:p_d} = c^{\pi}_{r_i:p_d}$ is called the *path-based TRE-visibility*, $vis^{TRE_p}_{p_d,u_m}$, because it considers the distinct paths via which the reviews are forwarded in the document reference network. It was firstly presented in Hess and Stein (2007a).

---

[2] At least, the contribution will decrease if the outdegree of each document on a path is greater than one, and the average outdegree is larger than the number of paths. This normally holds in document networks such as citation networks or the web.

The Distance-Based TRE-Visibility

The path-based TRE-visibility can be simplified by replacing the path-based contribution $c_{r_i:p_d}^{\pi}$ with a contribution based on the distance k_{r_i,p_d}, i.e., the number of edges along the shortest path from the review r_i to the document p_d to be ranked. A direct review r_i on p_d has the distance $k_{r_i,p_d} = 0$. The *distance-based TRE-visibility* $\mathrm{vis}_{p_d,u_m}^{\mathrm{TRE}_d}$ uses the contribution $c_{r_i:p_d} = \frac{1}{(\lambda k_{r_i,p_d}+1)^{\beta}}$ (firstly presented in Hess and Stein, 2007a). We use $\lambda k_{r_i,p_d} + 1$ in order to give direct reviews a contribution of 1. β and λ are used for fine-tuning the contribution of indirect reviews. The distance-based TRE-visibility is thus defined as:

$$\mathrm{vis}_{p_d,u_m}^{\mathrm{TRE}_d} = \frac{\mathrm{vc} \cdot \mathrm{vis}_{p_d}^{\circ} + \sum\limits_{i=1}^{n}\left(\dfrac{t_i}{(\lambda k_{r_i,p_d}+1)^{\beta}} \cdot r_i\right)}{\mathrm{vc} + \sum\limits_{i=1}^{n}\dfrac{t_i}{(\lambda k_{r_i,p_d}+1)^{\beta}}}$$

Algorithm 2 shows how to compute the distance-based TRE-visibility. It can easily be modified for computing the path-based TRE-visibility.

Comparing Path-based and Distance-based TRE-Visibility

The basic difference between path-based and distance-based TRE-visibility is that the path-based TRE-visibility takes the structure of the document reference network explicitly into account. That means that the number of cited papers has an impact: it makes a difference whether a document refers only to a single paper or to hundreds of papers because the review contribution is distributed among all referenced documents. So in the path-based TRE-visibility, the higher the branching factor, the smaller the impact of indirect reviews. This is reflected in the distance-based TRE-visibility by λ. Moreover, β is used to modulate the impact of indirect reviews based on the distance. Both parameters have to be determined on the basis of the network characteristics of the respective document reference network. I show how to determine these parameters in section 8.3.2.

With the path-based and the distance-based TRE-visibility, there are two approaches for ranking documents efficiently according to the user's personal web of trust. The computation is efficient because precalculated document visibilities are used. However, not only are the base visibilities computed offline but also the review contributions. At query time, the reviews have only to be weighted with the trust in them, because the trust t_i in a review r_i depends on the user's personal web of trust. These trust-weighted reviews are added to the document base visibilities. The documents are then sorted according to the TRE-visibilities for a personalized ranking.

Algorithm 2 Distance-Based TRE-Visibility

1: **function** D-TRE-VIS(User u, Document p, BaseVisibility vis_p, float vc, int λ, float β, int k, Graph $\mathcal{ML}_{\mathcal{I}_{\text{prop}} \cdot \mathcal{D}}) \rightarrow \text{vis}_{p,u}^{\text{TRE}_s}$

2: $\quad$ reviews $\leftarrow \emptyset$

3: $\quad$ citingDocs $\leftarrow \emptyset$

4: $\quad$ citingDocs $\leftarrow$ GETCITINGDOCUMENTS(p, k) $\quad \triangleright$ Get all predecessors of p at a maximum distance of k

5: $\quad$ **for all** (q, d) in citingDocs **do** $\quad\quad\quad\quad\quad \triangleright$ document q at distance d of p

6: $\quad\quad$ review-edges $\leftarrow \bigcup_{u_m \in U} \{(u_m, q, r) \in R\}$ $\quad\quad\quad \triangleright$ Get all reviews on p

7: $\quad\quad$ **for all** rev $= (u_m, q, r)$ in review-edges **do**

8: $\quad\quad\quad$ trust $= (u, u_m, t_{u \rightarrow u_m})$ $\quad\quad\quad\quad \triangleright$ Get the trust in the reviewer

9: $\quad\quad\quad$ t $= I(t_{u \rightarrow u_m})$ $\quad\quad\quad\quad\quad\quad\quad \triangleright$ Get the trust in the review

10: $\quad\quad\quad$ $c = \frac{1}{(\lambda d + 1)^\beta}$ $\quad\quad\quad\quad\quad\quad\quad \triangleright$ Get the review contribution

11: $\quad\quad\quad$ reviews $\leftarrow$ reviews $\cup \{(r, t, c)\}$

12: $\quad\quad$ **end for**

13: $\quad$ **end for**

14: $\quad$ $\text{vis}_{p,u}^{\text{TRE}_d} \leftarrow \dfrac{\text{vc} \cdot \text{vis}_p + \sum\limits_{(r,t,c) \in \text{reviews}} t \cdot r \cdot c}{\text{vc} + \sum\limits_{(r,t,c) \in \text{reviews}} t \cdot c}$

15: $\quad$ **return** $\text{vis}_{p,u}^{\text{TRE}_d}$

16: **end function**

17: **function** GETCITINGDOCUMENTS(Document p, int k) $\rightarrow$ citingDocs

18: $\quad$ documents $\leftarrow \{p\}$

19: $\quad$ predecessors $\leftarrow \emptyset$

20: $\quad$ citingDocs $\leftarrow \emptyset$

21: $\quad$ **for** $i \leftarrow 0, i++, i = k - 1$ **do**

22: $\quad\quad$ **for all** q in documents **do**

23: $\quad\quad\quad$ predecessors $\leftarrow$ predecessors $\cup \bigcup_{p_m \in D} \{(p_m, q) \in C\}$ $\quad \triangleright$ p_m cites q

24: $\quad\quad\quad$ **if** $\exists j : (q, j) \in$ citingDocs **then** $\quad \triangleright$ There is another path from q to p

25: $\quad\quad\quad\quad$ **if** i $<$ j **then**

26: $\quad\quad\quad\quad\quad$ citingDocs $\leftarrow$ citingDocs $\cup \{(q, i)\}$ $\quad \triangleright$ Replace (q, j) by (q, i) because this path is shorter

27: $\quad\quad\quad\quad$ **end if**

28: $\quad\quad\quad$ **end if**

29: $\quad\quad$ **end for**

30: $\quad\quad$ documents $\leftarrow$ predecessors

31: $\quad\quad$ predecessors $\leftarrow \emptyset$

32: $\quad$ **end for**

33: $\quad$ **return** citingDocs

34: **end function**

5.1.8 Overview on the TRE-Visibilities

Table 5.3 gives an overview of the presented TRE-visibility functions.

TRE-Vis	Name	Description
trv_{p_d,u_m}	trust-weighted review visibility	Takes the sum of the direct trust-weighted reviews $t_i r_i$ on a document p_d, with t_i depending on u_m's web of trust.
$\mathrm{vis}_{p_d,u_m}^{\mathrm{TRE}_s}$	simple TRE-visibility	Sums all direct, trust-weighted reviews $t_i r_i$ on document p_d and the document base visibility $\mathrm{vis}_{p_d}^{\circ}$.
$\mathrm{vis}_{p_d,u_m}^{\mathrm{TRE}_i}$	integrated TRE-visibility	Propagates trust-weighted reviews $t_i r_i$ as part of the visibility on the document network.
$\mathrm{vis}_{p_d,u_m}^{\mathrm{TRE}_{rp}}$	review-propagating TRE-visibility	Sums direct and indirect trust-weighted reviews and the document base visibility.
$\mathrm{vis}_{p_d,u_m}^{\mathrm{TRE}_p}$	path-based TRE-visibility	A review-propagating TRE-visibility that measures the contribution of an indirect trust-weighted review based on the spreading factor of the paths from the reviewed document to p_d.
$\mathrm{vis}_{p_d,u_m}^{\mathrm{TRE}_d}$	distance-based TRE-visibility	A review-propagating TRE-visibility that measures the contribution of an indirect trust-weighted review based on the distance of the reviewed document p_j to p_d, i.e., the number of steps in the shortest path from p_j to p_d.

Table 5.3: TRE-Visibility Measures

Although the integrated TRE-visibility offers the most appealing way to compute personalized TRE-visibilities as the trust-weighted reviews are propagated on the document network together with the structure-based visibilities, it is not appropriate for practical reasons. One has to compute everything at query time, leading to a delay in the presentation of the document ranking which would not be accepted by users. Therefore an efficient TRE-visibility measure, the review-propagating TRE-visibility, was developed, which preserves the essential characteristic of the integrated TRE-visibility, namely the consideration of indirect reviews. The review-propagating TRE-visibility has the following properties:

1. The impact of reviews on personalized document recommendations is determined on the basis of the user's personal web of trust. Reviews made by reviewers whom the requesting user highly trusts, modify the visibility of the recommended document (i.e., increase or decrease the document's base visibility). In contrast,

if a user is distrusted with respect to her or his ability to provide reviews and recommendations, this user's reviews have no impact on the visibility.

2. A review r_i on document p_d influences directly the TRE-visibility of p_d and indirectly the TRE-visibility of the documents referenced by p_d and the documents referenced by these documents and so on. The closer the review is to the document the higher is the level of influence.

3. The TRE-visibility generates recommendations even if no reviews were given at all, or only by distrusted users. This recommendation is based on the document base visibility computed on the document reference network.

4. Taking the weighted average of trust-weighted reviews and document base visibilities adjusts the impact of the unpersonalized document base visibilities depending on the trust in the reviews: if trustworthy reviews are available, the influence of the document base visibility is low.

Note that any reference-based visibility measure can be used in order to compute the document base visibilities that are used in the simple TRE-visibility and in the review-propagating TRE-visibility. The integrated TRE-visibility has to be modified depending on the visibility measure used. I have shown this adaptation for PageRank and for HITS. An extension to any derivation of PageRank and HITS is therefore easily feasible.

5.2 Author Trust Networks & Document Networks

Instead of having a reviewer trust network as discussed before, trust relationships can be set between authors. A trust value between authors expresses the trust in the evaluated user's capabilities as author. Assigning someone high trust means to consider this user to be a "good" author, i.e., to provide reliable information of a high quality, i.e. not to have any links to spam pages etc. As in the reviewer trust network, trust is expressed in a numerical value in [-1, 1], ranging from distrust to trust. Authors are connected with documents via 'author-of'-relationships. For the computations made in the following, I demand that each document has at least one author. This two-layer architecture is defined as follows.

Definition 7 *A two-layer network with an author trust network $\mathcal{T}$ and a document reference network $\mathcal{D}$ is a graph*

$$\mathcal{ML}_{\mathcal{T} \to \mathcal{D}} = (U \cup D, T \cup C \cup A)$$

with two subgraphs $\mathcal{T} = (U, T)$ and $\mathcal{D} = (D, C)$ and a set of edges $A \subseteq U \times D$ connecting authors and documents via the relationship "author-of".

There are three possibilities of using trust information in trust-enhanced document recommendations and rankings:

1. Modify document visibilities based on the trust in the author(s): if a user trusts an author, the visibility of the documents written by the trusted author should be high from the trusting user's perspective. Visibility measures that integrate subjective author trust – the author-trust-enhanced visibility measures – generate such personalized document rankings. Hess and Stein (2007b) firstly discussed this idea for PageRank. In section 5.2.1, I extend this approach to an author-trust-enhanced visibility to HITS. I'll include a discussion on how such measures can be computed efficiently.

2. Capture the semantics of references based on the trust of the citing author in the cited author: the trust information gives a hint as to whether a reference is supportive or rather depreciatory. The trust-enhanced link semantics was presented in Stein and Hess (2006), which extends Stein and Hess (2005), and measures were defined for PageRank. In section 5.2.2, I discuss this approach and extend it to HITS. Moreover, I look in more detail on the mapping of the trust values from the trust network to the references between documents.

3. Modify reference weights with trust information: references between documents can be weighted, whereby the weights define how the visibility is distributed among the outgoing references. Modulating these weights based on the trust relationships expressed between authors personalizes the document recommendations. Section 5.2.3 discusses this approach which was first presented in Hess and Stein (2007b).

Table 5.4 gives an overview on the definitions used in the following (note that the basic identifiers used are the same as for the TRE-visibility).

5.2.1 Author Trust-Enhanced Document Visibilities

The idea of the author-trust-enhanced visibility is that the visibility of a document is modified by the trust that is set in the document's author or the group of authors. This is realized by propagating trust values from the authors via the is-author-of-relationships to the documents and by integrating these trust values then in the reference-based visibility. In the example in figure 5.8, user u_1's trust in user u_5 changes the visibility of document p_4: if u_1 trusts u_5, who is the author of document p_4, the visibility of p_4 should increase from u_1's perspective. In contrast, if u_1 distrusts u_5, i.e., u_1 considers u_5 to write "bad" – uninteresting, badly investigated or even fraudulent – papers, then p_4 should lose visibility and decrease in the ranking. Similarly, u_1's trust in u_2 increases or decreases the visibility of document p_3.

Identifier	Description
p_d	document to be recommended
u_m	user for which the recommendation is generated
$t_{u_m \to u_n}$	u_m's (subjective) trust in user u_n
t_d	u_m's trust in the author(s) of p_d
P_{p_d}	set of documents referencing p_d
C_{p_d}	set of documents referenced by p_d
A_d	set of authors u_i of document p_d
$e_{i \to j}$	edge from document p_i to p_j
$\bar{e}_{i \to j}$	edge attribute for $e_{i \to j}$, results from mapping (and if necessary averaging) of trust $t_{u_m \to u_n}$ set by the author(s) of p_i in the author(s) of p_j to the references between the documents p_i and p_j
$w_{i \to j}$	edge weight for the edge $e_{i \to j}$, derived from the edge attribute $\bar{e}_{i \to j}$ by a mapping function I

Table 5.4: Definitions for the ATE-Visibility

Indirectly, u_1's trust in u_2 influences the visibilities of the documents p_1 and p_2 as illustrated in figure 5.9, because visibility measures in the style of PageRank propagate the trust-enhanced visibility of p_3 to all documents referenced by p_3. This has the effect that documents which are cited by an author whom u_1 trusts gain visibility, whereas the documents cited by an author whom u_1 distrusts lose visibility. This reflects the fact that readers would rather not follow links to other webpages or to cited publications if they distrust the author.

Using the trust information in this way personalizes the document visibilities from u_1's perspective. We call this personalized visibility *author-trust-enhanced visibility*: the ATE-visibility $\text{vis}^{\text{ATE}}_{p_d, u_m}$ calculates a recommendation for document p_d for user u_m.

Determining the Trust in the Author(s)

In order to measure the ATE-visibility $\text{vis}^{\text{ATE}}_{p_d, u_m}$, we have to determine, as a first step, u_m's trust t_d in the author or the author collective of document p_d based on u_m's trust $t_{u_m \to u_i}$ to these authors. The trust values $t_{u_m \to u_i}$ are either directly given by u_m or derived by some trust metric from the trust network. Trust values are, as in the case of the TRE-visibility in [-1,1] and $t_{\text{unknown}} = 0$ is set in users for whom neither a

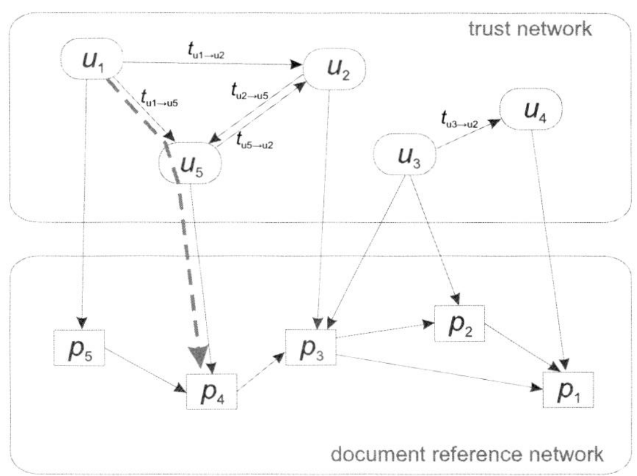

Figure 5.8: Modifying Visibilities by Subjective Trust in the Author

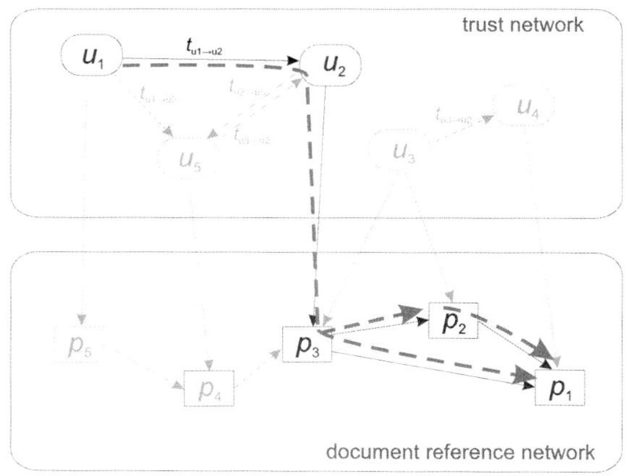

Figure 5.9: Indirect Influence of the ATE-Visibility

direct trust value is given nor a trust value can be inferred (because this user is not accessible by trust propagation, at least not at the maximum distance allowed). Note that by doing this, we have a trust value $t_{u_m \to u_i}$ in every author. As the visibility of a document should not become negative (this would have undesirable effects when propagating the visibility in the network), trust in the author collective has to be non-negative, i.e., $t_d \geq 0$. Therefore a mapping function has to be applied to the trust values $t_{u_m \to u_i} \in [-1, 1]$. The mapping can simply be achieved by shifting the trust values by $+1$ (note that in this setting, it is not required to have $t_d \in [0, 1]$ but $t_d \geq 0$). Certainly, other mapping functions could be used, too.

Let A_d be the set of authors u_i of document p_d. As in $\mathcal{ML}_{T \to D}$ every document must be connected with at least one author, the set A_d contains at least one element. For each user $u_i \in A_d$, a trust value $t_{u_m \to u_i}$ is given, either directly by u_m, inferred from the trust network or as t_{unknown}. The trust t_d in the author(s) of p_d is defined as:

$$t_d \;=\; \frac{\sum_{u_i \in A_d} t_{u_m \to u_i}}{|A_d|} \;+\; 1$$

Instead of using the average of the author trust, the minimum or maximum could also be taken.

The ATE-Visibility

The ATE-visibilities are computed with an extended visibility function. I will show how PageRank and HITS can be extended. I'll start with PageRank. It was defined in section 3.2.3 as:

$$\text{vis}_{p_d}^{\text{PR}} \;=\; (1 - \alpha) \;+\; \alpha \sum_{p_k \in P_{p_d}} \frac{\text{vis}_k^{\text{PR}}}{|C_{p_k}|}$$

with P_{p_d} being the set of documents referencing p_d and C_{p_k} being the set of documents referenced by document p_k. Then, α is the weight given to the reference-based part of the visibility and $1 - \alpha$ is the basic visibility given to each document regardless of whether it has any incoming links.

There are two intuitive modifications to the original PageRank so that it calculates ATE-visibilities. Firstly, I can modify the basic visibility $(1 - \alpha)$ of p_d by u_m's trust t_d in the author(s) of p_d.

$$\text{vis}_{p_d, u_m}^{\text{ATE}} \;=\; (1 - \alpha)\, t_d \;+\; \alpha \sum_{p_k \in P_{p_d}} \frac{\text{vis}_{p_k}^{\text{PR}}}{|C_{p_k}|}$$

Personalizing PageRank by adjusting the basic visibility has already been proposed by Page *et al.* (1998). In order to achieve a stronger personalization, I modify the entire PageRank with t_d:

$$\text{vis}_{p_d,u_m}^{\text{ATE}'} = t_d \, \text{vis}_{p_d}^{\text{PR}} = t_d \left((1 - \alpha) + \alpha \sum_{p_k \in P_{p_d}} \frac{\text{vis}_{p_k}^{\text{PR}}}{|C_{p_k}|} \right)$$

The trust t_d in the author(s) of document p_d affects in $\text{vis}_{p_d,u_m}^{\text{ATE}'}$ not only the basic visibility $(1 - \alpha)$ but also the reference-based visibility received from the incoming references. In the case that u_m totally distrusts the author(s) of p_d, the ATE-visibility of p_d is 0 regardless of number and impact of citations. Both functions have the property that the modified visibility is propagated to p_d's successors. The trust information has an indirect impact as sketched above.

In the case of HITS, only the second approach is feasible as HITS does not give to documents any basic visibility that can be modified by the trust in the authors. With a_{p_d} being the authority of a document p_d and h_{p_d} being the hub value computed, I define the ATE-visibility as:

$$h_{p_d,u_m}^{\text{ATE}} = t_d \, h_{p_d}, \qquad\qquad a_{p_d,u_m}^{\text{ATE}} = t_d \, a_{p_d}$$

We can ask – as in the case of the TRE-visibility defined on the basis of HITS – whether it is sensible to modify both hub and authority values by the trust in the author. This depends on what it means to trust someone as author. If this means to consider this user as someone who has in-depth knowledge of the topic on which he or she writes, it will be sensible to compute a_{p_d,u_m}^{ATE}. If a trustworthy author is also someone who has a good overview of a certain area, it is appropriate to compute h_{p_d,u_m}^{ATE}, too. In my opinion, trusting someone as an author comprises both these criteria and it is thus appropriate to compute the ATE-visibility for both hub and authority values.

Computing document rankings with the ATE-visibility has the drawback that the ATE-visibility must be computed at query time for all documents, because it is personalized and does not contain any user-independent part. Unfortunately, there is no straightforward way of using a precalculated document base visibility $\text{vis}_{p_d}^{\circ}$ as in the case of the TRE-visibility. However, a preprocessing step reduces considerably the computation load at query time. Offline computed document base visibilities can be used as initial values for the ATE-visibility. At query time, only few iterations with the ATE-visibility are then necessary. Page *et al.* have already mentioned that a good initial assignment speeds up the convergence so that only few iterations are required. The exact number of iterations depends on how big the indirect impact of the trust values should be. Defining that the trust in the author should influence the visibilities of the documents up to four steps away from the documents written by the trusted author (which is quite a lot) would lead to four iterations at query time. In an acyclic network, a single iteration is sufficient. If the recommendation is computed for a specific document, the computation load can be further reduced by considering only a fraction of the network. Only the documents that cite the requested document and the documents citing these documents and so on have to be considered. With HITS as reference-based measure on the document network, however, the proportion of the network would be bigger as for PageRank because HITS needs both citing and cited papers. This approach can certainly be applied to the integrated TRE-visibility, too.

Using only the above described ATE-visibility to determine rankings has the problem that the visibility is equally split among the outgoing edges (PageRank, for example, forwards $\frac{\mathrm{vis}^{\mathrm{PR}}_{p_d}}{|C_d|}$ along each outgoing edge of document p_d). References are thus always taken to be supportive, although this is not true. Assessing with the help of the information of the trust network whether a link is supportive or depreciatory addresses the problem. Here the second approach to propagate trust ratings to the document reference network comes into play.

5.2.2 Trust-Enhanced Link Semantics

References between documents are typically embedded in texts. In the text surrounding the link, authors can express their opinion on the cited document. In a positive expression of opinion, authors affirm, for example, the validity of a work by explaining that they were able to reproduce the results described in the cited paper. In contrast, authors might express disagreement or formulate in an extreme case even the suspicion that the information provided in the cited document is incorrect or faked. For the human reader of a document the semantics of a link, i.e., the opinion expressed in the link text, is obvious, whereas for a machine, the semantics is difficult to capture. Section 3.2.5 discussed this difficulty.

In the multi-layer architecture, we can use the information from the other layers in order to capture the semantics of the links between documents. The trust relationships are used to differentiate whether a link expresses trust or distrust: authors trusting each other will normally cite each other in a favorable way. It would be contradictory to cite someone in the context of scientific fraud and to assign her or him a high trust as author at the same time. In case of distrust between the authors, the link will more likely be deprecatory than supportive. These new edge weights, derived from the trust relationships, can then be used in reference-based visibility measures. A modified version of PageRank which considers edge weights, the *weighted PageRank*, makes use of the trust-based edge weights. The edge weights will influence the amount of visibility that is propagated to the cited documents. HITS can be modified in the same way. I discuss, in the following, the steps necessary to obtain such trust-based edge weights and their integration in a visibility measure.

Mapping Trust to Document References

The trust ratings between users, which are attributed to the edges in the trust network, are mapped to the edges between documents. This is illustrated for the trust relationships (direct or inferred) in figure 5.10. The trust value $t_{u_1 \to u_5}$ is attributed to the reference from document p_5, written by u_1, to document p_4, written by u_5. This new edge attribute gives a hint as to the semantics of the citation: if u_1 highly trusts u_5, then the citation will likely be supportive. Likewise, trust values $t_{u_3 \to u_4}$ and $t_{u_5 \to u_2}$ are propagated down to the references between p_2 and p_1, and between p_4 and p_3, respectively.

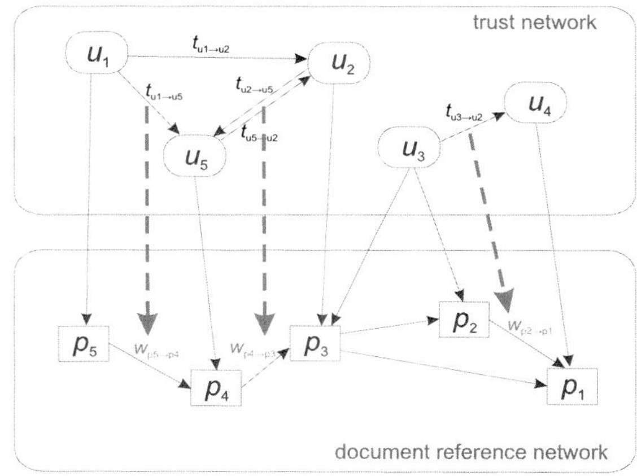

Figure 5.10: Trust-Enhanced Link Semantics

Generally formulated, the trust $t_{u_m \to u_n}$ of author u_m to the author u_n, whose document p_j is cited by document p_i written by u_m, is mapped to the edge $e_{i \to j}$ from document p_i to p_j. If documents are written jointly by several authors, more than one value will be mapped to the reference between the documents. A single edge attribute $\bar{e}_{i \to j}$ is obtained by averaging over all trust values that are mapped to this edge. The average is appropriate as long as trust values do not differ to much. This will likely be the case because coauthors normally have rather similar opinions on cited documents. For example, it is not likely that scientists coauthoring a scientific publication have completely diverging opinions on the literature in their field. If no value can be attributed to an edge $e_{i \to j}$, because there is no trust expressed between the authors of p_i and p_j, a fixed value $\bar{e}_{i \to j} = \bar{e}_{\text{default}} \in [t_{\min}, t_{\max}]$ is used. So exactly one edge attribute $\bar{e}_{i \to j}$ is determined for the edge between a document p_i and p_j.

Turning Attributed Trust into Edge Weights

Visibility measures in the style of PageRank require edge weights greater or equal to zero. The values $\bar{e}_{i \to j}$ that are attributed to each reference are turned into edge weights $w_{i \to j} \geq 0$ by applying a mapping function $I : [-1, 1] \to [0, m]$.

$$w_{i \to j} = I(\bar{e}_{i \to j})$$

Different mapping functions realize different trust semantics. Table 5.5 provides an overview of different mapping functions that could be applied and gives a short description on how I works.

Visibility Measures with Trust-Weighted Edges

Reference-based visibility measures can be defined for document networks with weighted references. Propagating document visibilities along the outgoing edges, PageRank splits a document's visibility equally among all referenced documents, whereas the weighted PageRank splits the visibility according to the weight $w_{i \to j}$ given to a reference:

$$\text{vis}_{p_d}^{\text{WPR}} = (1 - \alpha) + \alpha \sum_{p_i \in P_{p_d}} \frac{w_{i \to d} \; \text{vis}_{p_i}^{\text{WPR}}}{|C_{p_i}|}$$

In the same style, I can define a weighted version of HITS. Edge weights can be considered in the computation of the authority value: The more hubs reference to a document in a positive, supporting way the higher should be the authority value. The authority value $a_{p_d}^w$ that considers edge weights is thus defined as:

$$a_{p_d}^w = \gamma \sum_{p_l \in P_{p_d}} w_{l \to d} \; h_{p_l}$$

It is not sensible to modify the hub value, which is computed on the basis of the authority of those pages to which the hub links, by the trust that the author of the hub has in the author(s) of the authorities: linking to a document which I consider as bad (i.e. t_d is low) should not decrease my document's hub value if the corresponding text explains the reason for the citation, e.g. that the document is referenced in order to give an example for an opposite opinion.

In these modified versions of PageRank and HITS, the trust-based edge weights directly influence the visibility of a document. Here, we can now see what it means to use a certain mapping function I, i.e., we see its effect on the visibility.

I_+: $w_{i \to j} = \Delta + \bar{e}_{i \to j}$, with $\Delta \geq -t_{\min}$

I_+ guarantees that weights are non-negative. However, weights can be greater 1. If $\Delta = -t_{\min}$, then absolute distrust references will have zero weight. If $\Delta > -t_{\min}$, then all distrust references have at least some weight.

I'_+: $w_{i \to j} = \dfrac{\Delta + \bar{e}_{i \to j}}{\Delta + t_{\max}}$, with $\Delta \geq -t_{\min}$

I'_+ modifies I_+ so that all weights $w_{i \to j} \in [0, 1]$. This facilitates the interpretation of the resulting visibilities.

I_0: $w_{i \to j} = \max\{0, \bar{e}_{i \to j}\}$

I_0 gives no weight to all distrust references and is thereby more extreme than I'_+.

$I_{||}$: $w_{i \to j} = |\bar{e}_{i \to j}|$

In $I_{||}$, extremely high and low trust references give the highest weights. Neutral references are given zero weight.

I_λ: $w_{i \to j} = \begin{cases} \bar{e}_{i \to j} & \text{for } \bar{e}_{i \to j} \geq 0 \\ -\lambda \bar{e}_{i \to j} \quad (\lambda \in (0,1)) & \text{otherwise} \end{cases}$

I_λ modifies $I_{||}$ so that the weight of distrust references is lowered. For instance, with $\lambda = 0.5$, they contribute only half.

$I_\updownarrow$: $w_{i \to j} = 1 - |\bar{e}_{i \to j}|$

$I_\updownarrow$ is the contrary of $I_{||}$. High weight is only given to neutral references.

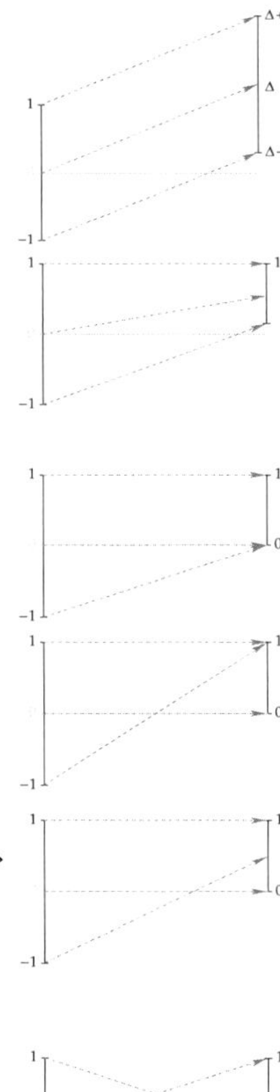

Table 5.5: Mapping Functions I

- I_+, I'_+ and I_0 give high weight to trust references and low (zero) weight to distrust references. This means that a cited document will no longer benefit from the visibility of the citing document if the citing author distrusts the cited work. Therefore, these mapping functions will be the ones that are normally used for generating document rankings. The difference between I_+ (I'_+) and I_0 is that I_0 gives zero weight to all distrust references. It considers only references with an at least slightly positive trust.

- $I_{\parallel}$ and I_{λ} give much weight to high trust and high distrust references. Documents that are very controversially cited – either they are really liked or hated – get the highest visibility. This visibility measure provides a very special view on the documents published in a certain area. This might be of interest, for instance, for researchers who analyze discussions and opinion-making processes in scientific communities. It can be a very helpful tool for an expert user who understands the underlying ranking mechanism and is thus able to interpret the results appropriately. I_{λ} is similar to $I_{\parallel}$ but gives less weight to the distrust references. So it modifies the ranking in such a way that a document needs to be more often cited positively than negatively.

- $I_{\updownarrow}$ gives high weight to neutral references. A high visibility will have those papers that are considered to be "just ok" and so are not controversially discussed. It may be considered as complementary to $I_{\parallel}$.

5.2.3 Modifying Reference Weights by Subjective Trust

Reference weights obtained, for example, by propagating trust information down to the edges in the document network or by extracting opinions with Natural Language Processing from link text, can be personalized based on trust information. Depending on the requesting user's subjective trust in the citing authors, the weights are adjusted: high trust in an author means also to trust the weights set by this author, whereas distrust in an author leads to distrust in this author's citations.

In figure 5.11, user u_1's trust in u_5 modifies the edge weight $w_{p_4 \rightarrow p_3}$. If $t_{u_1 \rightarrow u_5} = 1$, then the weight should be used as set by u_5 (or as derived from u_5's personal trust relationships). In case of distrust, however, no weight should be given to this reference. This means that the references by a distrusted author are not considered at all in the visibility calculation. This is fairly intuitive and corresponds to the random surfer model because people normally do not follow the links by someone they absolutely distrust. The trust information thus modifies the visibility support given via a reference.

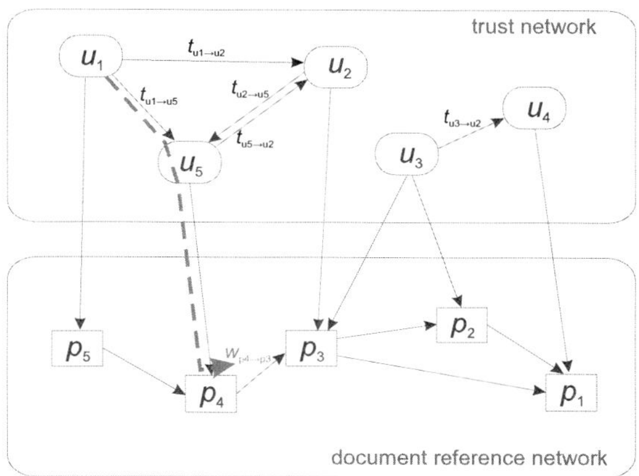

Figure 5.11: Author trust modifies reference weights

The personalized edge weights $w'_{i \to j}$ are defined as:

$$w'_{i \to j} \quad = \quad \frac{t_{u_m \to u_n} - t_{\min}}{t_{\max} - t_{\min}} w_{i \to j}$$

They are then used in the weighted PageRank $\mathrm{vis}^{\mathrm{WPR}}_{p_d}$ instead of the original non-personalized weights $w_{i \to j}$, giving a personalized weighted PageRank $\mathrm{vis}^{\mathrm{WPR}}_{p_d, u_m}$. The same holds true for the modified computation of HITS' authority value.

5.2.4 Integrating ATE-Visibility and Personalized Weights

There are two personalization strategies: the ATE-visibility and personalized trust-based edge weights. The ATE-visibility modifies directly the visibility of a document, i.e., it affects the nodes, based on the requesting user's personal trust in the author of the document. The personalized edge weights in the second approach affect the edges: edge weights are modified based on the trust in the author setting the reference. This, however, does not influence the visibility of the documents directly written by a particular trusted author but only the documents cited by this author. So a comprehensive personalization strategy can be achieved by integrating both ATE-visibility and personalized edge weights. They can easily be combined, as they are independent from each other: the ATE-visibility affects only the nodes, the personalized edge weights affect the edges. The weighted ATE-visibility $\mathrm{vis}^{\mathrm{ATE}_w}_{p_d,u_m}$ uses instead of PageRank the weighted PageRank with personalized edge weights $w_{i \to k}$. Including the trust-modified edge weights into both ATE-visibility measures $\mathrm{vis}^{\mathrm{ATE}}_{p_d,u_m}$ and $\mathrm{vis}^{\mathrm{ATE}'}_{p_d,u_m}$ then gives:

$$\mathrm{vis}^{\mathrm{ATE}_w}_{p_d,u_m} = t_d \, (1 - \alpha) + \alpha \sum_{p_i \in P_{p_d}} \frac{w'_{i \to d} \, \mathrm{vis}^{\mathrm{WPR}}_{p_i}}{|C_{p_i}|}$$

$$\mathrm{vis}^{\mathrm{ATE}'_w}_{p_d,u_m} = t_d \, \mathrm{vis}^{\mathrm{WPR}}_{p_d} = t_d \left((1 - \alpha) + \alpha \sum_{p_i \in P_{p_d}} \frac{w'_{i \to d} \, \mathrm{vis}^{\mathrm{WPR}}_{p_i}}{|C_{p_i}|} \right)$$

I use $\frac{w_{i \to d} \, \mathrm{vis}^{\mathrm{WPR}}_{p_i}}{|C_{p_i}|}$ instead of $\frac{w_{i \to d} \, \mathrm{vis}^{\mathrm{WPR}}_{p_i}}{\sum_{p_j \in C_{p_i}} w_{i \to j}}$ although this second alternative has the advantage that the overall amount of visibility that is propagated in the document reference network is not changed: it distributes more visibility than normal PageRank via the heavy-weighted references, while less visibility is propagated along the references with low weights. A normalization after each iteration as in the case of $\mathrm{vis}^{\mathrm{ATE}_w}_{p_d,u_m}$ is thus not required. However, this approach is here not appropriate. Consider an author Alice who cites two papers written by Bob. Alice highly trusts Bob so that the edge weights on the references from the document p_a written by Alice to documents p_{b_1} and p_{b_2} written by Bob is $w_{p_a \to p_{b_i}} = 1$. Dividing by the absolute number of references propagates $0.5 \, \mathrm{vis}_{p_a}$ on the edge from p_a to each p_{b_1} and p_{b_2}. Dividing by the sum of the edge weights propagates the same amount of visibility: $0.5 \, \mathrm{vis}_{p_a}$. Consider now the case that Alice distrusts Bob, and edge weights are $w_{p_a \to p_{b_i}} = 0.1$. Dividing by the absolute number of references gives $\frac{0.1}{2} \, \mathrm{vis}_{p_a} = 0.05 \, \mathrm{vis}_{p_a}$ whereas dividing by the sum of the edge weights gives $\frac{0.1}{0.2} \, \mathrm{vis}_{p_a} = 0.5 \, \mathrm{vis}_{p_a}$ – the same as in the case that Alice trusts Bob. The division by the sum of the edge weights is thus only sensitive to relative trust differences but not to absolute values.

In the case of HITS, the hub and the authority values are computed with the combined personalization strategy as:

$$h^{\mathrm{ATE}}_{p_d,u_m} = t_d \, h_{p_d}, \qquad a^{\mathrm{ATE}_w}_{p_d,u_m} = t_d \left(\gamma \sum_{p_l \in P_{p_d}} w_{l \to d} \, h^{\mathrm{ATE}}_{p_l,u_m} \right)$$

5.2.5 Overview on the ATE-Visibilities

Table 5.6 summarizes the ATE-visibility functions that are based on PageRank. For each of these measures, a corresponding measure was defined for the hub and authority value of HITS. Note here that in contrast to the different TRE-visibilities we do not have alternative functions, but functions that can be combined to form a comprehensive personalization approach.

TRE-Vis	Name	Description
$\text{vis}^{\text{ATE}}_{p_d,u_m}$	author-trust-enhanced visibility	Weights the visibility of a document p_d with u_m's trust t_d in its author(s).
$\text{vis}^{\text{WPR}}_{p_d}$	weighted PageRank	Extends PageRank by using edge weights derived from the trust network.
$\text{vis}^{\text{WPR}}_{p_d,u_m}$	personalized weighted PageRank	Uses in the weighted PageRank edge weights that are personalized for u_m.
$\text{vis}^{\text{ATE}w}_{p_d,u_m}$	weighted author-trust-enhanced visibility	Uses weighted edges in the author-trust-enhanced visibility $\text{vis}^{\text{ATE}}_{p_d,u_m}$ and thus combines $\text{vis}^{\text{ATE}}_{p_d,u_m}$ and $\text{vis}^{\text{WPR}}_{p_d,u_m}$.

Table 5.6: Overview on the ATE-Visibilities

5.3 Mixed Author and Reviewer Networks

Having looked at author and trust reviewer networks separately, I now consider those networks in which users can be both authors and readers. This is exactly the situation in the scientific community: researchers find themselves in the dual role of reader and writer. Papers are read by scientists either within the scope of their own work or as reviewers; both activities result in an opinion, i.e., in our terminology in a review, on the paper read. Scientific papers then include the citations to those papers that were used as a basis when working on the paper. On the web, the situation is similar: people maintaining homepages, writing blogs or contributing to wikis also visit other webpages in the role of a reader. I argue that it is not necessary to distinguish between different types of trust, e.g., to distinguish between trust in scientists with respect to their qualities as a reviewer and their ability to write good scientific papers. Reviewers for computer science conferences and journals, for instance, are normally scientists who enjoy a good reputation in the specific research area, i.e., who have high quality publications. As this works well in practice, a single trust value is sufficient. The two-layer architecture in this setting consists of a trust network between users who can be both authors and reviewers and of a document reference network. Both layers are interlinked by two types of edges, namely is-author-relationships and reviews on documents. While the reviews are weighted, the is-author edges are not weighted.

There are now different possibilities of generating recommendations within this two-layer architecture. Firstly, the is-author relationships could be transformed into reviews. Thereby, an edge weight has to be defined for the review edge. A very simplified approach would be to assign each edge the maximum review value, assuming that authors like their own papers and that they would give them a high review. This might work quite well except for cases in which authors distance themselves from their papers, for example, because they detected some unintentional mistake in it. The TRE-visibility can be directly computed on this newly transformed multi-layer network.

A second possibility is to derive two multi-layer networks from the mixed one. The first one contains all documents, all reviews and all users who provided at least one review. The second multi-layer network again includes all documents and all authors connected with their papers. On these multi-layer networks, the TRE-visibility and the ATE-visibility, respectively, can be computed. For the final result, both TRE- and ATE-visibility are combined, for instance, by taking the average. Alternatively, a weighted combination would be possible. This means that the portion of the TRE- or the ATE-visibility, respectively, depends on its "quality", e.g., on the degree of personalization or the number of direct reviews used for generating the recommendation.

5.4 Extending the Two-Layer to a Multi-Layer Approach

The previous sections discussed different extensions of a two-layer architecture, consisting of a document reference network and a trust network (authors and/or reviewers). I'll extend now such a two-layer architecture with an organization network. Basically, the organization network can be connected with the trust network or with the document reference network. In the following I will look at both combinations and at how to integrate the information from the organization network into trust-enhanced visibility measures.

5.4.1 Connecting Organization Networks and Trust Networks

When connecting the organization layer with the trust layer in order to enhance trust-based recommendations, the organizations and actors are typically connected via a member-of-relationship. This relationship is normally bidirectional (is-member-of and has-member, respectively) and non-weighted. Apart from member-of, completely different roles are viable, for instance, customer-of. However this relationship does not play a role for trust-enhanced document recommendations. The three-layer network with an organization network is defined as follows.

116

Definition 8 *A three-layer network with an organization network $\mathcal{O}$, an author trust network $\mathcal{T}$ and a document reference network $\mathcal{D}$ in which the organization network is connected with the trust network is a graph*

$$\mathcal{ML}_{\mathcal{O}\to\mathcal{T}\to\mathcal{D}} = (O \cup U \cup D,\ I \cup T \cup C \cup M \cup A)$$

with three subgraphs $\mathcal{O} = (O, I)$, $\mathcal{T} = (U, T)$ and $\mathcal{D} = (D, C)$, a set of edges $M \subseteq O \times U$ connecting organizations and authors via membership and a set of edges $A \subseteq U \times D$ between authors and documents.

In the same way, a three-layer architecture can be defined with a reviewer trust network instead of an author trust network. Note that trust and organization networks are irreducible. Neither interorganizational trust relationships nor cooperates-with relationships permit drawing conclusions about the relationships between the organizations' members. For instance, some members of two competing companies might be friends despite the competitive relationship between their organizations. In turn, an organization and its relationships do not represent the sum of the relationships of its members as discussed in section 3.1.6.

The organization network represents an additional source of information for the trust-based recommendations. Connecting organizations and persons, it provides further information on the person trust network. Following the two basic mechanisms for propagating information between distinct layers as described in section 4.3.2 and visualized in figure 4.2, information can be propagated on the one hand from the edges in the organization network to the edges in the trust network, and on the other hand directly from nodes to nodes, i.e., from the organizations to the persons in the trust network.

Propagating Organizations' Authority to Persons

Measures from social network analysis and reference-based measures such as PageRank can be applied to the reference structure of the organization network. This gives for each organization o_i a reputation value $rep^o_{o_i}$. An organization's authority can be propagated along the "has-member"-relationships to its members becoming by this an attribute of the nodes in the trust network. For a user u_m who is member of o_i, its organization-based reputation $rep^o_{u_m}$ is defined as:

$$rep^o_{u_m} = rep^o_{o_i}$$

An example from academia illustrates this: scientists benefit from the reputation of their university or their public granting organization in the sense that their credibility increases and thus the trust in them (Porter Liebeskind and Lumerman Oliver, 1998).

If global, non-personalized reputation values were computed for the persons in the trust network, the organization authority can be directly integrated into the personal authority and increase or decrease it, respectively. We denote with rep_{u_m} the new reputation of user u_m which is based on $rep^t_{u_m}$, the reputation inferred from the trust network by some global trust metric and $rep^o_{u_m}$, the reputation inferred from the organization network. All of these reputation values are in $[0,1]$. With α as weighting factor, the new reputation is defined as:

$$rep_{u_m} = \alpha \cdot rep^t_{u_m} + (1 - \alpha) \cdot rep^o_{u_m}$$

Alternatively, $rep^o_{u_m}$ might only be used if $rep^t_{u_m}$ is uncertain because, for example, it is based only on few trust statements and long trust chains. As the presented approach for trust-based recommendations works with interpersonal trust values (i.e. trust is a property of the edges in the trust network and not of the nodes), I do not go further into detail for the global reputation values but look at interpersonal trust.

The organization authority can be used to specify a trust value from a user u_m to an unknown user u_{unknown}. Unknown means that neither a direct trust value is given by u_m on u_{unknown} nor an indirect trust value can be computed (because there is no path from u_m to u_{unknown}, or because the distance between them is too big in order to apply a trust metric in a sensible way). Basically, the trust in an unknown user is defined as $t_{u_m \rightarrow u_{\text{unknown}}} = 0$. The reputation of the organization of which u_{unknown} is a member gives some additional information that can be used in order to replace zero with a more specific trust value:

$$t_{u_m \rightarrow u_{\text{unknown}}} = rep^o_{u_{\text{unknown}}}$$

Although the reputation is in $[0,1]$ while the trust value is in $[-1,1]$, this is still appropriate. As reputation is computed on the basis of the positive trust or cooperation edges, a reputation of zero denotes a low reputation (e.g. because this user's organization has only few cooperations with other organizations), and not a bad reputation. In the case that $rep^o_{u_{\text{unknown}}} = 0$, the unknown user would get assigned a trust of 0, i.e.: he or she would continue to be considered as unknown in the recommendation process. It might be argued that a trust of 1 is too high for someone unknown, only because the organization to which he or she belongs has such a high reputation. However, in reality this is often exactly what we are doing. Alternatively, the global reputation computed on the basis of the trust network can also be used:

$$t_{u_m \rightarrow u_{\text{unknown}}} = rep_{u_{\text{unknown}}}$$

Mapping Interorganizational Relationship Information on the Trust Network

Relationship information can be propagated from the edges in the organization network to the edges between the users who are members of the connected organizations. This information can be used analogous to the above case to set a trust value $t_{u_m \to u_{\text{unknown}}}$ from a user u_m to an unknown user that is more specific than zero. For instance, a (strong) trust between the organizations of which two non-connected users are members increases the unknown trust, whereas distrust might decrease the unknown trust. So u_m's trust in some user unknown user is

$$t_{u_m \to u_{\text{unknown}}} = t_{o_i \to o_j}$$

with $t_{o_i \to o_j}$ being the degree of trust between the organization o_i and o_j and u_m being member of o_i and u_{unknown} being member of o_j.

This trust value can then be used in the recommendation process. In the scope of the TRE-visibility, for instance, it would be used to weight the reviews provided by an unknown user. Note that these values are not inserted in the trust network (which would affect the trust propagation) but they are used only when computing recommendations.

Apart from estimating the trust in some unknown user based on the information from the organization network, the relationship information between two organizations can be used to refine the explicitly provided trust relationships. In trust networks that were extracted e.g. by web mining approaches, the trust values (also extracted) can be refined on the basis of the relationship information of the corresponding organizations, given that this information was not yet used during the extraction of the trust network. A strong cooperation relationship or a strong interorganizational trust relationship would then increase the trust value. When working with confidence values (i.e. the confidence in the trust asserted), the confidence would be strengthened.

The information from the organization network can help in clarifying cases in which it is problematic to infer trust values. I raised in section 3.1.5 the question on how to deal with cases in which contradictory trust values are assigned to a user, e.g., when a first user gave high trust and a second one high distrust. We proposed to give a degree of controversy as additional information to the user so that the user can decide by her-/himself. The interorganizational trust relationship information might explain such cases. For instance, if a user gets a very bad trust value only via one path but extremely good trust values via all other paths, the distrust value might be due to a strong competitive (or distrust) relationship between the corresponding organizations, which rubs off on its members.

Interorganizational Trust-enhanced Visibility Measures

Extending the two layer architecture for document recommendations to a multi-layer architecture, we may presuppose an organization network with research institutions and universities of which the persons in the trust network are members. The information that is propagated from the organization network to the trust network may modify the trust values on the edges between persons, especially for unknown users. These trust values can directly be included in the ATE- and the TRE-visibility. No modifications of the trust-enhanced visibility measures are required.

5.4.2 Connecting Organization Networks and Document Networks

An organization network can also be attached to the document reference network. Organizations are in this context, for instance, the journals or the publishers of scientific papers or the organizations that are responsible for a certain webpage. However, it is difficult to define a reference structure between these organizations on which reputation or authority can be computed. As the different layers in the multi-layer architecture have to be irreducible, we cannot simply infer the references between publishing journals from the citations between the papers contained, because this information is already used to generate the document reference network. A completely different approach would be to relate journals based on the topics they deal with. However, an authority value cannot be computed on such a topic network. Nevertheless, even without any reference structure, we might have some authority value for these organizations, which can then be used when measuring a document's trust-enhanced visibility. The documents then benefit from the authoritativeness of the journal (or the conference) in which they were published.

5.5 Overview on the Multi-Layer Approaches

In this chapter, I developed a set of measures for trust-based document recommendations. I focused on trust-enhanced document recommendations that were basically generated in a two-layer architecture consisting of a trust and a document reference network. The TRE-visibility measures use a reviewer trust network, while the set of ATE-visibility measures is defined on an author trust network. I have also shown how to generate document recommendations in a two-layer architecture in which the trust network comprises both reviewers and authors. Then, I extended the two-layer architecture with an organization network to a multi-layer architecture. Table 5.7 gives an overview on the approaches developed.

Architecture		Measures
$\mathcal{ML}_{\mathcal{T} \overset{\bullet}{\to} \mathcal{D}}$	Two-layer network with a reviewer trust network and a document reference network	Trust-review-enhanced (TRE-) visibility measures integrate trust-weighted reviews in reference-based visibility measures.
$\mathcal{ML}_{\mathcal{T} \to \mathcal{D}}$	Two-layer network with an author trust network and a document reference network	Author-trust-enhanced (ATE-) visibility measures modify reference-based visibility measures based on the requesting user's trust in the author(s). Weighted ATE-visibility measures use in addition (personalized) edge weights on the references.
$\mathcal{ML}_{\mathcal{O} \to \mathcal{T} \to \mathcal{D}}$	Three-layer network with an interorganizational trust network, a reviewer/ author trust network and a document network	TRE- and ATE-visibility measures are computed on the basis of an author or reviewer trust network which is enhanced with information from an organization network.

Table 5.7: Trust-enhanced Visibility Measures for Document Recommendations

6 Model of Uncertainty for Duplicates in Document Networks

6.1 Models of Uncertainty

Duplicate versions of one and the same document have to be considered in various settings, for instance, when performing searches across different document collections such as in the case of federated digital libraries or when search engines crawl the web. As discussed in section 2.1.5, these duplicates are a major source of uncertainty in the process of generating recommendations. Duplicates and near-duplicates provide difficulties when answering queries over document repositories. As the incoming and outgoing edges of duplicates are uncertain, the results by reference-based measures such as PageRank and by trust-enhanced visibility measures such as the TRE-visibility are distorted. Document recommender systems therefore have to deal with the duplicate versions of scientific papers and websites when computing recommendations and rankings. Before developing a model of uncertainty for this special type of uncertainty in document collections, a classification scheme for models of uncertainty is given.

6.1.1 Survey on Models of Uncertainty

The types of uncertainty that are frequently encountered in computer science can be classified into two models: models in which it is not known where the uncertainty is located and models in which this is known. As the first case corresponds to what most people think of when they face uncertainty in data, I call it *basic uncertainty*. A probability distribution can be associated with the uncertain data. An example for basic uncertainty is the transmission of data via a noisy channel. The probability that the received word does not contain any errors (or only up to x errors) can be indicated based on the quality of the channel. This probability does not say anything about the positions of the errors in the word, i.e., which bits may be flipped. I call the second type of uncertainty *cluster-based uncertainty* because a cluster of alternatives is offered. An example for cluster-based uncertainty is that there are two or more alternative representations of the word, e.g., the first alternative is the word 01101, and the second one 01111, i.e., the uncertainty is at position 4. In computer science, many approaches aim to eliminate uncertainty, or at least to minimize it. For instance, redundancy, e.g. check bits, may be introduced in messages before transmission. This permits decoding the signal received via a noisy channel.

Uncertainty is a current research topic in the area of databases[1]. In contrast to traditional deterministic databases, probabilistic databases are able to cope with inaccurate, imprecise or even missing data. Widom (2005) distinguishes in the accuracy model of the probabilistic database system TRIO three levels on which inaccuracy can be described: the attribute level, the tuple level and the relation level.

1. Uncertainty on the attribute level: an attribute value is the approximation of the exact (unknown) value. A probability is associated with the attribute value. In the case of basic uncertainty, the probabilities of the same attribute in different tuples are independent. In sensor networks, for instance, a value reported by a certain sensor, such as the temperature in a room, might be uncertain due to problems when measuring the value, or due to features inherent to the method of measurement (see e.g. Cheng and Prabhakar, 2003). The probability associated to a value in the database gives the likelihood that this value is the exact temperature in that room at the time of measurement. In digital document collections, the probability could indicate the likelihood that the author name is correctly parsed or that a certain reference is correctly extracted. The probability is based on general knowledge on the quality of the applied technique. Knowing this probability does not mean knowing where the error is. In contrast, cluster-based uncertainty on the attribute level means that there is a set of possible values and a probability distribution over this set. For example, when users fill in forms and the handwritten name should be recognized, the last letter might be ambiguous: with a probability of 0.7, it is an a and with a probability of 0.3, it is a d. This uncertainty type is, for instance, considered in TRIO (Benjelloun *et al.*, 2006) and by Re *et al.* (2006).

2. Uncertainty on the tuple level: the probability is associated with the tuple. In the case of basic uncertainty, the probability indicates the likelihood of this tuple being actually in the relation. In a digital document repository, it could be the probability that a document with this metadata exists at all. Another example is the tag-gene association in the Cancer Genome Anatomy Project in which the probability for a tuple to belong to the relation is based on uncertainties inherent in the experiments producing the association (Dalvi and Suciu, 2005). This type of uncertainty is considered in Benjelloun *et al.*, too. In databases with cluster-based uncertainty, duplicates of the same real-world object have a

---

[1]See e.g. the research projects TRIO `http://infolab.stanford.edu/trio/` and MystiQ `http://www.cs.washington.edu/homes/suciu/project-mystiq.html`.

certain probability of being the correct representation of this real-world object. In federating two document repositories, for example, the probabilities of the identified duplicates might depend on the quality of their source collection. For example, the version from a source collection with a reputation for high quality might have a probability of 0.7 and the version retrieved from one of the authors' homepages might have a probability of 0.3. Cluster-based uncertainty on the tuple level is, for instance, addressed by Andritsos *et al.* (2006)

3. Uncertainty on the relation level: Basic uncertainty on the relation level means that only a portion of the expected relation might actually be present, because the tuples does not completely correspond to the schema of the relation. For example, the tuples from some first source have 8 attributes, the tuples of some second source have 12 attributes but the schema of the relation defines 10 attributes. The probability hence indicates the coverage of the relation.

Uncertainty encountered in document collections can be classified in this framework of uncertainty types. Duplicate documents are a kind of *cluster-based uncertainty on the tuple level*. Duplicates can be identified by some duplicate detection mechanism. As they might originate from different sources with varying quality, they can have a certain probability of being correct. There is also a low *basic uncertainty on the tuple level*, namely that documents are not correctly assigned to a cluster. I do not consider this basic uncertainty further but assume to work on a "clean" document collection with all documents grouped correctly into clusters. I have described in section 3.2.6 how duplicates can be identified and be grouped into clusters. Additionally, *basic uncertainty on the attribute level* might affect all documents (and not only duplicates): attributes such as the author names, the titles, but also the reference lists may contain errors resulting from errors in the automatic process of extracting these information from the documents or from errors made by users or librarians when providing the metadata. However, it is not likely to have any information on this uncertainty type. As the uncertainty caused by the duplicates has the most impact on the quality of the document recommendations, the uncertainty model developed in this thesis addresses the cluster-based uncertainty in document networks. In the following, a database model for cluster-based uncertainty is presented and extended for document networks.

6.1.2 A Probabilistic Model for Cluster-based Uncertainty in Databases

Andritsos *et al.* (2006) presented a model for cluster-based uncertainty in relational databases. Query answering over these so-called "dirty databases" cannot proceed in the same way as query answering over databases without duplicates. A simple query over the small document collection shown in table 6.1 outlines the problem.

The relation gives for each document its metadata like authors, title and year of publication. The bibliographic entries are taken from CiteSeer but could also be the result of federating different document collections. Documents with the same *id* are duplicates, such as *doc*1 and *doc*2. They are slightly different versions of the same paper; one of them was published as a conference paper, the other one in a journal.

id	*docID*	*title*	*author*	*year*
d1	doc1	Authoritative sources in a hyperlinked environment	Kleinberg, J.	1998
d1	doc2	Authoritative sources in a hyper-linked environment	Kleinberg, J.M.	1999
d2	doc3	Artificial Intelligence: A Modern Approach	Russell, S., Norvig, P.	1994
d2	doc4	Articial Intelligence: Amodern Approach	Stuart J. Russell and Peter Norvig	1995

Table 6.1: A 'Dirty' Document Database

An example for a query to this database is now "get documents published in 1995 and later":

```
select id
from document d
where year > 1994
```

Standard query answering would return *d*1 and *d*2.[2] For *d*1, we know with certainty that it has been published after 1994. However, should *d*2 really be in the answer? To one of the sources, it has been published already in 1994.

Probabilistic Model

The probabilistic model by Andritsos *et al.* groups tuples t that refer to the same real-world entity into *clusters*. Each relation is hence partitioned into clusters. A probability $prob(t)$ is associated to each tuple. The probabilities of the tuples within a cluster sum to 1. In the case of digital libraries, the probability could indicate the quality of the document's source library. For instance, digital libraries that guarantee high quality metadata could be given a higher probability than the ones that extract metadata in a completely automated way. Table 6.2 extends the example database with a fictive probability[3] for each tuple. Additionally, a tuple identifier is given.

---

[2] Note that the query retrieves the ids, i.e., *d*1 and *d*2 and not *doc*1 and *doc*2.

[3] In the first cluster, the journal version *doc*1 is given a higher probability. In the second cluster, the probabilities are similar as the metadata of both duplicates contains errors.

	id	docID	prob
t1	d1	doc1	0.2
t2	d1	doc2	0.8
t3	d2	doc3	0.7
t4	d2	doc4	0.3

Table 6.2: Cluster-based Uncertainty with Probabilities

Query Answering in Probabilistic Databases

Andritsos *et al.* answer queries over databases containing duplicates with a probabilistic approach. They derive *probabilistic instances* ("candidate databases") from the database D. A probabilistic instance $\widehat{D}_i$ is a subset of D which takes exactly one tuple t out of each cluster C_j with probability $prob(t)$. In the above example, the probabilistic instances are obtained by choosing out of the first cluster either doc1 or doc2, and out of the second cluster either doc3 or doc4. This gives $\widehat{D}_1 = \{t1, t3\}$, $\widehat{D}_2 = \{t1, t4\}$, $\widehat{D}_3 = \{t2, t3\}$ and $\widehat{D}_4 = \{t2, t4\}$. In the next step, a probability distribution over the probabilistic instances is calculated. The probability is assigned to each $\widehat{D}_i$ by multiplying the probabilities of its tuples:[4]

$$Prob(\widehat{D}_i) \;=\; \prod_{t \in \widehat{D}_i} prob(t)$$

This gives for $\widehat{D}_1$ the probability $Prob(\widehat{D}_1) = 0.2 \cdot 0.7 = 0.14$. The answer to a query Q is now defined as a probabilistic measure on the tuples. Each tuple t is in the answer to Q with probability pr_t:

$$pr_t \;=\; \sum_{t \in Q(\widehat{D}_i)} Prob(\widehat{D}_i)$$

An answer is hence based on the results of querying all probabilistic instances and their probabilities. The answer to our example query is now as follows: $d1$ which has been published later than 1994 in every probabilistic instance is an answer to the query with probability 1. Document $d2$ is a result only in $\widehat{D}_2$ and $\widehat{D}_4$ and has thus the probability $pr_{d2} = Prob(\widehat{D}_2) + Prob(\widehat{D}_4) = 0.2 \cdot 0.3 + 0.8 \cdot 0.3 = 0.3$.

This approach has the drawback that the number of probabilistic instances may be exponential. An efficient query answering will only be realistic if the probability

---

[4]Tuples that represent the same real-world entity are conditionally dependent: if a tuple $t1$ is already in a probabilistic instance, the probability that a duplicate tuple $t2$ is in that instance is zero. Tuples that refer to different real-world entities are independent. (Andritsos *et al.*, 2006)

distribution is non-uniform, i.e., if only few probabilistic instances have a high probability and most of them have a low one. In this case, only the few highly probable instances have to be considered. If probabilities are uniformly distributed, the number of probabilistic instances cannot be restricted. Andritsos et al. present an approach that avoids deriving the probabilistic instances but instead answers the query directly on the dirty database. Queries are rewritten so that the tuples with the same id are grouped and their probabilities are summed. This, however, fails for some types of queries. Andritsos et al. pretend that their *class of rewritable queries* contains most queries relevant in practice. The example query is rewritten as:

```
select id, sum(prob)
from document d
where year > 1994
group by id
```

This uncertainty model can directly be applied to document collections as long as only metadata such as authors and titles are queried. Reference-based measures in the style of PageRank and the TRE- or ATE-visibility, however, analyze the references between documents. Therefore, the relational uncertainty model has to be extended to an uncertainty model for graphs. An efficient approach to computing the visibility measures is certainly required, too.

6.1.3 A Model for Cluster-Based Uncertain Graphs

A document collection without duplicates is a graph $G = (V, E)$ consisting of a set V of documents p_d and a set of directed links between the documents $E \subseteq V \times V$. The document graph for a collection that includes duplicate documents can now be defined as follows.

Definition 9 *A cluster-based uncertain graph is a structure*

$$GC = (V, E, C_1, ... C_m).$$

The documents p_d are grouped into the clusters $C_1, ..., C_m$. So C_i are partial functions from the set of documents V into $[0, 1]$ such that the domains of C_i partition V, whereby each element is in a unique cluster.

$C_i(p_d)$ gives the probability that some duplicate is the correct representation of the document and the probabilities of all duplicates within a cluster sum to 1, i.e. $\sum_{p \in C_i} C_i(p) = 1$. I define

$$p_d \in C_i :\Leftrightarrow C_i(p_d) > 0.$$

For the sake of simplicity, I denote in the following the probability of a node as $prob(p_d) = C_i(p_d)$. Note that a cluster may contain only a single node with $C_i(p_d) = 1$, namely in the case that it represents a document for which no duplicates were identified. The edges remain attached to the documents within the cluster. Table 6.3 extends the example collection by indicating the documents that an article cites. Figure 6.1 shows the corresponding cluster-based uncertain graph GC.

	id	docID	references	prob
$t1$	d1	doc1	doc3, doc5	0.7
$t2$	d1	doc2	doc5	0.3
$t3$	d2	doc3	doc5, doc6	0.2
$t4$	d2	doc4	doc5	0.8
$t5$	d3	doc5		1
$t6$	d4	doc6		1

Table 6.3: Document Relation with References

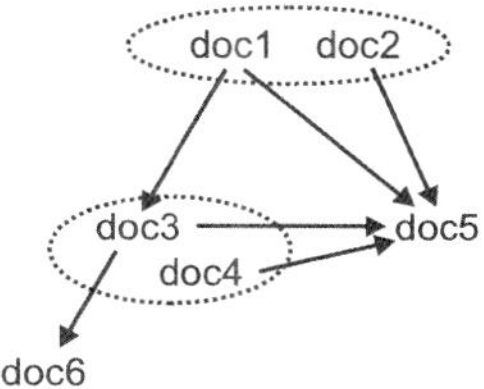

Figure 6.1: Document Graph GC with Clusters

Probabilistic Instances of Cluster-Based Uncertain Graphs

A probabilistic instance $\widehat{GC}_i$ is derived from the cluster-based uncertain graph GC by taking exactly one p_d out of each cluster C_j with probability $prob(p_d)$. $\widehat{GC}_i$ contains m nodes, i.e., the number of clusters. So there is a set $\widehat{GC} = \{\widehat{GC}_1, \widehat{GC}_2, ..., \widehat{GC}_n\}$ of probabilistic instances. Deriving these probabilistic instances, however, is not straightforward for graphs as the following example sketches. The document collection from table 6.3 gives four probabilistic instances, each of them inducing a graph: $\widehat{GC}_1 = \{t1, t3, t4, t5\}$, $\widehat{GC}_2 = \{t1, t4, t5, t6\}$, $\widehat{GC}_3 = \{t2, t3, t5, t6\}$ and $\widehat{GC}_4 = \{t2, t4, t5, t6\}$. Setting the references leads to the problem illustrated in figure 6.2. For $\widehat{GC}_1$, the document reference network is correct, whereas it is inconsistent for $\widehat{GC}_2$: doc1 cites with doc3 a document that does not exist in this probabilistic instance. The approach by Andritsos et al. can thus not directly be applied to graphs.

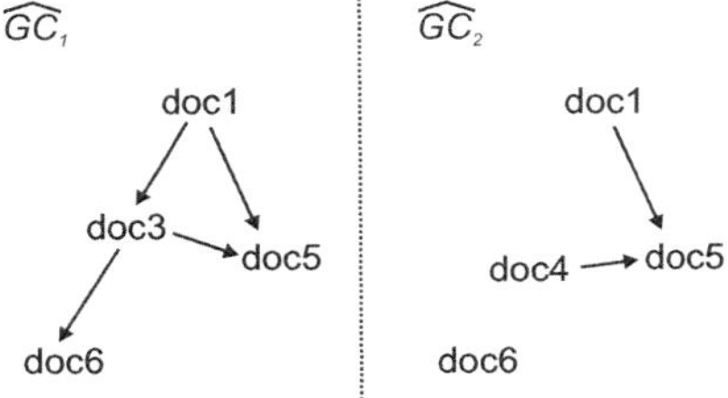

Figure 6.2: Probabilistic Instances of Graphs

The link structure of $\widehat{GC}_i$ is as follows: a link between selected duplicates $p_{k_i} \in C_k$ and $p_{l_j} \in C_l$ is set in $\widehat{GC}_i$ only if both p_{k_i} and p_{l_j} were connected in the original graph GC. The probability $Prob(\widehat{GC}_i)$ of a probabilistic instance $\widehat{GC}_i$ is:

$$Prob(\widehat{GC}_i) \;=\; \prod_{p_j \in \widehat{GC}_i} prob(p_j)$$

6.2 Queries to Uncertain Graphs

In the probabilistic approach by Andritsos et al., the answer to a query is determined on the basis of the answers computed on all probabilistic instances $\widehat{D}_i$ of an uncertain database D. In uncertain graphs, queries which evaluate to a measure can be answered in the same way: The respective query is answered on all probabilistic instances $\widehat{GC}_i$ of the cluster-based uncertain graph GC. The answer to the query is then again a probabilistic measure. There are two basic types of queries that analyze the reference structure of GC: *relational queries* and *functional queries*. A relational query on a document reference network is, for example, a query that defines the set of documents that are referenced by some document p_d. More generally, a relational query on a graph returns a relation of arity m. The answer to such a query on a probabilistic instance is a relation and these results are sorted by their probability. Thus, each document that satisfies some predicate U defined in the query is returned with its probability. This gives a sequence of documents, ordered according to their probability. Functional queries on graphs are measures on nodes and/or edges. Examples are reference-based visibility measures, measures from social network analysis, and the trust-enhanced visibility measures. In my thesis, I am interested in the measures defined in the multi-layer architecture. I focus hence on functional queries. Answering relational queries within this setting of uncertainty is described in Hess and de Rougemont (2007).

Functional Queries

A function f on a graph $G = (V, E)$ (without duplicates) takes the set of nodes $w = p_1, ..., p_k$ as arguments and returns a value $t \in \mathbf{R}$. The function f computes measures on a graph G. Measures such as centrality or PageRank are unary functions, i.e., they take one node as argument, whereas measures such as shortest-path are binary functions, i.e., they take two nodes as arguments.

Definition 10 *A function query f of arity k on the graph G is:*

$$f_G : V^k \to \mathbf{R}$$
$$f_G(w) = t$$

So f takes as parameters a set w of nodes, i.e., $w \in V^k$. In the case of PageRank, w is the document p_d for which the rank is computed, hence $f_G(w) = \mathrm{PR}_G(p_d)$. Such measures cannot directly be computed on the cluster-based uncertain graphs GC. Instead, these measures have to be computed on the distinct probabilistic instances $\widehat{GC}_i$. For instance, PageRank can be computed individually on all probabilistic instances. Doing this, however, we do not obtain a single value for the rank of document p_d but a set of values; in general, $\exists w : \widehat{f_{GC_i}}(w) \neq \widehat{f_{GC_j}}(w)$.[5] Based on this set of values, an expected value $E(\widehat{f_{GC_i}}(w))$ can be determined over all i. It is defined as:

$$f_{GC}(w) = E(\widehat{f_{GC_i}}(w)) = \sum_{i=1}^{n} Prob(\widehat{GC}_i) \cdot \widehat{f_{GC_i}}(w)$$

The expected value $E(\widehat{f_{GC_i}}(w))$ is computed as follows: computing $\widehat{f_{GC_i}}(w)$ over all probabilistic instances $\widehat{GC}_i$ gives a distribution (t, pr_t) of values t and their probabilities pr_t with

$$t \in \mathbf{R}, \qquad pr_t = \sum_{\widehat{f_{GC_i}}(w)=t} Prob(\widehat{GC}_i).$$

---

[5] If there is no such w, then the functions on both graphs are identical.

The probability of a value t is thus defined analogous to the probability of a tuple t on the basis of the probabilities of all probabilistic instances which give t as result.

6.3 Approximation

6.3.1 A Complete Instance of the Cluster-Based Uncertain Graph

Efficient query answering is crucial in the context of document rankings and other recommendation tasks: networks contain millions of millions of nodes and users are not willing to wait. So some approach is required which allows for computing the answer to a query without considering all probabilistic instances $\widehat{GC}_i$ of GC. Limiting the number of probabilistic instances considered is not feasible as their probabilities may be equally distributed. As reference-based queries analyze the network structure, the query rewriting proposed by Andritsos *et al.* is neither possible. So an alternative representation $\overline{GC}$ to the cluster-based uncertain graph GC is required which permits computing the answer directly on $\overline{GC}$. This representation and the corresponding query answering must ensure that the result obtained is in line with the results obtained by looking at all probabilistic instances $\widehat{GC}_i$. Before defining such an alternative representation, table 6.4 gives an overview of the notations used for the uncertain graphs that represent document reference networks.

Symbol	Name	Description
GC	cluster-based uncertain graph	A graph with duplicates. Duplicate nodes (documents) are grouped into multi-element clusters, unique documents are one-element clusters. References are identified with the distinct documents (not with the cluster). Probabilities are associated with the documents.
$\widehat{GC}_i$	probabilistic instance of GC	$\widehat{GC}_i$ contains one element out of each cluster in GC. The probability of a $\widehat{GC}_i$ is computed based on the probabilities of the documents contained.
$\widehat{GC}$	set of all probabilistic instances	$\widehat{GC} = \{\widehat{GC}_1, \widehat{GC}_2, ..., \widehat{GC}_n\}$, i.e. the set of all probabilistic instances that can be derived from GC.
$\overline{GC}$	complete instance of GC	Documents within a cluster are merged. Probabilities are assigned to the edges: the uncertainty is transferred from the nodes to the edges.

Table 6.4: Overview on Uncertain Graphs

The alternative representation, the so-called *complete instance* $\overline{GC}$ is derived from GC in three steps:

1. The duplicate nodes p_{k_1}, p_{k_2}, ...p_{k_n} within a cluster C_k are merged into a single node P_k.

2. All incoming and outgoing edges of the duplicate nodes p_{k_1}, p_{k_2}, ...p_{k_n} are attached to the new node P_k.

3. Probabilities are assigned to the edges: An edge e has a probability $prob(e) = 1$ only if it exists in all probabilistic instances $\widehat{GC}_i$, else $prob(e) < 1$. The uncertainty is thus transferred from the nodes to the edges.

Figure 6.3 shows the complete instance $\overline{GC}$ of a cluster-based uncertain graph GC. The node p_1 from GC is transformed into the node P_1 in $\overline{GC}$ and the duplicate nodes p_2 and p'_2 are merged into P_2. These new nodes P_1 and P_2 are connected by an edge because there is an edge between p_1 and p_2 in GC. As p_1 and p'_2 are not connected, the probability of the edge between P_1 and P_2 is $prob(e_{1\rightarrow2}) < 1$.

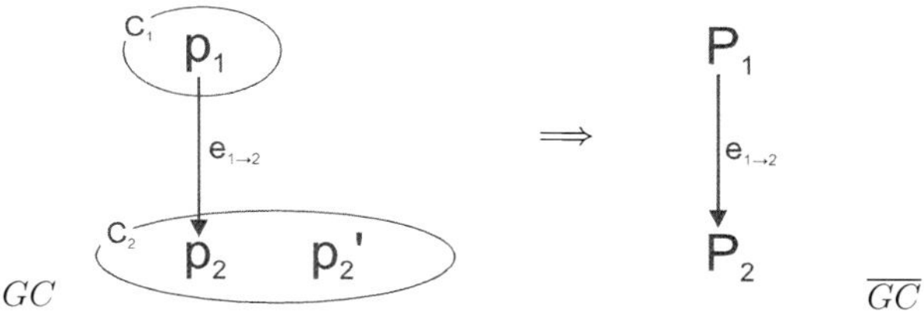

Figure 6.3: Uncertain Graph GC and its Complete Instance $\overline{GC}$

Probabilities on the Edges

Now the exact probabilities of all edges in $\overline{GC}$ have to be calculated. The probability of an edge $e_{F\rightarrow G}$ from a node p_F to a node p_G in $\overline{GC}$ is the sum of the probabilities of the instances $\widehat{GC}_i$ of GC in which an element p_{f_j} out of the component p_F (i.e., $p_{f_j} \in C_f$) is connected with an element p_{g_k} out of component p_G (i.e., $p_{g_k} \in C_g$).

$$prob(e_{F\rightarrow G}) = \sum_{\substack{e_{p_f \rightarrow p_g}, \\ p_f \in C_f,\ p_g \in C_g}} Prob(\widehat{GC}_i)$$

In the above example, the edge $e_{1\rightarrow2}$ is present in $\widehat{GC}_2 = \{p_1, p'_2\}$ while not in $\widehat{GC}_1 = \{p_1, p_2\}$; hence $prob(e_{1\rightarrow2}) = 0.5$ assumed that $Prob(\widehat{GC}_1) = Prob(\widehat{GC}_2)$.

In this way, we can naively attach probabilities to all edges. However, as the following example shows, edges cannot be taken as independent. Consider two slightly different cluster-based uncertain graphs GC_1 and GC_2 as shown in figure 6.4. For both GC_1 and GC_2, the complete instance $\overline{GC}$ is identical. It is shown in figure 6.5.

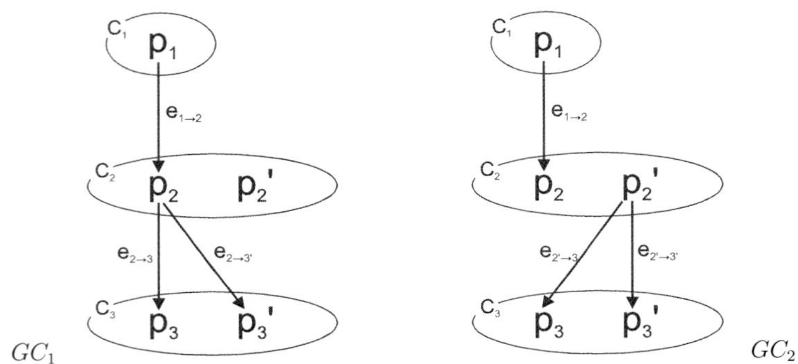

Figure 6.4: Two Cluster-Based Uncertain Graphs GC_1 and GC_2

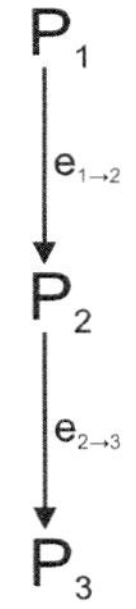

Figure 6.5: Complete Instance $\overline{GC}$ of GC_1 and GC_2

Assuming again that all probabilistic instances are equally probable, the edge probabilities are $prob(e_{1\rightarrow2}) = 0.5$ and $prob(e_{2\rightarrow3}) = 0.5$. While this is correct for GC_1, it is not for GC_2. The probabilistic instances are for both GC_1 and GC_2 as follows: $\widehat{GC}_1 = \{p_1, p_2, p_3\}$, $\widehat{GC}_2 = \{p_1, p_2, p_3'\}$, $\widehat{GC}_3 = \{p_1, p_2', p_3\}$, $\widehat{GC}_4 = \{p_1, p_2', p_3'\}$. In the case of GC_1, the path from p_1 to all elements of component P_3 is present in two instances, namely $\widehat{GC}_1$ and $\widehat{GC}_2$. The probability of the path from P_1 to P_3 in $\overline{GC}$

is hence positive. In the case of GC_2, there is no probabilistic instance in which p_1 is connected with any element of P_3. $\overline{GC}$, however, shows such a connection. The result t to a query would thus differ from the result obtained by querying all probabilistic instances independently. In order to address this problem, conditional probabilities must be considered.

Conditional Probabilities

The conditional probability $prob(e_{D \to F} \mid e_{F \to G})$ is defined as:

$$prob(e_{D \to F} \mid e_{F \to G}) = \sum_{\substack{e_{p_d \to p_f} \wedge e_{p_f \to p_g}, \\ p_d \in C_d, \; p_f \in C_f, \; p_g \in C_g}} Prob(\widehat{GC}_i)$$

I consider here only the conditional probabilities of adjacent edges although the problem of conditional probabilities also exists for arbitrary pairs of edges and for chains of edges. A complete instance $\overline{GC}$ can thus be defined as follows:

Definition 11 *A complete instance $\overline{GC}$ is the graph that is obtained from a cluster-based uncertain graph GC by merging the duplicate nodes $p_{k_1}, p_{k_2}, \dots p_{k_n}$ within each cluster C_k into a single node P_k. Edges are set between two nodes P_k and P_l if there is an edge between two duplicates p_{k_i} and p_{k_l}. All probabilities $prob(e_{P_k \to P_l})$ and all conditional probabilities $prob(e_{P_k \to P_l} \mid e_{P_l \to P_m})$ are attributed to the edges.*

6.3.2 Approximation of Functional Queries

Computing measures such as a document's visibility over all probabilistic instances $\widehat{GC}_i$ gives a distribution of values $\widehat{f}_{\widehat{GC}_i}(w)$. Using the probabilities of the probabilistic instances, let $f_{GC}(w) = E(\widehat{f}_{\widehat{GC}_i}(w))$. As it may be very expensive to compute the expected value $E(\widehat{f}_{\widehat{GC}_i}(w))$, we want to approximate it. We know that the expected value is in the interval

$$I_w^{\widehat{GC}} = [\gamma, \; \delta] \qquad \text{with} \qquad \gamma = \min \left\{ \widehat{f}_{\widehat{GC}_i}(w) : \; \widehat{GC}_i \in \widehat{GC} \right\} \qquad \text{and}$$

$$\delta = \max \left\{ \widehat{f}_{\widehat{GC}_i}(w) : \; \widehat{GC}_i \in \widehat{GC} \right\},$$

given by the distribution of values, i.e., $f_{GC}(w) \in I_w^{\widehat{GC}}$. On the complete instance $\overline{GC}$, we can efficiently approximate the interval $I_w^{\widehat{GC}}$ without considering all instances $\widehat{GC}_i$. By such approximation, we obtain an interval $I_w^{\overline{GC}} = [\alpha, \; \beta]$, such that $\widehat{f}_{\widehat{GC}_i}(w) \in I_w^{\overline{GC}}$ for all i. Thus, $f_{GC}(w) \in I_w^{\overline{GC}}$.

Definition 12 *An algorithm $\mathcal{A}$ which outputs (α, β) ε-approximates $f_{GC}(w)$ if:*

$$(a) \quad \alpha - \varepsilon \leq \min_{\widehat{GC}_i} \widehat{f_{\widehat{GC}_i}}(w) \leq \alpha + \varepsilon$$

$$(b) \quad \beta - \varepsilon \leq \max_{\widehat{GC}_i} \widehat{f_{\widehat{GC}_i}}(w) \leq \beta + \varepsilon$$

From (a) and (b) follows that $\widehat{f_{\widehat{GC}_i}}(w) \in [\alpha - \varepsilon, \ \beta + \varepsilon]$ for all $\widehat{GC}_i$.

We want to efficiently approximate the interval $I_w^{\overline{GC}}$, possibly with randomized algorithms. In this case, the conditions (a) and (b) should be true with high probability over the probabilistic space associated with the algorithm. We consider ε as a measure for the quality of the approximation. Ideally, $\varepsilon = 0$.

The size of the interval I gives a measure for the precision of the answer. The smaller the interval, the more precise is the answer. A small interval means that the different probabilistic instances provide rather similar results.

Table 6.5 gives an overview on the function queries on the different graphs and their approximation.

Symbol	Description
$f_G(w)$	function f on a graph G without duplicates; takes as parameter a sequence of nodes $w \in V^k$ with V being the set of nodes
$\widehat{f_{\widehat{GC}_i}}(w)$	function $\widehat{f}$ on a the probabilistic instance $\widehat{GC}_i$ of a cluster-based uncertain graph GC
$E(\widehat{f_{\widehat{GC}_i}}(w))$	expected value of $\widehat{f_{\widehat{GC}_i}}(w)$, computed over all $\widehat{GC}_i$, i.e., $f_{GC}(w) = E(\widehat{f_{\widehat{GC}_i}}(w))$
$I_w^{\widehat{GC}} = [\gamma, \delta]$	interval given by the distribution of the $\widehat{f_{\widehat{GC}_i}}(w)$; $f_{GC}(w) = E(\widehat{f_{\widehat{GC}_i}}(w)) \in I_w^{\widehat{GC}}$
$I_w^{\overline{GC}} = [\alpha, \beta]$	interval that approximates $I_w^{\widehat{GC}}$ such that $\widehat{f_{\widehat{GC}_i}}(w) \in I_w^{\overline{GC}}$ for all i; hence $f_{GC}(w) \in I_w^{\overline{GC}}$

Table 6.5: Overview on Function Queries and their Approximation

6.3.3 Approximation of the TRE-Visibility

In the following, I develop an approximation of the TRE-visibility, more precisely, of the distance-based TRE-visibility (see section 5.1.7). In order to approximate the distance-based TRE-visibility $\text{vis}^{\text{TRE}_d}_{p_d, u_m}$, I will firstly have to approximate the length of the shortest path between the reviewed document and the document p_d (for which the recommendation is computed). The length of the shortest path is required in other measures, too. For instance, the closeness centrality of an actor is based on the lengths of the shortest paths to other actors.

Shortest Path Approximation

We want to approximate on the complete instance $\overline{GC}$ of an uncertain graph GC the length of the shortest path $\text{SP}_{GC}(p_s, p_n)$ from a node p_s to a node p_n in GC. I aim to give a small interval $I^{\overline{GC}}_{p_s \to p_n}$ in which the length of the shortest path is for all probabilistic instances $\widehat{GC}_i$, i.e., such that $\widehat{\text{SP}}_{\widehat{GC}_i}(p_s, p_n) \in I^{\overline{GC}}_{p_s \to p_n} = [\alpha, \ \beta]$.

Interval Propagation Rules The length of the shortest path from a starting point p_s to some target node p_n is approximated by forwarding intervals in $\overline{GC}$ in a naive way.[6] Let $I(p_n) = [\alpha_n, \ \beta_n]$ be $I^{\overline{GC}}_{p_s \to p_n}$ i.e. the interval for the length of the shortest path from p_s to p_n, when p_s and $\overline{GC}$ are fixed. Similarly, let $I(p_n/p_{m_i}) = [\alpha_{n/m_i}, \ \beta_{n/m_i}]$ be the interval of the length of the shortest path reaching p_n through the predecessor p_{m_i} of p_n, when p_s and $\overline{GC}$ are fixed.

The interval $I(p_n)$ should be so that $\widehat{\text{SP}}_{\widehat{GC}_i}(p_s, p_n) \in I(p_n)$ for all i. Propagating the intervals from p_s to p_n, the starting interval is $I(p_s) = [\alpha_s, \ \beta_s] = [0, 0]$. With each step via an edge in the graph $\overline{GC}$, the length of the shortest path increases by 1. So if there is a single incoming edge to a node p_m, namely the edge $e_{l \to m}$ from a node p_l, and this edge is set in all probabilistic instances, and $I(p_l) = [\alpha_l, \ \beta_l]$, then $I(p_m) = [\alpha_l + 1, \ \beta_l + 1] = [\alpha_m, \ \beta_m]$. However, the edge $e_{l \to m}$ may be set only in some of the probabilistic instances. The length of the shortest path can thus also be ∞. The possibility that edges may not be available in some probabilistic instances has to be considered by the interval propagation rules.

I now consider a node p_n with k ancestors p_{m_i} where each p_{m_i} has a set of predecessors p_{l_i}. The intervals $I(p_{m_i}/p_{l_i}) = [\alpha_{m_i/l_i}, \ \beta_{m_i/l_i}]$ are given for each p_{m_i}. I cannot simply obtain $I(p_n)$ based on taking the minimum $\alpha_{m_i/l_i} + 1$ and the minimum of all $\beta_{m_i/l_i} + 1$ because the edges $e_{l_i \to m_i}$ and $e_{m_i \to n}$ are not independent as it is indicated by the

---

[6] In order to facilitate reading, I use here lower case letters for the nodes in $\overline{GC}$.

conditional probabilities on the edges. The lower bound α_n and the upper bound β_n of the interval $I(p_n) = [\alpha_n,\ \beta_n]$ are determined as follows. Clearly, they may occur in different probabilistic instances.

- In order to compute the lower bound for the interval $I(p_n)$, only the intervals $I(p_{m_i}/p_{l_i})$ from such p_{m_i} are considered so that there is a path between p_{l_i} to p_n in at least one $\widehat{GC}_i$, i.e. the conditional probability of the edges $e_{l_i \to m_i}$ and $e_{m_i \to n}$ has to be positive: $prob(e_{m_i \to n} \mid e_{l_i \to m_i}) > 0$. Now, α_n is computed on the basis of the α_{m_i/l_i} that satisfy this property: $\alpha_n = \min_{m_i}\{\alpha_{m_i/l_i}\} + 1$. If there does not exist such a p_{m_i}, the interval propagation stops and the length of the shortest path is ∞.

- The upper bound β_n of the interval $I(p_n)$ is again defined on the basis of all $I(p_n/p_{m_i})$. So we compute in the first step $I(p_n/p_{m_i})$ for all predecessors p_{m_i} of p_n. The upper bound β_{m_i} is given as it was computed in a previous step. Now, β_{n/m_i} depends on the probability $prob(e_{m_i \to n})$: if this edge is certain, i.e. $prob(e_{m_i \to n}) = 1$, then $\beta_{n/m_i} = \beta_{m_i} + 1$, else it is ∞. β_n is then computed on the basis of all β_{n/m_i}.

Before defining the interval propagation rules, I'll outline this first step with the help of the example shown in figures 6.6 and 6.7. $\overline{GC}$ is derived from GC as described before. The edge probabilities are indicated based on the assumption that all probabilistic instances have equal probability. Now $I(P_8) = [\alpha_8,\ \beta_8]$ should be computed based on the already determined intervals $I(P_5/P_1)$, $I(P_6/P_2)$, $I(P_6/P_3)$, $I(P_6)$ and $I(P_7/P_4)$ as shown in figure 6.7.

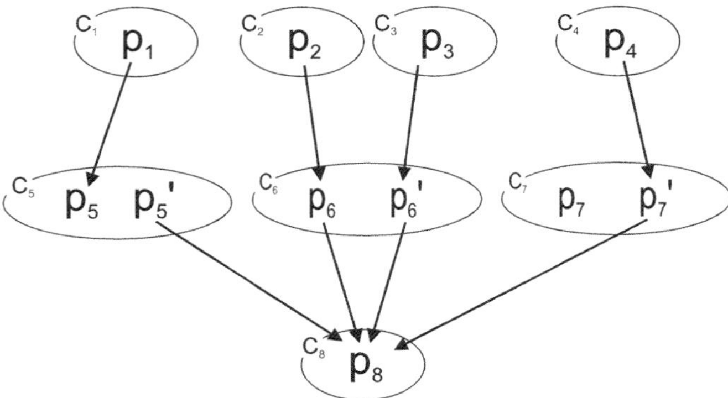

Figure 6.6: Propagating Intervals in the Case of Several Ancestors: GC

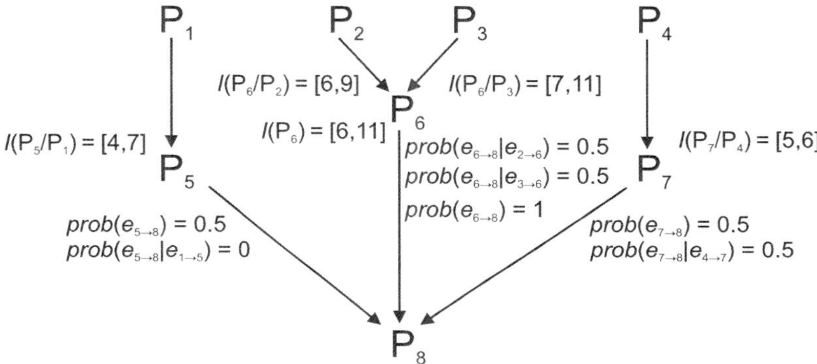

Figure 6.7: Propagating Intervals in the Case of Several Ancestors: $\overline{GC}$

The lower bound is $\alpha_8 = \alpha_7 + 1 = 5 + 1$ because this is the minimum α over all predecessors of P_8 that have an edge with a conditional probability greater than zero to P_8. α_5 is thus not considered: as one can see in GC, there is no probabilistic instance in which P_1 is connected with P_8. The upper bound is $\beta_8 = \beta_6 + 1 = 11 + 1$ because it is determined on the basis of the edges that are certain, i.e. only on the basis of edge $e_{P_6 \to P_8}$. Thus, $I(P_8) = [\alpha_8, \ \beta_8] = [6, 12]$. Obviously, the lower as well as the upper bound are reached in a probabilistic instance. There is no probabilistic instance, in which the length of the shortest path is shorter or longer as indicated by $I(P_8)$.

The interval $I(p_n/p_{m_i})$ can now be inductively defined on the depth n in the graph $\overline{GC}$ from p_s where p_s and p_n are clusters.

Definition 13 *For p_s at distance 0 from p_s:*

$$I(p_s) = [\alpha_s, \ \beta_s] = [0, 0].$$

For p_1 at distance 1 from p_s:

$$\begin{aligned}
I(p_1/p_s) &= [1, 1] \ \textit{if } prob(p_s \to p_1) = 1, \ \textit{else} \\
I(p_1/p_s) &= [1, \infty]
\end{aligned}$$

At a node p_n at distance n from p_s, with k ancestors p_{m_i} where $I(p_{m_i}/p_l) = [\alpha_{m_i/l}, \ \beta_{m_i/l}]$ has been defined, we let:

Case 1: $prob(e_{m_i \to n}) < 1$, i.e. the edge $e_{m_i \to n}$ is uncertain:

$$I(p_n/p_{m_i}) = [\min_{l:\; prob(e_{m_i \to n}|e_{l \to m_i})>0} \{\alpha_{m_i/l}\} + 1,\; \infty]$$

$$= [\alpha_{n/m_i},\; \beta_{n/m_i}] \text{ if there exist such a } l,\; else$$

$$I(p_n/p_{m_i}) = [\infty,\; \infty]$$

$$= [\alpha_{n/m_i},\; \beta_{n/m_i}]$$

Case 2: $prob(e_{m_i \to n}) = 1$, i.e. the edge $e_{m_i \to n}$ is certain.

$$I(p_n/p_{m_i}) = [\min_{l:\; prob(e_{m_i \to n}|e_{l \to m_i})>0} \{\alpha_{m_i/l}\} + 1,\; \beta_{m_i} + 1]$$

$$= [\alpha_{n/m_i},\; \beta_{n/m_i}]$$

Finally, $I(p_n)$ is defined along 2 cases:

Case 1: all edges $e_{m_i \to n}$ are globally uncertain, i.e. there is an instance where none of these edges exists, i.e. $prob(\bigwedge_i \neg e_{m_i \to n}) > 0$ for all m_i:

$$I(p_n) = [\min_{m_i}\{\alpha_{p_n/m_i}\}, \infty].$$

Case 2: for each probabilistic instance, some set S of predecessors p_{m_i} is such that the edges $\{e_{m_i \to n}\}$ exist, i.e. $prob(\bigwedge_S e_{m_i \to n}) > 0$:

$$I(p_n) = [\min_{m_i}\{\alpha_{n/m_i}\}, \max_{S}\; \min_{m_i \in S,\; p_l:\; prob(e_{m_i \to n}|e_{l \to m_i})>0} \{\beta_{m_i/l}\} + 1]$$

Shortest Path Interval Propagation Algorithm (SPIP) The algorithm SPIP computes the length of the shortest path from a node p_s to a node p_t on the complete instance $\overline{GC}$ of a cluster-based uncertain graph GC. SPIP computes the intervals $I(p_i/p_l)$ and $I(p_i)$ for p_i connected at distance $1, 2, ...d$ from p_s by using the rules given in definition 13. Algorithm 3 shows SPIP.

This algorithm generalizes the classical Dijkstra's Shortest Path algorithm, in this uncertainty model. Notice that if a cluster point p_d is at distance d in $\overline{GC}$, it may be at distance larger than d in all probabilistic instances $\widehat{GC_i}$. SPIP returns an interval $[\alpha,\; \beta]$ which may be defined at some stage $j > d$. It is possible that α is defined at stage j_1 and β at stage j_2, with $j_1 < j_2 < 2.n$.

We now prove that SPIP approximates $SP_{GC}(p_s, p_t)$, after exploring at most $O(n)$ nodes of the graph with $\varepsilon = 0$. The exact value $SP_{GC}(p_s, p_k)$ for a node p_k at depth d from p_s is within the interval $I(p_k) = [\alpha_k,\; \beta_k]$ and satisfies the approximation conditions with $\varepsilon = 0$.

Algorithm 3 SPIP Algorithm (p_t)

Let $V = \{p_s\}$.

Stage $j = 1$.

Until all reachable nodes p_i have a complete fixed-point ($I(p_i)$ is defined and stable)

{

1. Let W the set of successors nodes in V,

2. For $p_i \in W$: compute $I(p_i/p_l)$ when $I(p_l)$ is defined, compute $I(p_i)$,

3. $V = W$,

4. $j = j + 1$

}

If p_t was reached, Output $I(p_t)$ else Output $[\infty, \infty]$.

Theorem 1 *For each node p_d at depth d from p_s, SPIP approximates $\mathrm{SP}_{GC}(p_s, p_k)$ with $\varepsilon = 0$, after exploring at most n nodes.*

Proof 1 We prove that the Output $[\alpha,\ \beta]$ satisfies the properties (a) and (b) stated in definition 12. Namely, $\mathrm{SP}_{\widehat{GC}_i}(p_s, p_d) \in [\alpha,\ \beta]$ for each $\widehat{GC}_i$ and α (resp. β) is the minimum (resp. maximum) value attained for some $\widehat{GC}_i$. Let $SP(p_n) = SP(p_s, p_n)$ when p_s is fixed.

We first consider condition (a). Let us prove by induction on j, the stage of the SPIP algorithm, that if j is the first stage where α_n is defined and finite in $I(p_n) = [\alpha_n, \beta_n]$, then there is an instance $\widehat{GC}_i$ where $SP(p_n) = j$ and for all other instances $SP(p_n) \geq j$. For $j = 0$, it is true for $I(p_s)$, the only point at distance 0. Suppose it is true at stage j, and consider a point p_n in the next stage $j + 1$, i.e. the successor of some point p_{m_i}. By definition α_{p_n} is the minimum of a set $\{\alpha_{p_n/m_i}\}$ corresponding to $\{I(p_n/p_{m_i})\}$, for which a conditional probability $prob(e_{m_i \rightarrow n} \mid e_{l \rightarrow m_i})$ is non-zero. By induction hypothesis, there is an instance $\widehat{GC}_i$ where $SP(p_{m_i}) = j$ and for all other instances $\widehat{GC}_k$, $SP(p_{m_i}) \geq j$. Because the conditional probability $prob(e_{m_i \rightarrow n} \mid e_{l \rightarrow m_i})$ is non zero, we can extend $\widehat{GC}_i$ into $\widehat{GC}'_i$ such that $SP(p_n) = j + 1$ and for all other instances $\widehat{GC}_k$, $SP(p_n) \geq j + 1$. We conclude that condition (a) is satisfied.

Consider condition (b) on instances where $SP(p_n)$ is maximum. Let us prove by induction on j, the stage of the SPIP algorithm, that if j is the first stage where β_n is defined and finite in $I(p_n) = [\alpha_n, \beta_n]$, then there is an instance $\widehat{GC}_i$ where $SP(p_n) = j$ and for all other instances $SP(p_n) \leq j$. It is true for $j = 0$, and suppose it is true at stage j. Take p_n for which β_n is defined at stage $j + 1$. There is an instance for which p_n is connected, i.e. there is a set S of predecessors p_{m_i} such that the edges $\{e_{m_i \rightarrow n}\}$ exist, because $prob(\bigwedge_S e_{m_i \rightarrow n}) > 0$. For each such $m_i \in S$, consider its predecessors p_l such that $prob(e_{m_i \to n} \mid e_{l \to m_i}) > 0$. There is an instance $\widehat{GC}_i$ which realizes both S and the edges $e_{m_i \to n} \mid e_{l \to m_i}$. Its shortest path to p_n is $\min_{m_i \in S, \ p_l:\ prob(e_{m_i \to n} \mid e_{l \to m_i}) > 0} \{\beta_{m_i/l}\} + 1$, as $\beta_{m_i/l}$ is an upper bound by the induction hypothesis. We now take the Maximum over all such S, as we look for the worst case over all probabilistic instances and therefore satisfy (b).

$\square$

Notice that the algorithm SPIP is deterministic and approximates with 0 error. Although exploring at most $O(n)$ nodes, it may take more than O(n) time if the indegree of the nodes is not bounded. If the indegree is bounded, the algorithm is also $O(n)$ in time.

TRE-Visibility Approximation

Now, the TRE-visibility $\text{vis}_{GC}^{\text{TRE}}(p_d, u_m)$ from the perspective of a user u_m for a document p_d is approximated on the complete instance $\overline{GC}$ of a cluster-based uncertain graph GC. The approximation should give a small interval $I_{p_d,u_m}^{\overline{GC}} = [\gamma_{p_d,u_m}, \ \delta_{p_d,u_m}]$ in which the TRE-visibility is for all $\widehat{GC}_i$ such that $\text{vis}_{GC}^{\text{TRE}}(p_d, u_m) \in I_{p_d,u_m}^{\overline{GC}}$. The impact of reviews decreases as the distance between p_q and p_d increases: the trust-weighted review $t_j r_j$ is divided by $(k_j + 1)^b$, with k_j being the length of the shortest path of p_q to p_d.

In the following, a simplified version of the distance-based TRE-visibility function is used, which does not consider precomputed document base visibilities, i.e. the trust in the reference-based part is $t_0 = \text{vc} = 0$, and which averages by n, the number of reviews. It takes both the reviews r_j which are directly on p_d and those which are on documents p_q referencing p_d directly or indirectly. A review r_j is weighted both with the trust t_j in the review and the distance of the reviewed document p_q to the document to be recommended p_d. This is called the review contribution c_j. The simplified TRE-visibility that is approximated in the following is thus defined as:

$$\text{vis}_{GC}^{\text{TRE}}(p_d, u_m) \;=\; \frac{\displaystyle\sum_{i=1}^{n} \left(\frac{t_i}{(k_{i,d} + 1)^b} \cdot r_i \right)}{n}$$

In a cluster-based uncertain graph, the uncertainty affects only the distance k_j which is the length of the shortest path from p_q to p_d, i.e., $SP_{GC}(p_q, p_d)$. In the previous section, we provided an approximation for the length of the shortest path: $SP_{GC}(p_q, p_d) \in I_{p_d \to p_q}^{\overline{GC}} = [\alpha, \beta]$. It can now directly be used as part of the TRE-visibility function.

When computing the TRE-visibility for p_d, the review contribution c_j has to be computed for each review r_j on a document p_s. Firstly, the interval for the length of the shortest path from p_q to p_d is determined:

$$k_j = SP_{GC}(p_q, p_d) \in I^{\overline{GC}}_{p_d \to p_q} = [\alpha_j, \ \beta_j]$$

This then gives the interval for the trust-weighted review $R(r_j)$:

$$R(r_j) = \left[\frac{t_j r_j}{(\beta_j + 1)^b}, \ \frac{t_j r_j}{(\alpha_j + 1)^b} \right]$$

Note that α_j now determines the upper bound and β_j the lower bound: if $\beta_j = \infty$, i.e., there is no path from p_s to p_d, then the contribution of the review is zero. The interval for the TRE-visibility of a document p_d from the perspective of a user u_m is thus

$$I^{\overline{GC}}_{p_d, u_m} = \left[\frac{\displaystyle\sum_{j=1}^{n} \frac{t_j r_j}{(\beta_j + 1)^b}}{n}, \ \frac{\displaystyle\sum_{j=1}^{n} \frac{t_j r_j}{(\alpha_j + 1)^b}}{n} \right] = [\gamma_{p_d, u_m}, \ \delta_{p_d, u_m}]$$

TRE-Visibility Approximation Algorithm (TAP)   Let TAP be the algorithm that takes the graph structure, p_d and u_m as input and computes the interval I for the TRE-visibility $\mathrm{vis}^{TRE}_{GC}(p_d, u_m)$ as follows. For each of the n reviews r_j, it computes the interval $R(r_j)$ and outputs $I^{\overline{GC}}_{p_d, u_m} = \left[\frac{\sum_{j=1}^{n} \frac{t_j r_j}{(\beta_j + 1)^b}}{n}, \ \frac{\sum_{j=1}^{n} \frac{t_j r_j}{(\alpha_j + 1)^b}}{n} \right]$.

Definition 14 *The algorithm TAP ε-approximates* $\mathrm{vis}^{TRE}_{GC}(p_d, u_m)$ *if:*

$$(a) \quad \gamma_{p_d, u_m} - \varepsilon \leq \min_{\widehat{GC}_i} \ \mathrm{vis}^{TRE_d}_{\widehat{GC}_i}(p_d, u_m) \leq \gamma_{p_d, u_m} + \varepsilon$$

$$(b) \quad \delta_{p_d, u_m} - \varepsilon \leq \max_{\widehat{GC}_i} \ \mathrm{vis}^{TRE_d}_{\widehat{GC}_i}(p_d, u_m) \leq \delta_{p_d, u_m} + \varepsilon$$

(a) and (b) give $\mathrm{vis}^{TRE_d}_{\widehat{GC}_i}(p_d, u_m) \in [\gamma_{p_d, u_m} - \varepsilon, \ \delta_{p_d, u_m} + \varepsilon]$ *for all* $\widehat{GC}_i$.

Theorem 2 *The algorithm TAP approximates the TRE-visibility* $\mathrm{vis}^{TRE}_{GC}(p_d, u_m)$ *for a document p_d from the perspective of a user u_m with $\varepsilon = 0$.*

Proof 2   Each trust-weighted review $\widehat{R(r_j)}_{\widehat{GC}_i} = \frac{t_j r_j}{(\widehat{SP}_{\widehat{GC}_i}(p_q, p_d)+1)^b}$ (with r_j being the review on p_q, and p_d being the document to which visibility r_j contributes) is in any probabilistic instance $\widehat{GC}_i$ in the interval given by the approximation:

$$\widehat{R(r_j)}_{\widehat{GC}_i} \in \left[\frac{t_j r_j}{(\beta_j + 1)^b}, \ \frac{t_j r_j}{(\alpha_j + 1)^b}\right]$$

because

- there is no uncertainty on the reviews and the trust values t_j and r_j are identical in all probabilistic instances $\widehat{GC}_i$ and in the graph $\overline{GC}$ on which the approximation is computed, and

- $\widehat{SP}_{\widehat{GC}_i}(p_s, p_d) \in [\alpha_j, \ \beta_j]$ according to theorem 1 and

- the function is continuous of the inverse of SP.

So $\widehat{R(r_j)} \in \left[\frac{t_j r_j}{(\beta_j+1)^b}, \ \frac{t_j r_j}{(\alpha_j+1)^b}\right]$.

The TRE-visibility $\widehat{vis}_{GC}^{TRE}(p_d, u_m)$ calculated in any probabilistic instance is in the interval given by the approximation, because the same number of review contributions is considered, and $\widehat{R(r_j)} \in \left[\frac{t_j r_j}{(\beta_j+1)^b}, \ \frac{t_j r_j}{(\alpha_j+1)^b}\right]$ as shown before.

$\square$

Applying the Interval Propagation to other Measures

Reference-based measures that compute the visibility of a document based on the visibility of the citing documents such as PageRank, or extensions of PageRank that are adapted to the typically acyclic document networks of scientific publications can be approximated in the same style as the shortest path. Instead of forwarding the interval with the current shortest path, an interval with the minimum and maximum visibility is propagated. Where required, an interval for the number of outgoing links may additionally be forwarded.

7 SPRec – A Multi-Layer Recommender System for Scientific Papers

7.1 Overview on SPRec

The web-based Scientific Paper Recommender system SPRec is a multi-layer recommendation system that implements the TRE-visibility framework. Recommendations are based on a joint analysis of a document reference network and a reviewer trust network. Reviews by the users connect both layers. SPRec aims to support users browsing digital repositories of academic publications by offering different types of recommendations and rankings.

7.1.1 Document Recommendations and Rankings

Users can benefit from SPRec in several ways. On the one hand, using reviews by trusted users means that it is possible to advise efficiently against those scientific publications that are either just uninteresting to the user's particular community or are considered to be untrustworthy e.g. because they are declared as fakes following official investigations. On the other hand, papers are recommended that are of special interest to the user but that might only be known to a small research community and hence seldom cited. SPRec generates two types of recommendations:

- Recommendation for a particular scientific paper: "Should I buy this pay-per-view article?" or "Is this article worth reading?".

- Ranking of a set of scientific papers: the papers that match the search terms given in the user's query are ranked according to the visibility of the articles.

7.1.2 The Document Reference Network in SPRec

While the web of trust is established within the community of SPRec users, the document reference network is based on the metadata on scholarly papers provided by organizations such as CiteSeer. CiteSeer as well as document repositories maintained by universities or other research organizations often grant access to their metadata by using the Open Archives Initiative (OAI) Protocol for Metadata Harvesting (OAI-PMH)[1]. In the OAI terminology, they are called *data providers*. SPRec, in contrast, acts as a *service provider*. Its service, i.e. the trust-based recommendations, builds on the metadata harvested from the data providers. OAI-PMH is a harvesting protocol that facilitates sharing metadata between data providers and service providers. Items in a digital document repository, such as scholarly papers or other types of media, are described in a record. OAI-PMH defines the different parts of a record. Records are provided in XML (Extensible Markup Language). Unqualified Dublin Core, the metadata standard developed by the Dublin Core Metadata Initiative (DCMI), is used for describing the metadata. Dublin Core specifies a set of elements for the description of digital objects. For example, there are elements for the title (dc:title), the creator (dc:creator) and the subject (dc:subject) of the document.[2] This guarantees a basic level of interoperability. Additionally, metadata can also be provided in other formats, e.g., MARC (MAchine-Readable Cataloging). The MARC format is widely used in libraries for the bibliographic description of library items.[3]

SPRec requires metadata that contains, apart from basic information such as title and author names, reference information. The references between the articles are needed to build the document reference network, which is one of the basic components of the recommendation mechanism of SPRec. Currently, SPRec uses the CiteSeer metadata[4], which offers for each article the list of references to other indexed articles. CiteSeer automatically extracts the reference lists for each article from the text. Referenced articles which are not yet in the CiteSeer database are – if possible – added to the database, too (Giles *et al.*, 1998). SPRec is not limited to using CiteSeer as data provider. Its import routine can easily be adapted for the metadata provided by other OAI compliant repositories of scholarly papers. SPRec contains the metadata of more than 700,000 documents with around 1.5 million references between the articles. The papers are primarily from the computer science literature, and were published in journals or conference proceedings.

---

[1]See the website of the OAI: `http://www.openarchives.org/`. For a brief introduction to OAI-PMH see the tutorial `http://www.oaforum.org/tutorial/`.

[2]For more information on Dublin Core see `http://dublincore.org/`.

[3]For more information on MARC see `http://www.loc.gov/marc/`.

[4]The CiteSeer metadata is available for download at `http://citeseer.ist.psu.edu/oai.html`.

7.2 The SPRec Website

The web-based recommendation service SPRec is available at `http://www.kinf.wiai.uni-bamberg.de/SPRec/`. Figure 7.1 shows a screenshot of the website.

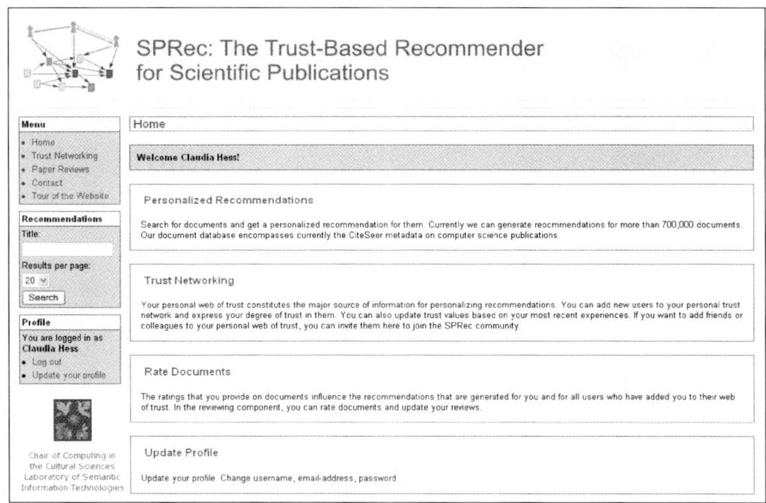

Figure 7.1: Screenshot of SPRec

SPRec is a web-based recommendation service that can easily accessed by the users with a web browser. Table 7.1 gives an overview on the technical details of the implementation of the application.

Programming language	Java 5
Application server	Apache Tomcat 5.5
Database	MySQL Server 5
Framework	Apache Struts 1.2.8
Further technologies	JSP, Log4J

Table 7.1: Implementation of SPRec

7.2.1 User Profile

SPRec can be used by registered users. A registration at the SPRec website is necessary in order to identify the user and to then generate personalized recommendations. In order to register, the name of the user is asked for as well as additional information. The user profile can be modified at any time by the user. The user's last and first name are made public within the SPRec community, i.e., only to registered users. This is necessary in order to be able to find other users in the community and to include them in the own web of trust. Email addresses and further information are not published.

7.2.2 Trust Networking Component

The user's personal web of trust represents the major source of information for personalizing the document recommendations. In the trust networking component, the users establish this web of trust. With the help of a basic search functionality, they can search in the user profiles. Alternatively, they may browse the user community. If the user searched for is not yet a member of the SPRec community, he or she can be invited by simply sending an automatically generated email via the SPRec interface.

Trust values indicate a user's degree of trust in other users. The degree of trust evaluates (as discussed in the context of the multi-layer architecture with reviewer trust networks) whether this user applies similar criteria when reviewing documents. Trust is expressed on a scale ranging from distrust to full trust. If a user Alice declares that she highly trusts a user Bob this means that she regards Bob's reviews as useful. Concretely, if Bob highly recommends an article, it is very likely that Alice agrees with him. In contrast, articles considered by Bob as not interesting or even as containing false information are not appreciated by Alice either.

The web of trust and the trust values specified are hidden, i.e., users know only about the trust relationships indicated by themselves. They do not know to which user's web of trust they were added. This is to guarantee privacy, especially, because users should feel free to assign distrust – which should normally not be known by the distrusted user. Alternatively, it would be possible to display only the positive relationships (as does epinions.com). This, however, might also lead to problems because users might feel offended by not being in the trust network of some colleague. Therefore, SPRec keeps all trust-related information secret.

7.2.3 Reviewing Component

A document recommendation is based on those reviews provided by users deemed as trustworthy. The reviews are provided in the reviewing component. A high rating means that the user recommends the article because it is interesting, novel etc. A low rating, in contrast, is given to articles that are simply not interesting or even faked. The review clearly reflects the user's personal opinion, similar to the ratings in the context of FilmTrust where users specify how much they liked a certain movie. Technically, the reviews are in [0,1].

7.3 Recommendations with SPRec

Personalized recommendations are generated for a distinct paper or for a set of papers in the form of a ranking. The search interface offers a simple key word based search on the titles and the authors of the documents contained in the local database. In response to a user query, a list of documents matching the search term(s) is returned and presented in decreasing order of the document visibilities computed by PageRank. A personalized recommendation can then be computed for selected papers, in the sense: "Should I cite this article?" or "Should I buy this pay-per-view article?". This personalized recommendation is generated with the TRE-visibility. Figure 7.2 shows an example for a personalized document recommendation.

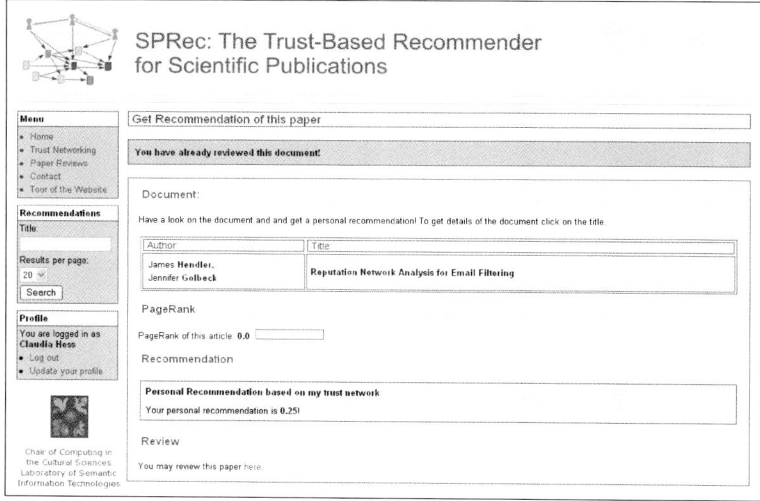

Figure 7.2: Screenshot of the Recommendation Component of SPRec

In SPRec, all recommendations and rankings are generated on the basis of reference-based visibility measures. It does not seem to be sensible to generate recommendations with collaborative filtering because the number of reviews tends to be very small compared to the number of documents.

Technically, SPRec is closely connected with Comte, the simulation environment used for the analysis of the trust-enhanced visibility measures (see section 8.1). Comte implements the TRE- and the ATE-visibility measures as well as PageRank. SPRec uses Comte as a library which offers a high flexibility in the choice of the ranking algorithms.

7.3.1 PageRank as Baseline

SPRec uses PageRank as a basic visibility measure for the document ranking. Although the Age PageRank would be more appropriate for this mainly acyclic network of scientific papers, the "normal" PageRank has to be used because the year of publication is often missing in the CiteSeer metadata available for download; around 40% of the documents do not have the year indicated. Rankings and recommendations computed with PageRank are clearly not personalized because SPRec has neither additional information on the user nor on the context of the search query. The PageRank algorithm is run offline on the complete document reference network. At query time, precalculated PageRank values are used.

7.3.2 Personalized TRE-Visibility

Generating recommendations with the TRE-visibility, some decisions have to be made. Firstly, an appropriate metric for the trust propagation has to be selected. Secondly a mapping function is required in order to map trust between users to trust in reviews. Last but not least, the concrete TRE-visibility function has to be chosen.

Trust Metric

The trust metric predicts the degree of trust between two indirectly connected users on the basis of the explicitly declared trust relationships. The indirect trust values are precomputed offline in order to reduce the computation load at query time. As the degree of trust may change and new trust values are added, the indirect trust values are updated regularly. SPRec uses MoleTrust (Avesani *et al.*, 2005) as trust metric which was briefly discussed in the context of path-based metrics in section

3.1.5. MoleTrust was originally designed for trust values in [0, 1], with 0 for distrust and 1 for trust. Here, I adapt it to trust values in [-1, 1] (with -1 for distrust). This is easily feasible because a threshold indicates which trust statements are considered: trust propagation stops at users to which the source user has a trust below a certain threshold. This user's trust statements are not used. MoleTrust sets this threshold to 0.6. In SPRec, this threshold is decreased to 0, which stands for a neutral opinion (and not for distrust). That means that all trust expressions by users who are at least a little bit trusted are considered. Trust statements by distrusted users do not influence the indirect trust values at all. This evades the question whether two successive distrust statements should lead to high trust or to absolute distrust. Regarding the trust propagation horizon, i.e., the number of steps via which trust is propagated, SPRec follows the recommendation by Avesani *et al.*, who compute indirect trust for all users at a maximum distance of 3 to the source user.

The algorithm 4 shows how to apply MoleTrust in order to transform a trust network $\mathcal{T}$ into its propagated version $\mathcal{T}_{\text{prop}}$. Note that for the sake of simplicity, in the algorithm as described below, the average is taken if there are several paths of the same length. The original version and the implementation for SPRec takes the weighted average. $\mathcal{T}_{\text{prop}}$ contains for each user her or his directly given trust values (which are in the original trust network $\mathcal{T}$) and the inferred trust values. Only when weighting the reviews with the trust, the default trust in unknown users is set for each pair of users for which no trust value is given in $\mathcal{T}_{\text{prop}}$. This is exactly the result of steps 1 and 2 described in 5.1.3.

Mapping Function

The impact of a review is computed based on the direct and the predicted trust relationships. So the trust between users is mapped to trust in reviews t_j. The mapping function defines thus a mapping from the trust values $t_{u_m \to u_n}$ in [-1,1] to a value t_j in [0, 1]. The mapping function has to be monotonic increasing. SPRec applies the following mapping function to direct and inferred trust values. It is shown in figure 7.3.

$$t_j \;=\; \frac{1}{4}\, t^2_{u_m \to u_n} \;+\; \frac{1}{2}\, t_{u_m \to u_n} \;+\; \frac{1}{4}$$

This particular mapping function was chosen because it fulfills the following requirements:

- -1 is mapped to 0 so that the impact of a review by a distrusted user is 0,

- 1 is mapped to 1, i.e., the review of a trusted user is given full impact,

---

Algorithm 4 Trust Propagation

1: **function** TRUST-PROP(Graph $\mathcal{T} = (U, T)$, int horizon) $\rightarrow \mathcal{T}_{\text{prop}}$
2:      inferredTrust $\leftarrow \emptyset$
3:      **for all** u in U **do**
4:          accessibles $\leftarrow [\{u\}, \{u_m : (u, u_m, t_{u \rightarrow u_m}) \in T\}, ...\{\}_{horizon}]$
5:          edges $\leftarrow [\emptyset, \{(u, u_m, t_{u \rightarrow u_m}) \in T\}, \{\}_2, ...\{\}_{horizon}]$
6:          visitedNodes $\leftarrow$ accessibles[0] $\cup$ accessibles[1]
7:          **for** (dist=2, dist $\leq$ horizon, dist++) **do**
8:              Hash H $\leftarrow \emptyset$ $\triangleright$ keys: users, values: list of trust values
9:              **for all** $v \in \{v' : (u, v', t_{u \rightarrow v'}) \in$ edges[dist-1]$\}$ **do**
10:                 **if** $t_{u \rightarrow v'} > 0$ **then** $\triangleright$ Trust propagation only for trusted users
11:                     **for all** $u_m \in \{u' : (v, u', t_{v \rightarrow u'}) \in T\}$ **do**
12:                         **if** $u_m \notin$ visitedNodes **then** $\triangleright$ no shorter path to u_m
13:                            accessibles[dist] $\leftarrow$ accessibles[dist] $\cup \{u_m\}$
14:                            **if** $u_m \notin$ H **then** $\triangleright$ u_m is not key in H, there is (not yet) an alternative path of the same length to u_m
15:                                H[u_m] $\leftarrow \{(t_{u \rightarrow v} \cdot t_{v \rightarrow u_m})\}$
16:                            **else** $\triangleright$ alternative path of the same length
17:                                H[u_m] $\leftarrow$ H[u_m] $\cup \{(t_{u \rightarrow v} \cdot t_{v \rightarrow u_m})\}$
18:                            **end if**
19:                         **end if**
20:                     **end for**
21:                 **end if**
22:              **end for**
23:              **for all** $\langle u_m \Rightarrow \tau \rangle \in$ H **do** $\triangleright$ Collect new edges
24:                 edges[dist] $\leftarrow$ edges[dist] $\cup \left\{ \left(u, u_m, \frac{\sum_{t \in tv} t}{|\tau|}\right) \right\}$
25:              **end for**
26:              visitedNodes $\leftarrow$ visitedNodes $\cup$ accessibles[dist]
27:              inferredTrust $\leftarrow$ inferredTrust $\cup$ edges[dist] $\triangleright$ inferredTrust contains for each user u all inferred trust relationships
28:          **end for**
29:      **end for**
30:      $T_{\text{prop}} \leftarrow T \cup$ inferredTrust $\triangleright$ Update T with all inferred trust values
31:      **return** $\mathcal{T}_{\text{prop}} = (U, T_{\text{prop}})$
32: **end function**

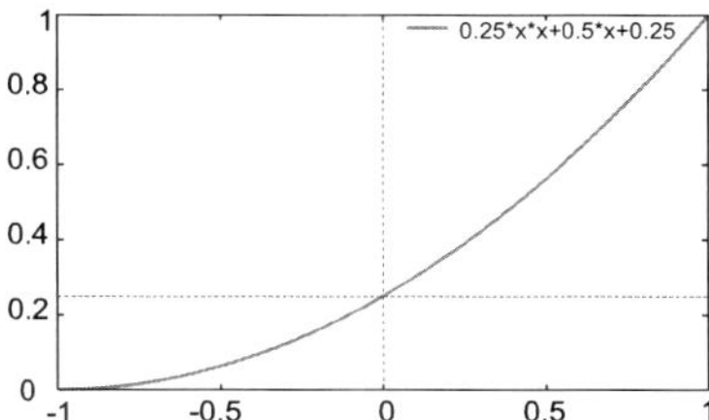

Figure 7.3: Mapping Function used in SPRec

- 0 is mapped to 0.25 and thereby some impact is given to the reviews by unknown users and in the case of neutrality.

Giving some impact to the reviews by unknown users is appropriate in the case of document recommendations because the risk involved is rather low. This mapping function can easily be applied at runtime.

TRE-Visibility Measure

The recommendations are now generated with a TRE-visibility measure, more precisely with the distance-based TRE-visibility. I have selected the distance-based TRE-visibility as a review-propagating TRE-visibility that uses document base visibilities which are precomputed offline with PageRank. This reduces the computation load at query time considerably.

7.4 Outlook on Future Developments of SPRec

Concerning the basic functionality of SPRec, a number of things could be improved. First of all, the document collection could be enlarged, i.e., the metadata from more or other metadata providers should also be considered, in order to deal with the rather low quality of the CiteSeer metadata. The search functionality on the documents could be improved, too, for instance, by allowing for more complex queries. With respect to the recommendations, the response time should be minimized, especially for the TRE-visibility. In a usability study, the usability of the SPRec website could be analyzed and then improved. This leads directly to the question on additional functionality that could be provided by SPRec. This includes, for instance, a visualization of the networks and the possibility of navigating in these networks in order to find known users in the community or to explore related literature.

The main point that should be addressed in future versions is to facilitate the trust networking and the reviewing, i.e., to decrease the effort required by the user. Future versions of SPRec could implement different approaches that facilitate establishing the trust network. On the one hand, the use of FOAF data would be straightforward, i.e., to permit users including their personal FOAF file, either by uploading it at the SPRec website or simply by specifying its URL. On the other hand, SPRec could suggest trust relationships, or at least possible connections on the basis of web mining approaches. For example, a list of users could be presented who are in some previous relationship with the user, such as coauthors and colleagues. Concerning the reviewing component, it is conceivable that users are allowed to import their bibtex files and to indicate a default review for these documents. The reviewing component would display those documents (i.e., their metadata) that are contained in SPRec's database. The default review given could then directly be modified.

These measures would facilitate using SPRec. In contrast to the rankings provided for example by CiteSeer or Google Scholar, the users can actively influence their personal document rankings by providing reviews and by extending their personal web of trust. Such a recommender system builds on the collaborative work of a user community such as can be seen in many Social Web applications in which users actively participate, for example, by tagging web resources and pictures or by contributing to wiki articles.

SPRec can be generalized from a scientific paper recommender to a website recommender system, e.g., for websites in a certain context, such as webpages on health care. In this case, some adaptations would be necessary with respect to the visibility measures used and the basic functionality. When dealing with websites, additional information can be used that facilitate the networking and the reviewing. Reviews on websites, for example, can be derived from the user's bookmarks and browsing history. Such information is analyzed in the context of usage mining, a sub area of web mining.

8 Evaluation and Discussion

The trust-enhanced measures for personalized recommendations in multi-layer architectures are analyzed in simulation. A simulation offers the possibility of testing the visibility measures on large-scale document collections that highly differ in their structure, e.g. that have the properties of scientific paper networks or of wikis. This avoids being restricted to a single collection with certain properties. After an introduction to the simulation environment, I will describe how the multi-layer networks for the simulation studies are generated. Then I'll perform several studies for the TRE- and the ATE-visibility, respectively.

8.1 Simulation Environment for the Multi-Layer Architecture

The simulations are done with Comte, a simulation tool developed in the project *Communication-Oriented Modeling* (COM) in the Laboratory for Semantic Information Technology at the University of Bamberg; hence the name COM Test Environment[1]. The objective of this project was the communication-oriented (in contrast to agent-oriented) modeling and analysis of large-scale communication processes such as newsgroups, scholar communication via scientific publications or webpages. This analysis was supported by the simulation environment.

Comte provides basic mechanisms for simulating and analyzing mass communication. To reflect the time line of the communication process, Comte generates new documents in distinct time steps which reference the documents generated in previous steps. The number of documents generated and the number of references set by the documents are determined by the parameterization of the distribution function. As new documents link to older documents, it has to be defined which documents are referenced. In reality, often those documents are cited that already have a high visibility (see the discussions on the rich-get-richer effect in scale-free networks in section 3.2.2).

---

[1] For more information on COM and to download of the simulation tool (in Java) see the project website at `http://www.kinf.wiai.uni-bamberg.de/COM/`.

Various visibility functions are implemented in Comte. Combined with the distribution functions, they can be used for generating different types of networks. This gives document networks that show a specific citation pattern, namely either a modernist, a classicist or a historicist citation pattern. Modernist means that papers tend to cite recent papers. This citation behavior is typical for computer science. Other disciplines, in contrast, mostly cite classics or historic literature, leading to a different structure of the document reference network. Comte offers a statistical analysis of the simulation results as well as different visualizations. Comte 2 extends the basic functionality of Comte 1 to better fit the requirements imposed by the analysis of distinct networks combined in a multi-layer architecture. It implements various trust-enhanced visibility functions. An important aspect was to implement these measures in such a way that Comte could be used as library for SPRec. The development of both SPRec and Comte 2 was therefore strongly interwoven.

Figure 8.1 shows a screenshot of the graphical interface of Comte. On the left side, the tab showing the visualization of the generated message graph is selected. The graph shows a modernist citation pattern: the most visible nodes (the darker the color of the message, the higher its visibility) are in the five newest generations displayed on the top. The right side shows the parameterization of the selected distribution and visibility functions, the legend for the visualization as well as the number of steps in which the message graph is generated.

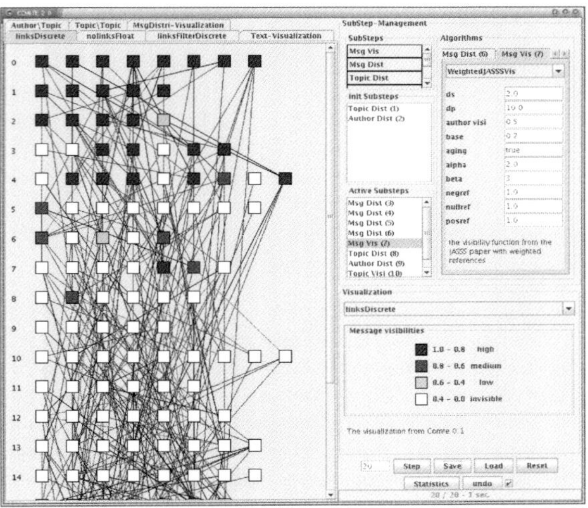

Figure 8.1: Comte

8.2 Multi-Layer Networks for the TRE-Visibility Simulation Studies

8.2.1 Generating Document Reference Networks

The document networks used in the simulation studies are generated with Comte. I use in the simulation small and medium-sized networks. The medium-sized networks D_m contain around 10,000 documents, a number which likely corresponds to the size of a document reference network for a specific research area in a certain discipline, e.g. web mining as a special area in computer science. The small networks D_s encompass around 2,000 documents and are generated in order to analyze whether results hold true for smaller networks. If results are in the same order of magnitude for D_m and D_s, future simulations could be run on the small networks. For instance, when the optimal parameterization of some trust-enhanced visibility measure is determined for a certain document collection, using small-sized document networks would save computation time.

Comte generates a document network stepwise in order to simulate the growth of real document networks over a certain time span. At each step, a set of papers is generated. This is fairly intuitive, because in reality a set of papers is published in the same conference proceedings or journal. For the networks used in the simulation, between 8 and 12 documents are generated at each time step s_i, i.e. there are in average 10 documents per generation. This might be approximately the number of papers on a certain topic published in a conference or a workshop. These documents link to the documents that were generated in previous time steps $s_1, ..., s_{i-1}$. Citations between scientific papers normally go back in time. Cyclic references are rare because two papers would have to be published at the same conference or in the same journal and both authors must be aware of the respective other author's work. As this is unusual, the simulation uses acyclic networks.

I define for the simulation three basic types of networks with respect to the number of references per document. The first type of network contains documents with 6 to 14 references, i.e. in average 10 references per document. This is quite realistic for scientific papers. In order to analyze whether the results are stable when the number of references is increased or decreased, i.e. for networks with a different type of citation behavior, networks with a lower and a higher number of references are generated. In the second type of network, the average number of citations is 5, while the minimum of citations set by a document is 2 and the maximum is 8. The third type of network has documents with 10 to 20 references, so on average 15 references. So there are three types of networks with a different number of references per document: D^{2-8}, D^{6-14} and D^{10-20}.

The documents to be cited are now selected: documents that have a high visibility at the current time step are more intensively cited. This reflects real citation behavior. The visibility of a document is computed by an extended version of PageRank, namely Age PageRank, which considers the aging of documents (see section 3.2.3). In contrast to PageRank, Age PageRank avoids referencing only the first generated documents. In fact, it favors recently generated documents (in reality, recently published papers). It is here defined as

$$\text{vis}^{\text{APR}}_{p_d} = \frac{(1 - \alpha) + \alpha \cdot \sum_{p_k \in R_{p_d}} \frac{\text{vis}^{\text{APR}}_{p_k}}{|C_{p_k}|}}{a_{p_d} + 50}$$

with $\alpha = 0.85$, and a_{p_d} being the age of document p_d. I use $a_{p_d} + 50$ in order to smooth the decrease in visibility with increasing age. After 1000 steps, the document reference network contains around 10,000 documents and shows a modernist citation pattern. I use only document networks with a modernist citation pattern in the simulation studies. The simulations, however, are not specific for a particular citation pattern. Table 8.1 gives an overview of the characteristics of the basic types of networks used in the simulation studies.

	Type of Network	
	Small-Sized ($\mathbf{D}_s$)	Medium-Sized ($\mathbf{D}_m$)
# of documents	$\approx$ 2,000 documents	$\approx$ 10,000 documents
# of generation steps	200	1,000
# of documents per step	8 – 12	8 – 12
# of references per document		
2– 8 references	$\mathbf{D}_s^{2-8}$	$\mathbf{D}_m^{2-8}$
6–14 references	$\mathbf{D}_s^{6-14}$	$\mathbf{D}_m^{6-14}$
10–20 references	$\mathbf{D}_s^{10-20}$	$\mathbf{D}_m^{10-20}$
citation pattern	modernist, i.e. documents attract references based on their visibility computed with Age PageRank	

Table 8.1: Properties of the Basic Networks

8.2.2 Generating Trust and Reviews

The trust-review enhanced visibility – the TRE-visibility – is computed in a multi-layer architecture that combines a reviewer trust network with a document reference network. For much of the analysis of the TRE-visibility, such as the comparison of the different TRE-visibility measures, it is sufficient to compute visibilities from the perspective of a single user. This allows for abstracting from a concrete trust network. The reviews r_j and the trust t_j in them can thus directly be generated from the perspective of some test user u. Normally, the trust in the reviews is determined on the basis of the interpersonal trust values (directly given or inferred) and the default trust given to unknown users. This gives a trust value for all reviews: there is a t_j for each r_j.

The reviews and the trust in the reviews are generated en bloc for all documents. Reviews are not directly generated at each time step because this would favor old documents. Reviews r_j, which are randomly in [0,1], are randomly distributed over all documents. In a real document reference network, it is conceivable that reviews tend to focus rather on documents that have a high visibility (because such documents are more often read) than being randomly distributed. As this simulation study is interested in the differences between TRE-visibility measures, this, however, does not matter. The trust t_j in the reviews r_j is randomly distributed in [0,1]. I generate the set of reviews on the documents so that the number of reviews corresponds to ten percent of the documents. As a document can be reviewed more than once, around 9.5% of the documents are reviewed. For the medium-sized networks D_m (which contain around 10,000 document), 1000 reviews are generated in total. In the case of the small-sized networks D_s, 200 reviews are set on the 2000 documents. This gives the multi-layer networks $ML_{s,10}$ and $ML_{m,10}$. The number of reviews can clearly be changed. For instance, with a number of reviews corresponding to five percent of the documents, multi-layer networks $ML_{s,5}$ and $ML_{m,5}$ are obtained.

Table 8.2 shows the characteristics of the multi-layer networks with a reviewer trust network. Technically, the result of generating multi-layer networks with Comte are XML files, one for each multi-layer network. The XML file lists the documents, their references and the reviews on them, including the trust in the reviews.

	Small-Sized Networks (ML_s)	Medium-Sized Networks (ML_m)
document networks	D_m^{2-8}, D_m^{6-14}, D_m^{10-20}	D_s^{2-8}, D_s^{6-14}, D_s^{10-20}
# of reviews	1,000	200
	reviews on $\approx$ 9.5% of the documents	
$r_i \in [0,1]$	reviews r_i are randomly in [0,1]	
$t_i \in [0,1]$	trust t_i in a review r_i is for a test user u randomly in [0,1]	
multi-layer networks	$ML_{m,10}^{2-8}$, $ML_{m,10}^{6-14}$, $ML_{m,10}^{10-20}$	$ML_{s,10}^{2-8}$, $ML_{s,10}^{6-14}$, $ML_{s,10}^{10-20}$

Table 8.2: Multi-Layer Networks with Reviews and Trust

8.3 Evaluation of the TRE-Visibility

In order to evaluate the TRE-visibility measures, several simulation studies will be performed and some analysis of their properties will be done. The first step will be the parameterization of the TRE-visibility measures. The evaluation then continues with a thorough comparison, also in comparison with PageRank. The essential difference between the mere structure-based visibility measures such as PageRank and the TRE-visibilities is the trust-weighted reviews. Therefore, I will analyze the impact of the reviews on the recommendations while varying the number of reviews and the average review values. This analysis also shows how TRE-visibilities change for users with different preferences. Moreover, the studies will demonstrate how the TRE-visibility develops for a paper detected to be based on faked data. As the reviews are so important for the TRE-visibility, the last simulation study is concerned with the percentage of documents that have to be reviewed in order to compute TRE-visibilities that differ from PageRank.

8.3.1 Parameterization of the TRE-Visibility Measures

I use in the following analysis PageRank as visibility measure. PageRank has the advantage over HITS that it can be computed directly for all documents regardless of the user query. PageRank $\mathrm{vis}_{p_d}^{\mathrm{PR}}$ is computed with $\alpha = 0.85$ and the basic visibility is set as $\frac{1-\alpha}{k}$ with $k = 100$ so that the impact of trust-weighted reviews and document base visibility is in the same range. In the review-propagating TRE-visibility measures $\mathrm{vis}_{p_d,u_m}^{\mathrm{TRE}_p}$ and $\mathrm{vis}_{p_d,u_m}^{\mathrm{TRE}_d}$, the document base visibility is computed with PageRank and contributes with $\mathrm{vc} = 0.5$. The path-based and the distance-based TRE-visibility consider reviews up to a distance of 3; i.e. reviews influence the visibilities of those documents that are at maximum three steps away. This, however, does not mean that these reviews fully contribute. Both distance-based and path-based TRE-visibility decrease the impact of reviews at distance 2 and 3. The parameterization of the distance-based TRE-visibility is more complicated than that of PageRank and of the other TRE-visibility measures. I therefore discuss it in the next section. For the following discussions, it is necessary to know the order of magnitude in which the (TRE-)visibilities are. For instance, an average difference of 0.1 would be negligible for values in $[0, 10]$ but considerable for values in $[0, 1]$. On the types of networks used in the simulation study, PageRank and the TRE-visibilities are in $[0, 1]$.

8.3.2 Fine-tuning the Distance-Based TRE-Visibility

As the distance-based TRE-visibility does not directly consider the outdegree of the documents (in contrast to the path-based and the integrated TRE-visibility) and as the impact of a review should decrease with increasing distance to the document at issue, the parameters β and λ have to be set. For they depend on a number of factors, ranging from the network size and the number of references per document to the number of documents generated in each step, they have to be determined in simulation for a particular type of network.

> ▶ **Aim:** Finetune the distance-based TRE-visibility for different types of document networks and give – if possible – general methods. ◀

I determine β and λ for basic types of multi-layer networks. The simulation is performed both on the medium-sized networks $\mathrm{ML}_{m,10}^{2-8}$, $\mathrm{ML}_{m,10}^{6-14}$, $\mathrm{ML}_{m,10}^{10-20}$ and the small-sized networks $\mathrm{ML}_{s,10}^{2-8}$, $\mathrm{ML}_{s,10}^{6-14}$ and $\mathrm{ML}_{s,10}^{10-20}$. The properties of these networks were summarized in table 8.2. Ten multi-layer networks are generated for each type of medium-sized network. As the simulation on the small-sized networks is only meant to verify results on networks with a smaller number of documents, a single multi-layer network is generated of each type of small-sized network. Different combinations of β and λ are tested on these networks. By λ, the distance-based visibility measure takes into account that the path-based TRE-visibility splits the review contribution among all outgoing references of a document. I use $\lambda \in \{1, 3, ..., 22\}$. The parameter β regulates the impact of indirect reviews; I use $\beta \in \{1.0, 1.5, ..., 4.0\}$. Varying λ and β in this way gives 42 simulation runs for each multi-layer network.

As the distance-based TRE-visibility simplifies the path-based TRE-visibility, it is sufficient to compare them directly. If the combination of a certain β and λ is good, the difference between $\mathrm{vis}_{p_d,u}^{\mathrm{TRE}_d}$ and $\mathrm{vis}_{p_d,u}^{\mathrm{TRE}_p}$ will be low for any document p_d and any user u. Comparing the results, I distinguish between documents that have at least one direct review and documents with only indirect reviews. The difference in $\mathrm{vis}^{\mathrm{TRE}_d}$ and $\mathrm{vis}^{\mathrm{TRE}_p}$ is computed for all documents. Then, the average is taken for the set of directly reviewed documents and for the set of indirectly reviewed ones. This is feasible as the standard deviation is very small (s < 0.01) in all networks. The average differences between the indirectly reviewed documents are of special interest because here, the differences between the path-based and the distance-based TRE-visibility measure become obvious. The visibilities $\mathrm{vis}^{\mathrm{TRE}_d}$ and $\mathrm{vis}^{\mathrm{TRE}_p}$ of the directly reviewed documents are very similar as both give direct reviews an impact of 1 ($c_{r_i:p_d} = 1$ for a review r_i directly on p_d). They thus differ for directly reviewed documents only in the amount of visibility that is contributed by additional indirect reviews. With the respective parameterization of $\mathrm{vis}^{\mathrm{TRE}_d}$, this difference should be very low. Table 8.3 gives an overview of the approach for fine-tuning the distance-based TRE-visibility. I present and discuss the results separately for networks with 2 to 8, with 6 to 14 and with 10 to 20 references. Table 8.9 then summarizes the findings of this simulation study.

types of networks	$ML_{m,10}^{2-8}$, $ML_{m,10}^{6-14}$, $ML_{m,10}^{10-20}$, $ML_{s,10}^{2-8}$, $ML_{s,10}^{6-14}$, $ML_{s,10}^{10-20}$
# of networks	10 networks of each medium-sized network type, 1 network of each small-sized network type
# of simulation runs	42 for each network
parameterization	$\lambda \in \{1, 4, 7, 10, 13, 16, 19, 22\}$
	$\beta \in \{1.0, 1.5, 2.0, 2.5, 3.0, 3.5, 4.0\}$
TRE-visibilities	vis^{TRE_d} and vis^{TRE_p} on indirectly reviewed documents
benchmark	low average difference between the computed TRE-visibilities

Table 8.3: Fine-Tuning of the Distance-based TRE-Visibility

Fine-Tuning vis^{TRE_d} on Networks with 2–8 References per Document

Table 8.4 shows the results of the simulation on medium-sized networks with 2 to 8 references per document. A low average difference for the indirectly reviewed documents indicates a good parameterization. The best results are achieved with $\lambda = 1$ and $\beta = 3.5$: the visibilities $vis_{p_d,u}^{TRE_d}$ and $vis_{p_d,u}^{TRE_p}$ differ in average only by 0.023. Results are only slightly worse for $\lambda = 1$ and $\beta = 3.0$. Fairly good results are obtained with $\lambda = 7$ and $\beta = 1.5$, too. For $\lambda \geq 10$, the average differences are considerably higher; they need hence not to be considered further. This result suggests that λ is related to the branching factor, although it is not so simple that we can just take the average. I focus in the following analysis on the results obtained with $\lambda \in \{1, 4, 7\}$. Figure 8.2 shows the corresponding graphs. We can see that the higher λ is chosen, the lower has to be β: for $\lambda = 1$, $\beta = 3.0$ and $\beta = 3.5$ give lowest average differences whereas for $\lambda = 7$, $\beta = 1.5$ has to be used in order to obtain average differences of roughly the same quality. This is due to the fact that both λ and β decrease for a review at a distance $k \geq 1$ its contribution. A higher λ compensates a lower β and vice versa.

The lowest average difference is currently 0.023. The question is now whether lower average differences can be achieved with a better parameterization. Looking at the graph for $\lambda = 1$, there might be a lower difference for β between 3.0 and 3.5. For $\lambda = 4$, lower average difference might be obtained by using a β between 1.5 and 2.0. Moreover, it would be interesting to look at results obtained by varying λ, namely $\lambda = 5, 6, ..., 9$ and a fixed $\beta = 1.5$. I run a further simulation for $\lambda = 1$, $\beta \in \{3.1, 3.2, 3.3, 3.4\}$ and for $\lambda = 4$, $\beta \in \{1.6, 1.7, 1.8, 1.9\}$. As we can see in table 8.5, results can be improved by modifying β at a very fine granular level. The average difference decreases to 0.021 by using $\lambda = 1$ and $\beta \in \{3.2, 3.3\}$. For $\lambda = 4$, the average difference decreases, too.

$\lambda \backslash \beta$	1.0	1.5	2.0	2.5	3.0	3.5	4.0
1	0.185	0.141	0.096	0.054	**0.026**	**0.023**	0.040
4	0.103	0.034	0.038	0.065	0.076	0.081	0.082
7	0.068	**0.029**	0.063	0.078	0.082	0.083	0.084
10	0.049	0.042	0.072	0.081	0.083	0.084	0.084
13	0.039	0.053	0.077	0.082	0.083	0.084	0.084
16	0.033	0.059	0.079	0.083	0.084	0.084	0.084
19	0.030	0.064	0.080	0.083	0.084	0.084	0.084
22	0.029	0.067	0.081	0.083	0.084	0.084	0.084

Table 8.4: Av. Differences between $\mathrm{vis}^{\mathrm{TRE}_d}$ and $\mathrm{vis}^{\mathrm{TRE}_p}$ for Indirectly Reviewed Documents ($\mathrm{ML}_{m,10}^{2-8}$)

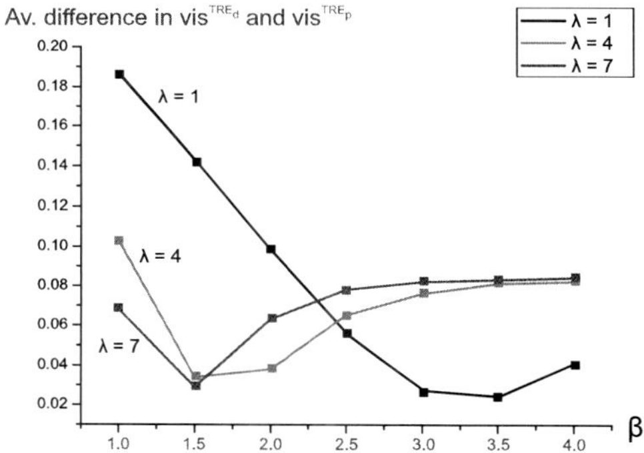

Figure 8.2: Av. Differences between $\mathrm{vis}^{\mathrm{TRE}_p}$ and $\mathrm{vis}^{\mathrm{TRE}_d}$ ($\mathrm{ML}_{m,10}^{2-8}$)

The results on the medium-sized networks comply with the results on the small-sized network: the lowest average differences (here around 0.03) are obtained for $\lambda = 1$ and $\beta \in \{3.0, 3.5\}$. Average differences are also similar on networks in which a lesser number of documents is generated per step. In Hess and Stein (2007a), in which the document networks encompassed around 12,000 documents generated in 3300 generations with only 3.5 documents in average and 2 to 7 references per document, $\lambda = 1$ and $\beta = 3.0$ were best suited. Finding the optimal parameterization in simulation might be very time consuming, depending on the size of the network. It is a pragmatic solution for networks with a small (i.e. < 10) number of references per document to use $\lambda = 1$ and to adjust only the parameter β with $\beta \approx 3.5$.

$\lambda\,^\beta$	3.0	3.1	3.2	3.3	3.4	3.5
1	0.026	0.023	0.021	0.021	0.022	0.023

$\lambda\,^\beta$	1.5	1.6	1.7	1.8	1.9	2.0
4	0.034	0.028	0.025	0.027	0.032	0.038

Table 8.5: Refining Results with finer granular β or λ ($\mathrm{ML}_{m,10}^{2-8}$)

Fine-Tuning $\mathrm{vis}^{\mathrm{TRE}_d}$ on Networks with 6–14 References per Document

Table 8.6 presents the results for medium-sized networks with 6 to 14 references per document. With a first glance at the results, we can see that the lowest average differences are now achieved for $\lambda \in \{7, 10, 13\}$, which is around the number of outgoing references per document. The corresponding graphs are shown in figure 8.3. The range of β can also be narrowed down: for $\lambda \in \{7, 10, 13\}$, only β between 2.5 and 3.5 give interesting results. The distance-based TRE-visibility is the closest to the path-based TRE-visibility for $\lambda = 13$, $\beta = 2.5$ and for $\lambda = 7$, $\beta = 3.0$. Both parameterizations are quite different. With $\lambda = 7$, a value is used that is almost the minimal number of references per document. In contrast, $\lambda = 13$ is close to the maximal number of references per document.

$\lambda\,^\beta$	1.0	1.5	2.0	2.5	3.0	3.5	4.0
1	0.315	0.291	0.262	0.230	0.197	0.166	0.140
4	0.266	0.202	0.140	0.100	0.078	0.060	0.050
7	0.238	0.158	0.099	0.069	0.050	0.056	0.075
10	0.219	0.131	0.079	0.053	0.055	0.076	0.085
13	0.204	0.114	0.067	0.048	0.069	0.083	0.087
16	0.193	0.101	0.058	0.053	0.077	0.086	0.088
19	0.182	0.092	0.052	0.061	0.081	0.087	0.088
22	0.174	0.084	0.048	0.067	0.084	0.088	0.089

Table 8.6: Av. Differences between $\mathrm{vis}^{\mathrm{TRE}_d}$ and $\mathrm{vis}^{\mathrm{TRE}_p}$ for Indirectly Reviewed Documents ($\mathrm{ML}_{m,10}^{6-14}$)

For the currently considered combinations of λ and β, the average differences between $\mathrm{vis}^{\mathrm{TRE}_d}$ and $\mathrm{vis}^{\mathrm{TRE}_p}$ are larger than for the networks with 2 to 8 references. This might be because the optimal parameterization is not yet found. As it can be seen in figure 8.3, it is possible that average differences can be decreased by modifying β,

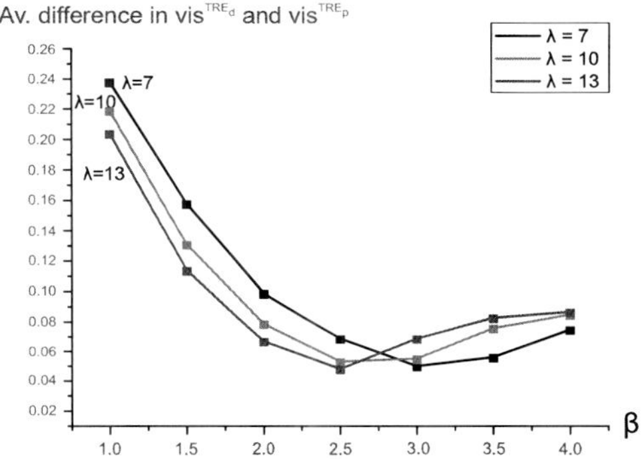

Figure 8.3: Av. Differences between vis^{TRE_p} and vis^{TRE_d} ($\text{ML}_{m,10}^{6-14}$)

namely to consider $\lambda = 7$ with $\beta = 3.0, 3.1, ..., 3.5$, and $\lambda = 13$ with $\beta = 2.0, 2.1, ..., 2.5$. A better parameterization might also be achieved for $\lambda = 10$ by varying β between 2.5 and 3.0. The results for $\lambda = 10$ are shown in table 8.7. The lowest average difference is now 0.048, which is identical with the previous best results.

λ β	2.5	2.6	2.7	2.8	2.9	3.0
10	0.053	0.050	0.048	0.049	0.051	0.055

Table 8.7: Refining Results with finer granular β or λ ($\text{ML}_{m,10}^{6-14}$)

A fairly good result that is not achieved with $\lambda \in \{7, 10, 13\}$, is obtained for $\lambda = 22$, $\beta = 2.0$. The higher λ compensates the lower β. As results do not give any hint on a potential optimization by fine-tuning β, this combination is not considered further.

Having rather equal average differences for two parameterizations, such as for $\lambda = 7$, $\beta = 3.0$ and $\lambda = 13$, $\beta = 2.5$, we have to select one of them to be used in the further simulation studies. This decision can be supported by looking at the average differences to PageRank and to the integrated TRE-visibility. Not wanting to anticipate the detailed comparison of the TRE-visibility measures, the average differences to PageRank are bigger for $\lambda = 7$, $\beta = 3.0$ than for $\lambda = 13$, $\beta = 2.5$, while the differences to the integrated TRE-visibility are highly similar.[2] As a bigger

---

[2]For indirectly reviewed documents, the average difference between PageRank and vis^{TRE_d} is 0.065 with $\lambda = 7$, $\beta = 3.0$ and 0.054 with $\lambda = 13$, $\beta = 2.5$. Between vis^{TRE_d} and vis^{TRE_i}, it is 0.052 for $\lambda = 7$, $\beta = 3.0$ and 0.047 for $\lambda = 13$, $\beta = 2.5$.

difference is a desirable property because it indicates that reviews have much impact, I use for simulations on $\mathrm{ML}_{m,10}^{6-14}$ $\lambda = 7$, $\beta = 3.0$.

On the small-sized networks, lowest average differences are obtained by using λ as above, but with a β smaller by 0.5, i.e. with $\lambda = 13$ and $\beta = 2.0$, and with $\lambda = 7$ and $\beta = 2.5$, respectively. This is to say that the same range of λ is of interest, independent from the network size.

Fine-Tuning $\mathrm{vis}^{\mathrm{TRE}_d}$ on Networks with 10–20 References per Document

Table 8.8 shows the simulation results on networks with 10 to 20 references per document. The lowest average differences are here achieved with λ between 7 and 19. The corresponding graphs are displayed in figure 8.4. As we have already seen for the networks with 6–14 references per document, very low average differences are obtained with λ being the minimal and the maximal number of references per document, respectively. Again, β has to be decreased with increasing λ. So the average difference between path-based and distance-based TRE-visibility is 0.035 for $\lambda = 19, \beta = 2.5$ as well as for $\lambda = 10, \beta = 3.0$. A very low average difference is obtained with $\lambda = 7$, $\beta = 3.5$.

λ \ β	1.0	1.5	2.0	2.5	3.0	3.5	4.0
1	0.346	0.335	0.321	0.307	0.292	0.277	0.262
4	0.322	0.290	0.254	0.215	0.169	0.116	0.063
7	0.308	0.263	0.210	0.147	0.076	0.034	0.056
10	0.297	0.242	0.174	0.092	0.035	0.058	0.079
13	0.289	0.225	0.143	0.054	0.044	0.075	0.085
16	0.281	0.209	0.116	0.036	0.061	0.082	0.088
19	0.275	0.195	0.093	0.035	0.071	0.085	0.089
22	0.269	0.183	0.074	0.042	0.077	0.087	0.089

Table 8.8: Av. Differences between $\mathrm{vis}^{\mathrm{TRE}_d}$ and $\mathrm{vis}^{\mathrm{TRE}_p}$ for Indirectly Reviewed Documents ($\mathrm{ML}_{m,10}^{10-20}$)

Analyzing the graphs for $\lambda = 10$ and $\lambda = 19$ in figure 8.4, it can be expected that the average difference decreases for finer granular β. Alternatively, $\lambda = 13 \pm 1$ could be considered with a finer granular β, namely with $\beta = 2.5, 2.6, ..., 3.0$. However, as the above presented parameterization already gives low average differences, we can spare ourselves further time spent carrying out intensive simulations. Nevertheless, the concrete parameterization for the following studies has to be chosen. Looking at both $\lambda = 19, \beta = 2.5$ and $\lambda = 10, \beta = 3.0$ in depth, we can see that the average difference

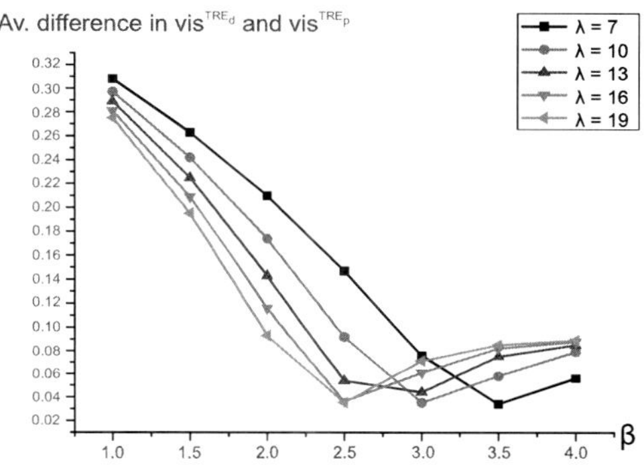

Figure 8.4: Av. Differences between $\mathrm{vis}^{\mathrm{TRE}_p}$ and $\mathrm{vis}^{\mathrm{TRE}_d}$ ($\mathrm{ML}^{10-20}_{m,10}$)

to PageRank is higher for the smaller λ, too, such as in the case of the networks with 6 to 14 references per document.[3] The parameterization $\lambda = 10, \beta = 3.0$ is therefore well suited for the simulation study.

Results on the small-sized network $\mathrm{ML}^{10-20}_{s,10}$ are similar to the results on the medium-sized networks. The smallest average differences were achieved with $\lambda = 10$ and $\lambda = 19$ and, as already in the case of the networks with 6 to 14 references per document, with a decreased β, i.e. with $\beta = 2.5$ (instead of 3.0) and $\beta = 2.0$ (instead of 2.5).

Summing Up: Parameterization

Table 8.9 shows the parameterization of the distance-based TRE-visibility that gives the lowest average differences on the indirectly reviewed documents on medium-sized networks. This parameterization is used in the following simulation studies. For the small-sized networks, the parameterization is quite similar as in the case of the medium-sized networks: λ is identical while β tends to be slightly smaller.

The question is now how to find a good parameterization of the distance-based TRE-visibility for a certain document reference network, either generated in a simulation environment or a real network such as the CiteSeer network. These multi-layer networks differ in size, in the number of outgoing references per document etc. Is it

---

[3]For indirectly reviewed documents, the average difference between PageRank and $\mathrm{vis}^{\mathrm{TRE}_d}$ is 0.083 with $\lambda = 10, \beta = 3.0$ and 0.067 with $\lambda = 19, \beta = 2.5$. Between $\mathrm{vis}^{\mathrm{TRE}_d}$ and $\mathrm{vis}^{\mathrm{TRE}_i}$, it is 0.061 for $\lambda = 7, \beta = 3.0$ and 0.052 for $\lambda = 13, \beta = 2.5$.

# of references	λ	β
$\mathrm{ML}_{m,10}^{2-8}$	1	3.3
$\mathrm{ML}_{m,10}^{6-14}$	7	3.0
$\mathrm{ML}_{m,10}^{10-20}$	10	3.0

Table 8.9: Parameterization of the Distance-Based TRE-Visibility

possible to give some general advice for the parameterization? As I used networks with a modernist citation pattern, the following considerations apply only to these networks.

In networks with a small branching factor, the parameterization is quite straightforward as discussed above. 'Small' means that documents have in average five outgoing references. I recommend using $\lambda = 1$ and to adjust only β with $\beta \in [3.0, 3.5]$. For networks with a higher branching factor, the parameterization is more complex. As results on the medium-sized networks comply with the results on the small-sized networks, one might think of simulating the parameterization on a small network that is similar to the network at issue with respect to its structure (references and reviews). If such a network exists, it is possible to narrow down the range of λ and β for which low average differences can be achieved. However, in most cases, a smaller network with the same properties will rarely be available. Taking a section out of the original network is unlikely to result in a network with similar structural properties.

However, as seen in the above simulations, it is not necessary to test the full range of λ and β. It was sufficient to consider λ in the range of the minimal and the maximal number of outgoing references per document. However, references in real networks are likely to be not uniformly distributed as in $\mathrm{ML}_{m,10}^{2-8}$ and $\mathrm{ML}_{s,10}^{2-8}$, but there will be documents which reference to many other documents and documents that cite only one or two other documents. Starting with the average number of citations is more appropriate than taking the absolute minimum and maximum. The precise value for β has then only to be tested for a limited range of λ. Moreover, based on the simulation results, only $\beta \in [2.5, 3.5]$ have to be considered. So a first simulation might be run for λ equals and plus/minus 5 of the average number of citations, and $\beta = 2.5, 3.0, 3.5$. This considerably reduces the number of simulation runs.

▶ **Result of the Fine-tuning:** I have parameterized the distance-based TRE-visibility for different types of document reference networks by systematically varying the parameters λ and β. As expected, it is necessary to fine-tune the distance-based TRE-visibility for a particular document network. However, I could considerably narrow down the range in which the parameters λ and β have to be for different types of networks. ◀

8.3.3 Comparison of (TRE)-Visibility Measures

A simulation study offers the means to learn more about the differences in the visibilities computed by the distinct TRE-visibility functions. In such a simulation, TRE-visibilities should also be compared with PageRank, in order to analyze how much the reviews influence the TRE-visibility. With respect to the TRE-visibility measures, the differences between the integrated TRE-visibility and the efficient review-propagating TRE-visibility functions are of special interest. The integrated TRE-visibility can be considered as a type of baseline as it constitutes the most intuitive way of propagating trust-weighted reviews on a document network. In the comparative analysis of the TRE-visibility functions, particular attention is paid to the impact that indirect reviews have on the recommendation. According to how I designed the measures, the path-based, the distance-based and the integrated visibilities should be close to each other. In other words, the average differences should be low.

▶ **Aim:** Analyze the differences between PageRank and the TRE-visibility measures. Based on the differences between the TRE-visibility measures, determine which TRE-visibility measure to use in a multi-layer-based document recommendation system. ◀

The simulation study is meant to deepen the understanding of differences between the TRE-visibility measures – it does not deal with the differences in the visibilities computed by a certain function for different users. So the multi-layer networks as generated before can be used, which abstract from a concrete trust network. Table 8.10 summarizes the approach taken in the comparative simulation study.

types of networks	$\mathrm{ML}_{m,10}^{2-8}$, $\mathrm{ML}_{m,10}^{6-14}$, $\mathrm{ML}_{m,10}^{10-20}$, $\mathrm{ML}_{s,10}^{2-8}$, $\mathrm{ML}_{s,10}^{6-14}$, $\mathrm{ML}_{s,10}^{10-20}$
# of networks	10 networks of each medium-sized network type, 1 network of each small-sized network type
# of simulation runs	1 for each network
(TRE)-visibilities	$\mathrm{vis}_{p_d}^{\mathrm{PR}}$, $\mathrm{vis}_{p_d,u}^{\mathrm{TRE}_s}$, $\mathrm{vis}_{p_d,u}^{\mathrm{TRE}_i}$, $\mathrm{vis}_{p_d,u}^{\mathrm{TRE}_p}$, $\mathrm{vis}_{p_d,u}^{\mathrm{TRE}_d}$
average differences	between documents with direct reviews, documents with only indirect reviews and over all documents

Table 8.10: Comparison of (TRE)-Visibility: Approach

For each of the thirty medium-sized networks, the different types of visibilities are computed from the perspective of the test user u for all documents. In order to verify whether results are in the same order of magnitude on small-sized networks, the simulation is also run on the small networks. The visibility measures are parameterized as described in section 8.3.1. For the distance-based TRE-visibility, the parameterization is summarized in table 8.9.

Results of the Comparative Simulation

The resulting (TRE)-visibilities of all documents, i.e. $\mathrm{vis}^A_{p_d,u}$ and $\mathrm{vis}^B_{p_d,u}$, respectively, are compared pairwise for two TRE-visibility measures A and B. The average differences between these visibility values are computed for three groups of documents: firstly, the directly reviewed documents (Δ_{direct}), i.e., all documents with at least one direct review; secondly, the indirectly reviewed documents ($\Delta_{\mathrm{indirect}}$), i.e., all documents without direct review; and thirdly, all documents (Δ_{total}). The average on all networks can be computed due to the small standard deviation ($s < 0.01$). Results are shown in tables 8.11, 8.12 and 8.13. The first four lines of table 8.12 show the average differences between document visibilities computed with one of the TRE-visibility measures and with PageRank. The remaining six lines present the average differences between the visibilities computed with the distinct TRE-visibility functions.

PageRank as well as the TRE-visibilities are for these types of networks in general in $[0,1]$. In the medium-sized networks used in this simulation, the maximal PageRank that a document achieves is around 0.64 while the minimum is 0.001, i.e. the basic visibility given to a document that is not cited at all.

Alg. A	Alg. B	Δ_{direct}	$\Delta_{\mathrm{indirect}}$	Δ_{total}
PageRank	$\mathrm{vis}^{\mathrm{TRE}_s}$	0.226	0.0	0.021
PageRank	$\mathrm{vis}^{\mathrm{TRE}_i}$	0.266	0.076	0.094
PageRank	$\mathrm{vis}^{\mathrm{TRE}_p}$	0.257	0.084	0.100
PageRank	$\mathrm{vis}^{\mathrm{TRE}_d}$	0.255	0.077	0.094
$\mathrm{vis}^{\mathrm{TRE}_s}$	$\mathrm{vis}^{\mathrm{TRE}_i}$	0.040	0.076	0.073
$\mathrm{vis}^{\mathrm{TRE}_s}$	$\mathrm{vis}^{\mathrm{TRE}_p}$	0.034	0.084	0.079
$\mathrm{vis}^{\mathrm{TRE}_s}$	$\mathrm{vis}^{\mathrm{TRE}_d}$	0.031	0.077	0.073
$\mathrm{vis}^{\mathrm{TRE}_i}$	$\mathrm{vis}^{\mathrm{TRE}_p}$	0.026	0.050	0.047
$\mathrm{vis}^{\mathrm{TRE}_i}$	$\mathrm{vis}^{\mathrm{TRE}_d}$	0.024	0.044	0.042
$\mathrm{vis}^{\mathrm{TRE}_d}$	$\mathrm{vis}^{\mathrm{TRE}_p}$	0.011	0.021	0.019

Table 8.11: Av. Differences in TRE-Visibilities ($\mathrm{ML}^{2-8}_{m,10}$)

Interpretation of the Results from the Comparative TRE-Visibility Simulation

Several small tables repeat in the following parts of the data from the above tables 8.11, 8.12 and 8.13 in order to facilitate the comparison. The average differences

Alg. A	Alg. B	Δ_{direct}	Δ_{indirect}	Δ_{total}
PageRank	$\text{vis}^{\text{TRE}_s}$	0.227	0.0	0.022
PageRank	$\text{vis}^{\text{TRE}_i}$	0.269	0.075	0.094
PageRank	$\text{vis}^{\text{TRE}_p}$	0.259	0.089	0.105
PageRank	$\text{vis}^{\text{TRE}_d}$	0.252	0.065	0.083
$\text{vis}^{\text{TRE}_s}$	$\text{vis}^{\text{TRE}_i}$	0.042	0.075	0.072
$\text{vis}^{\text{TRE}_s}$	$\text{vis}^{\text{TRE}_p}$	0.035	0.089	0.084
$\text{vis}^{\text{TRE}_s}$	$\text{vis}^{\text{TRE}_d}$	0.027	0.065	0.061
$\text{vis}^{\text{TRE}_i}$	$\text{vis}^{\text{TRE}_p}$	0.027	0.052	0.050
$\text{vis}^{\text{TRE}_i}$	$\text{vis}^{\text{TRE}_d}$	0.030	0.052	0.050
$\text{vis}^{\text{TRE}_d}$	$\text{vis}^{\text{TRE}_p}$	0.022	0.050	0.048

Table 8.12: Av. Differences in TRE-Visibilities ($\text{ML}_{m,10}^{6-14}$)

Alg. A	Alg. B	Δ_{direct}	Δ_{indirect}	Δ_{total}
PageRank	$\text{vis}^{\text{TRE}_s}$	0.226	0.0	0.021
PageRank	$\text{vis}^{\text{TRE}_i}$	0.266	0.075	0.093
PageRank	$\text{vis}^{\text{TRE}_p}$	0.259	0.089	0.106
PageRank	$\text{vis}^{\text{TRE}_d}$	0.256	0.083	0.100
$\text{vis}^{\text{TRE}_s}$	$\text{vis}^{\text{TRE}_i}$	0.040	0.075	0.072
$\text{vis}^{\text{TRE}_s}$	$\text{vis}^{\text{TRE}_p}$	0.035	0.089	0.084
$\text{vis}^{\text{TRE}_s}$	$\text{vis}^{\text{TRE}_d}$	0.031	0.083	0.078
$\text{vis}^{\text{TRE}_i}$	$\text{vis}^{\text{TRE}_p}$	0.026	0.053	0.051
$\text{vis}^{\text{TRE}_i}$	$\text{vis}^{\text{TRE}_d}$	0.030	0.061	0.058
$\text{vis}^{\text{TRE}_d}$	$\text{vis}^{\text{TRE}_p}$	0.016	0.035	0.033

Table 8.13: Av. Differences in TRE-Visibilities ($\text{ML}_{m,10}^{10-20}$)

between the (TRE-)visibilities are rounded off to two decimal places.

Differences between PageRank and TRE-Visibility Tables 8.14 and 8.15 show the average differences between PageRank and the TRE-visibility measures on directly and indirectly reviewed documents, respectively.

PageRank vs.	$\text{vis}^{\text{TRE}_s}$	$\text{vis}^{\text{TRE}_i}$	$\text{vis}^{\text{TRE}_p}$	$\text{vis}^{\text{TRE}_d}$
$\text{ML}_{m,10}^{2-8}$	0.23	0.27	0.26	0.26
$\text{ML}_{m,10}^{6-14}$	0.23	0.27	0.26	0.25
$\text{ML}_{m,10}^{10-20}$	0.23	0.27	0.26	0.26

Table 8.14: PageRank versus TRE-Visibility (Δ_{direct})

The visibilities computed with the simple TRE-visibility $\mathrm{vis}^{\mathrm{TRE}_s}$ differ considerably from PageRank for those documents that have at least one direct review. They differ on average by around 0.23. The integrated, the path-based and the distance-based TRE-visibility differ from PageRank for directly reviewed documents in the same order of magnitude as the simple TRE-visibility. The small difference – around 0.26 instead of 0.23 – comes from the fact the directly reviewed documents also have indirect reviews, which influence the visibility.

PageRank vs.	$\mathrm{vis}^{\mathrm{TRE}_s}$	$\mathrm{vis}^{\mathrm{TRE}_i}$	$\mathrm{vis}^{\mathrm{TRE}_p}$	$\mathrm{vis}^{\mathrm{TRE}_d}$
$\mathrm{ML}_{m,10}^{2-8}$	0.00	0.08	0.08	0.09
$\mathrm{ML}_{m,10}^{6-14}$	0.00	0.08	0.09	0.07
$\mathrm{ML}_{m,10}^{10-20}$	0.00	0.08	0.09	0.08

Table 8.15: PageRank versus TRE-Visibility ($\Delta_{\mathrm{indirect}}$)

As the simple TRE-visibility is composed by the document base visibility (i.e. Page-Rank) and the direct, trust-weighted reviews, it is identical to PageRank for those documents that do not have any direct review. The other TRE-visibility measures should differ from PageRank as they consider indirect reviews. In the case of the integrated TRE-visibility, the propagation of the trust-weighted reviews as part of PageRank leads to an average difference between $\mathrm{vis}^{\mathrm{TRE}_i}$ and mere PageRank of around 0.08 for the indirectly reviewed documents. The path-based TRE-visibility differs from PageRank by around 0.09, and the distance-based TRE-visibility by around 0.08. So the difference between $\mathrm{vis}^{\mathrm{TRE}_p}$ and PageRank as well as between $\mathrm{vis}^{\mathrm{TRE}_d}$ and PageRank are in the same order of magnitude as the one between $\mathrm{vis}^{\mathrm{TRE}_i}$ and PageRank. Summing up, the TRE-visibility differs considerably from PageRank. Both direct and indirect reviews have an impact on the TRE-visibility. This, however, does not yet say whether the different TRE-visibility measures are close to each other. This requires comparing them directly.

Differences between TRE-Visibilities The average differences between the simple TRE-visibility and the other TRE-visibility functions are summarized in table 8.16.

$\mathrm{vis}^{\mathrm{TRE}_s}$ vs.	$\mathrm{vis}^{\mathrm{TRE}_i}$	$\mathrm{vis}^{\mathrm{TRE}_p}$	$\mathrm{vis}^{\mathrm{TRE}_d}$
$\mathrm{ML}_{m,10}^{2-8}$	0.04	0.03	0.03
$\mathrm{ML}_{m,10}^{6-14}$	0.04	0.04	0.03
$\mathrm{ML}_{m,10}^{10-20}$	0.04	0.04	0.03

Table 8.16: $\mathrm{vis}^{\mathrm{TRE}_s}$ versus $\mathrm{vis}^{\mathrm{TRE}_i}$, $\mathrm{vis}^{\mathrm{TRE}_p}$ and $\mathrm{vis}^{\mathrm{TRE}_d}$ (Δ_{direct})

Looking at the directly reviewed documents, one might expect that the integrated, the path-based and the distance-based TRE-visibility are identical for the directly reviewed documents. Instead, they are only fairly similar. This is due to the influence of indirect reviews. So we see here the amount of visibility that is changed by additional indirect reviews. The average differences in directly reviewed documents are between the simple TRE-visibility and the integrated, the path-based and the distance-based TRE-visibility, respectively, between 0.03 and 0.04. For the indirectly reviewed documents, $\text{vis}^{\text{TRE}_s}$ is identical with PageRank. Thus the differences between the other TRE-visibility functions and the simple TRE-visibility correspond to the differences to PageRank, namely between 0.07 and 0.09.

The comparison of the integrated TRE-visibility with the review-propagating TRE-visibility functions is shown in tables 8.17 and 8.18. We can see that the path-based TRE-visibility and the distance-based TRE-visibility differ from the integrated TRE-visibility by around 0.03 for directly reviewed documents and by around 0.05 for indirectly reviewed documents. Both differ thus from the integrated TRE-visibility much less than from PageRank. The path-based and the distance-based TRE-visibility are quite similar.

vs.	$\dfrac{\text{vis}^{\text{TRE}_i}}{\text{vis}^{\text{TRE}_p}}$	$\dfrac{\text{vis}^{\text{TRE}_i}}{\text{vis}^{\text{TRE}_d}}$	$\dfrac{\text{vis}^{\text{TRE}_p}}{\text{vis}^{\text{TRE}_d}}$
$\text{ML}_{m,10}^{2-8}$	0.03	0.02	0.01
$\text{ML}_{m,10}^{6-14}$	0.03	0.03	0.02
$\text{ML}_{m,10}^{10-20}$	0.03	0.03	0.02

Table 8.17: Pairwise Differences between $\text{vis}^{\text{TRE}_i}$, $\text{vis}^{\text{TRE}_p}$ and $\text{vis}^{\text{TRE}_d}$ (Δ_{direct})

vs.	$\dfrac{\text{vis}^{\text{TRE}_i}}{\text{vis}^{\text{TRE}_p}}$	$\dfrac{\text{vis}^{\text{TRE}_i}}{\text{vis}^{\text{TRE}_d}}$	$\dfrac{\text{vis}^{\text{TRE}_p}}{\text{vis}^{\text{TRE}_d}}$
$\text{ML}_{m,10}^{2-8}$	0.05	0.04	0.02
$\text{ML}_{m,10}^{6-14}$	0.05	0.05	0.05
$\text{ML}_{m,10}^{10-20}$	0.05	0.06	0.04

Table 8.18: Pairwise Differences between $\text{vis}^{\text{TRE}_i}$, $\text{vis}^{\text{TRE}_p}$ and $\text{vis}^{\text{TRE}_d}$ (Δ_{indirect})

Summing Up: Differences between (TRE-)Visibility Measures

Results are consistent over the three types of medium-sized networks. This also holds true for the small-sized networks: the data is not only consistent across the small-sized networks but is in line with the results on the medium-sized networks. As the experiments done for Hess and Stein (2007a) gave similar results, the discussed differences and similarities, respectively, between the visibility measures are valid in a more general way. Summing up, I can say that the TRE-visibility, regardless of whether the integrated, the path-based or the distance-based TRE-visibility is computed, differs considerably from PageRank. The simple TRE-visibility differs from PageRank only for the directly reviewed documents, which is evident as it does not take into account indirect reviews. On the above used networks, differences are of around 0.2 to 0.3 on the directly reviewed documents and of around 0.1 on the indirectly reviewed documents. Given that the maximum PageRank is at around 0.6., the TRE-visibility provides a view on the network that heavily depends on the reviews and the users' personal trust in these reviews. This also applies for those documents that do not have any review at all because their visibility is modified by the indirect reviews.

The integrated, the path-based and the distance-based TRE-visibility are quite close to each other. Now the question is, which of them should be used. The integrated TRE-visibility is not efficiently computable on large scale networks. However, it can be considered as base line because it is technically the closest to PageRank. Which of the review-propagating TRE-visibility is now better suited? The findings from the simulation study give a slight preference to the distance-based TRE-visibility over the path-based TRE-visibility: average differences are lower on all medium-sized networks.

> ▶ **Result of the Comparison:** In contrast to PageRank, the TRE-visibility of a document strongly depends on the reviews (i.e. by reviews that are made by users in whom the user asking for the document ranking has high personal trust). The TRE-visibilities provide thus a personalized view. Based on the results as well as on the efficiency of its computation, I suggest using the distance-based TRE-visibility. ◀

8.3.4 The Influence of Reviews: Varying the Number of Reviews and the Average Review Value

I am now interested in the question of the influence that the reviews have on the visibility of a document. Therefore, I compute the TRE-visibility for a certain document from the perspective of a user with a different number of reviews. The average value of these reviews is also varied. A simulation study is not required for this question because it can be directly answered from the TRE-visibility formula.

> ▶ **Aim:** Analyze the increase and decrease, respectively, of the TRE-visibility for a document depending on the number of reviews and on the average review value. ◀

Here I use the integrated TRE-visibility $\mathrm{vis}_{p,u}^{\mathrm{TRE}_i}$, which is based on the reference-based visibility $\mathrm{vis}_{p,u}'$ received via the incoming links and on the direct reviews. Indirect reviews are already part of the reference-based visibilities of all citing documents. Therefore results hold true for any document reference network and any reference-based visibility measure. The results also apply to the other TRE-visibility measures. In this case, the reference-based visibility consists only of the visibility computed with PageRank or any other visibility measure.

The following analysis focuses on a document p from user u's perspective. Its reference-based visibility $\mathrm{vis}_{p,u}'$ is modified by n direct reviews. The trust in all reviews r_i is $t_i = 1$. The average review value is $\bar{r} = \frac{\sum_{i=1}^{n} r_i}{n}$. I measure the TRE-visibility for different average review values. Table 8.19 gives the concrete setting of this study.

reference-based visibility of p	$\mathrm{vis}_{p,u}'$	$\in \{0.1, 0.5, 0.9\}$
# of reviews	n	$\in \{1, 2, 5, 10, 20\}$
average review value $\bar{r}$	$\bar{r}$	$\in \{0.0, 0.1, ..., 0.9, 1.0\}$
trust in the review	$\forall r_i : t_i$	$= 1$

Table 8.19: Studying the Influence of Reviews

Increase and Decrease in Visibility

Figures 8.5, 8.6 and 8.7 show the TRE-visibilities of document p with a reference-based visibility of 0.1, 0.5 and 0.9, respectively. In each figure, five graphs show the modification of the TRE-visibility depending on the average review value $\bar{r}$. The reference-based visibility is indicated as baseline.

First of all, I can state that the TRE-visibility increases with an increasing average review value. This shows that the reviews have an impact as intended by the definition of the TRE-visibility measures. The TRE-visibility and the reference-based visibility are equal when the average on all direct review values is identical with the reference-based visibility. Consider for instance figure 8.5 where $\mathrm{vis}_{p,u}' = 0.1$. With 10 reviews on p which give in average 0.1 (e.g. $r_1, ..., r_9 = 0$, $r_{10} = 1$ or $r_1, ..., r_{10} = 0.1$): $\mathrm{vis}_{p,u}^{\mathrm{TRE}_i} = \mathrm{vis}_{p,u}'$.

The more direct reviews are on a document, the less important is the reference-based visibility. In the extreme case that the TRE-visibility consists only of the reviews, an increasing average review value gives a straight line from (0,0) to (1,1). In the other extreme case, the TRE-visibility is based only on the reference-based visibility. There is then a straight line from (0, vis$'$) to (1, vis$'$). Combining the reference-based visibility

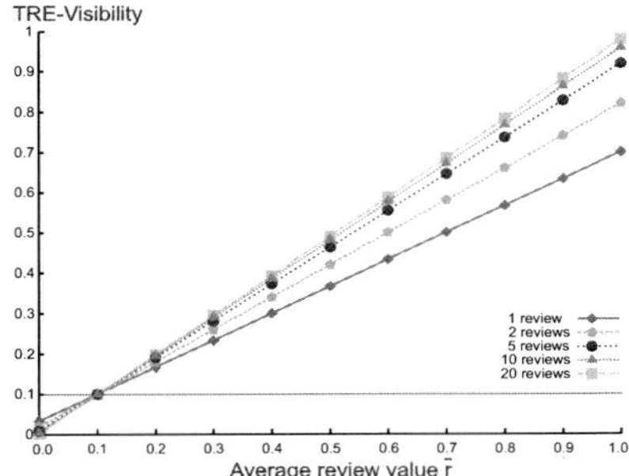

Figure 8.5: The Influence of Reviews: $\text{vis}'_{p,u} = 0.1$

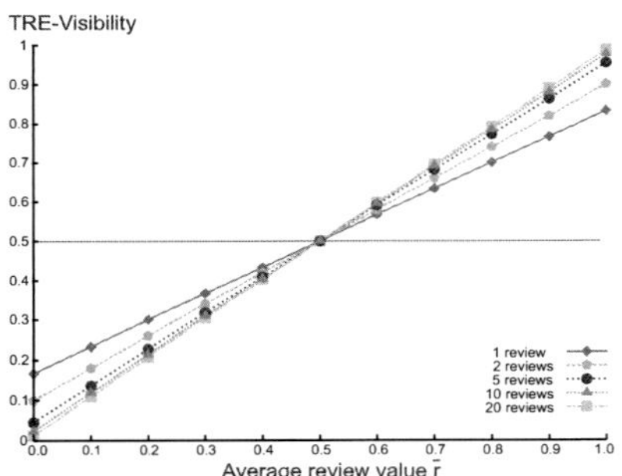

Figure 8.6: The Influence of Reviews: $\text{vis}'_{p,u} = 0.5$

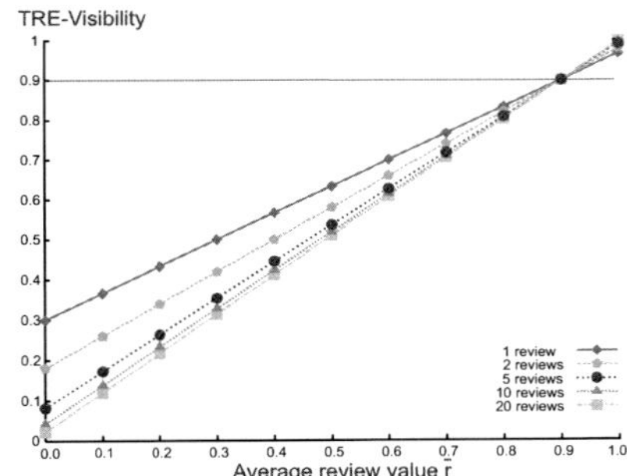

Figure 8.7: The Influence of Reviews: $\text{vis}'_{p,u} = 0.9$

and the direct reviews in the integrated TRE-visibility gives a straight line between these extreme cases. In each figure, the higher the number of reviews, the higher is the slope of the straight lines. For $n \geq 5$, it is close to the case that the TRE-visibility is exclusively based on the reviews. This result is appropriate as I defined the TRE-visibility so that the impact of the reference-based visibility on the recommendation will be low if there are many reviews by trustworthy users available. Moreover, with the visibility contribution vc $= 0.5$, the "trust" in the reference-based visibility is only 0.5 whereas the trust in the users' reviews is 1. If the reference-based visibility should have a higher impact in some setting, then vc has to be increased.

In order to analyze the impact that a single review has on the TRE-visibility, we look at the graphs for $n = 1$ across the three figures. This single review has maximal impact on the TRE-visibility if it is 0 or 1, i.e. $\bar{r} \in \{0.0, 1.0\}$. For a low document base visibility, the impact of a single positive review is much higher than for a document that has a high reference-based visibility. For instance, if $\text{vis}'_{p,u} = 0.1$, a single positive review (i.e., $n = 1$ and $r_1 = 1$ giving $\bar{r} = 1$) is sufficient for increasing the visibility to $\text{vis}^{\text{TRE}_i}_{p,u} = 0.7$. In contrast, a single positive review on a document with $\text{vis}'_{p,u} = 0.9$ gives a TRE-visibility of $\text{vis}^{\text{TRE}_i}_{p,u} = 0.97$. The inverse holds true for adverse reviews: they have more impact on a document with a high reference-based visibility. For instance, a single review $r = 0$ on p decreases a reference-based visibility of 0.9 to 0.3 whereas a reference-based visibility of 0.1 is decreased to 0.03.

> ▶ **Results of Varying the Number of Reviews and the Average Review Value:** Having only five reviews by users in whom the user asking for the document recommendation has high trust (i.e. $t_i = 1$) leads to the fact that the TRE-visibility is completely dominated by the reviews. The recommendation thus depends completely on the user's personal web of trust and on the trusted users' reviews. The TRE-visibility increases (decreases) with an increasing (decreasing) average review value. TRE-visibility and reference-based visibility are identical when the average over the reviews equals with the reference-based visibility. ◀

8.3.5 Opposite Opinions on Documents

As the previous studies have shown, the TRE-visibility differs considerably from PageRank due to the influence of trust-weighted reviews. Now, the question is on how the TRE-visibilities differ for two users u_A and u_B who are from two rivaling communities $\mathcal{A}$ and $\mathcal{B}$ with different, even opposite opinions on the documents.

> ▶ **Aim:** Analyze the difference in the TRE-visibilities for two users from two rivaling communities with opposite opinions on the documents. ◀

Users within a community have high mutual trust whereas users from community $\mathcal{A}$ highly distrust users from community $\mathcal{B}$ and vice versa. This means that only the reviews by users within community $\mathcal{A}$ (or $\mathcal{B}$, respectively) influence the TRE-visibilities for user u_A (u_B). Users from both communities differ in their reviews, i.e. they often have opposite opinions on the same document. Consider now a document p. For the sake of simplicity, its reference-based visibility is $\mathrm{vis}'_{p,u_A} = \mathrm{vis}'_{p,u_B}$ (e.g. p has just been published and has not yet any indirect reviews because the few citing papers – if there are any – have not yet been reviewed). This document is rated by users from u_A's community with in average $\bar{r}_A < \mathrm{vis}'_{p,u}$ and by users from u_B's community with in average $\bar{r}_B > \mathrm{vis}'_{p,u}$. This means that community $\mathcal{A}$ rather dislikes p whereas community $\mathcal{B}$ rather likes p. The higher $|\bar{r}_A - \bar{r}_B|$, the more controversial is the opinion. The TRE-visibility is now computed for p.

I start with a concrete example, namely $\mathrm{vis}'_{p,u} = 0.5$, and analyze how the TRE-visibilities differ for u_A and u_B. If there are no reviews, neither from users within u_A's community nor from users within u_B's community, then $\mathrm{vis}^{\mathrm{TRE}_i}_{p,u_A} = \mathrm{vis}^{\mathrm{TRE}_i}_{p,u_B}$. However, we have stated that users from both communities provided diverging ratings. Table 8.20 shows for several combinations of review values the resulting TRE-visibilities and the differences between them.

	Community $\mathcal{A}$		Community $\mathcal{B}$			
n	$\bar{r}_A$	$\mathrm{vis}^{\mathrm{TRE}_i}_{p,u_A}$	$\bar{r}_B$	$\mathrm{vis}^{\mathrm{TRE}_i}_{p,u_B}$	$\|\bar{r}_A - \bar{r}_B\|$	$\|\mathrm{vis}^{\mathrm{TRE}_i}_{p,u_A} - \mathrm{vis}^{\mathrm{TRE}_i}_{p,u_B}\|$
1	0.4	0.43	0.6	0.57	0.2	0.14
1	0.0	0.17	1.0	0.83	1.0	0.66
5	0.4	0.41	0.6	0.59	0.2	0.18
5	0.0	0.05	1.0	0.95	1.0	0.90

Table 8.20: Opposite Views

With a single trusted review and a still similar view (a difference of 0.2), the TRE-visibilities differ by 0.14. With a single completely opposite review, the difference is already 0.66. Increasing the number of reviews, the differences increase. With five trusted reviews which are opposite, the differences is 0.9. This can also be seen in figure 8.6. With an increasing difference in the average reviews of both communities, the TRE-visibilities computed for u_A and u_B move on the straight line for $n = 5$ in opposite directions. If users from communities $\mathcal{A}$ and $\mathcal{B}$ provided a different number of reviews, we have to look at the respective graphs in figure 8.6.

In general, I can say that as the differences between the average reviews get higher, so, too, do the differences in the TRE-visibility. In reality, there would normally also be reviews by users who are neither members of community $\mathcal{A}$ nor of community $\mathcal{B}$. If users u_A or u_B have some trust in these users, these reviews would also influence the

TRE-visibility. They would possibly smooth the difference between the views of both communities.

In a simulation study with an early version of the integrated TRE-visibility (not considered here) in Hess *et al.* (2006), we analyzed a similar setting. However, we used a generated trust network (i.e. trust is not either -1 or 1 as above) and computed the average differences in TRE-visibilities for all documents for the users of two different communities. In simulation, we have shown that the average differences in TRE-visibilities are low for users within the same community and high for users of different communities (as the measure is different from the one used in the thesis, the exact differences are hardly to interpret here).

> ▶ **Result: TRE-visibilities for users from two rivaling communities:** The opposite opinions of two communities are reflected in the TRE-visibilities computed for members of these communities. TRE-visibilities thus differ not only from PageRank but differ for users with a different view on the documents. ◀

8.3.6 Flipping Reviews on Fraudulent Papers

A requirement derived from the use cases was to deal in the recommendation process with faked publications. As references in published papers cannot be modified, a fraudulent paper continues to have the same incoming references and thus the same reference-based visibility. The TRE-visibility addressed this problem by considering trust-weighted reviews. I'm now interested in the question of how efficiently the TRE-visibility downgrades such papers. Therefore, I look at a certain document p which is well-known in its community but which is then detected to be based on faked data or to contain false information. If this becomes public, reviews on this paper will change to strong reject, i.e. reviews will be flipped from 1 to 0. I look at how the TRE-visibility of p changes over the time when the reviews are flipped.

> ▶ **Aim:** Analyze how the TRE-visibility of a document changes if reviews on this document are flipped from $r_i = 1$ to $r_i = 0$. ◀

I consider a paper p that has a high visibility compared with the other papers in its community. It is not only often cited (relative to the other papers in its community) but it has also received excellent reviews. I compute the integrated TRE-visibility $\text{vis}_{p,u}^{\text{TRE}_i}$. Starting with n appreciating reviews $r_i = 1$, I increase the percentage of adverse reviews $r_i = 0$ ($\forall r_i : t_i = 1$). After each flip, the TRE-visibility is re-computed. This setting is from a technical point of view similar to the one in section 8.3.4. Having 9 out of 10 reviews being negative is identical to on average $\bar{r} = 0.9$. Flipping reviews changes the average review value. The graphs in figures 8.5, 8.6 and 8.7 can thus simply be mirrored, and on the x-axis, the increasing percentage of negative reviews is displayed (however, data points are different as only reviews of 0 and 1 are allowed). As example, I show in figure 8.8 the graph for $\mathrm{vis}'_{p,u} = 0.9$, i.e. for a highly cited document.

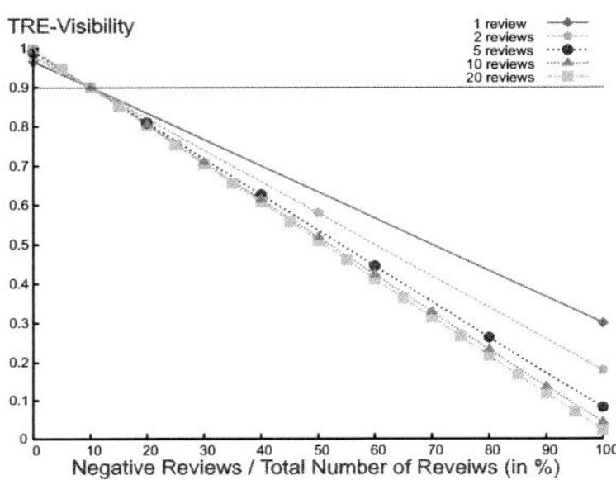

Figure 8.8: Flipping Reviews: $\mathrm{vis}'_{p,u} = 0.9$

Starting with 100% positive reviews, the TRE-visibility is higher than the reference-based visibility (remember that $\mathrm{vis}^{\mathrm{TRE}_i}_{p,u} > \mathrm{vis}'_{p,u}$ if $\bar{r} > \mathrm{vis}'_{p,u}$). The TRE-visibilty now decreases with increasing percentage of adverse reviews. The higher the reference-based visibility, the fewer rejecting reviews are required in order to decrease the TRE-visibility below the reference-based visibility, i.e., below the visibility that would be used in a normal reference-based ranking. For instance, the TRE-visibility is for a document with a reference-based visibility of $\mathrm{vis}'_{p,u} = 0.9$ already below 0.9 if more than 10% of the reviews are negative. This is to say that highly cited papers can be efficiently downgraded in their rank by using the TRE-visibility. If all reviews are rejecting, the TRE-visibility even goes down to almost zero when the total number of review is five or more, even with a reference-based visibility of 0.9. Moreover, the more reviews that are on p, the lower will be the proportion of adverse reviews required for obtaining the same TRE-visibility. For $\mathrm{vis}'_{p,u_m} = 0.9$, for instance, $\mathrm{vis}^{\mathrm{TRE}_i}_{p,u} = 0.0.26$ if 75% of 20 reviews are adverse. If there are only 5 reviews, 80% of them must be adverse in order to obtain the same TRE-visibility.

> ► **Result of the Study on Fraudulent Documents:** The TRE-visibility is well suited for downgrading the visibility of papers that are considered untrustworthy and thus decreasing efficiently their position in a ranking. This also holds true for extremely often-cited documents. ◄

8.3.7 Percentage of Reviews Required for Network Coverage

Recommendation techniques such as collaborative filtering suffer from the cold-start problem, which means that a personalized recommendation cannot be made for an item unless it has been rated at least once. This is especially critical for the starting phase of a recommender system when the number of reviews is still low. Although the TRE-visibility measures are based on reviews, too, the cold-start problem should be eased significantly by the fact that reviews are propagated on the document network. There is now the question on the relative number of reviews required to compute personalized TRE-visibilities for most documents.

▶ **Aim:** Analyze the relative number of reviews required for a thorough personalization of document recommendations with the TRE-visibility. ◀

According to the design of the TRE-visibility, it should be possible to make personalized recommendations with a quite low percentage of documents being reviewed. In a simulation study, I look at the proportion of documents for which the TRE-visibility differs from PageRank due to the influence of direct or indirect reviews. I add reviews step-by-step in order to simulate the activity and the growth of the reviewer community and I compute the coverage of the network at each time step.

In the simulation study, I use the medium-sized networks as in the other simulations. At each time step s_i, a set of randomly distributed reviews is generated (note that by distributing reviews randomly, a document may be reviewed more than once). The number of reviews generated in a step s_i corresponds to one percent of the number of documents. As the document reference networks encompass around 10,000 documents, 100 reviews are generated in each step. At each step s_i, I determine for a document reference network D the sets P^k of documents with $k \in \{0, 1, 2, 3\}$. P^0 contains those documents that have at least one direct review (i.e. the review is at distance $k = 0$). The set P^1 includes in addition to the documents in P^0 those documents with reviews at a distance $k = 1$, i.e., the documents that are cited by at least one directly reviewed document. The sets P^2 and P^3 contain all documents with reviews at distance $k \leq 2$ and $k \leq 3$, respectively. So reviews at a distance of maximum 3 are considered, just as in the previous simulations. P^k is defined as:

$$P^0 := \{p_d : \exists r_i \text{ on } p_d\}$$
$$P^i := P^{i-1} \cup \{p_d : \exists p_j \in P^{i-1} : e_{j \to d}\}$$

The network coverage cov_D^k is the proportion of documents in D that is reached by a review at a maximum distance of k. It is defined as:

$$cov_D^k = \frac{|P^k|}{|D|}.$$

Table 8.21 summarizes the setting for the simulation study on the network coverage.

types of networks	D_m^{2-8}, D_m^{6-14} and D_m^{10-20}
# of networks	10 networks of each network type
# number of reviews	100 reviews in each step s_i
# number of steps	15
coverage	proportion of documents with at least one review at distance k
distance	$k \in \{0, 1, 2, 3\}$; for $k = 0$, the document is directly reviewed, for $k \geq 1$, the document is indirectly reviewed

Table 8.21: Coverage by Reviews: Simulation Approach

Network Coverage

The network coverage gives the proportion of documents for which the TRE-visibility differs from PageRank due to the influence of direct and indirect reviews. Tables 8.22, 8.23 and 8.24 show the coverage for an increasing number of reviews on the three types of medium-sized networks. As the standard deviation is very small, the average can be taken over the 10 networks of each type.

number of reviews	k 0	1	2	3
100	1.0	5.7	22.8	49.0
200	2.0	11.0	37.7	63.2
300	3.0	16.1	47.2	69.7
400	3.9	20.8	55.0	74.3
500	4.9	24.8	59.5	76.7
600	5.8	28.7	64.0	79.0
700	6.8	32.6	67.6	80.8
800	7.7	35.8	70.2	81.7
900	8.6	39.0	72.7	83.1
1000	9.6	41.9	74.8	84.1
1100	10.4	44.8	77.0	85.4
1200	11.3	46.9	77.8	85.5
1300	12.3	49.8	79.8	86.7
1400	13.1	51.9	80.8	87.0
1500	14.0	54.1	82.0	87.6

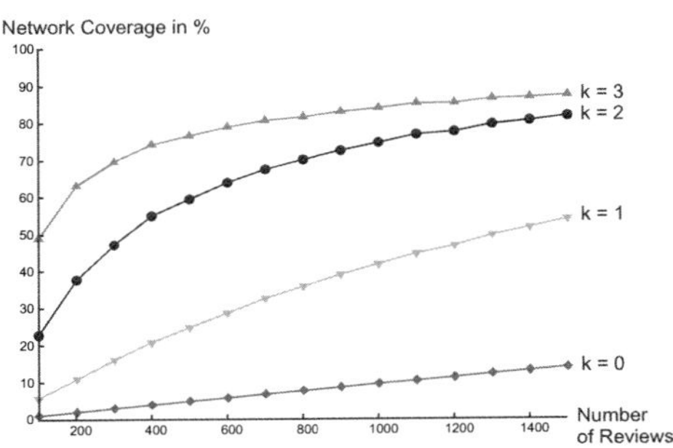

Table 8.22: Network Coverage (ML_m^{2-8})

number of reviews	k			
	0	1	2	3
100	1.0	10.2	52.3	80.9
200	2.0	19.2	68.9	87.4
300	3.0	26.7	76.1	89.1
400	3.9	33.4	81.2	90.7
500	4.8	39.1	84.5	91.9
600	5.8	44.2	86.1	92.3
700	6.8	49.2	87.9	92.9
800	7.7	53.0	89.1	93.3
900	8.6	56.8	90.1	93.8
1000	9.5	60.3	91.1	94.3
1100	10.4	63.1	91.8	94.7
1200	11.4	66.3	92.5	94.9
1300	12.2	68.4	92.6	94.9
1400	13.1	70.5	93.1	95.0
1500	13.9	72.5	93.4	95.2

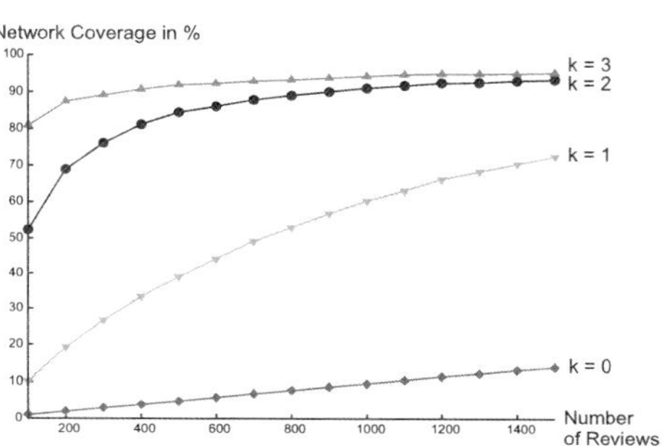

Table 8.23: Network Coverage (ML_m^{6-14})

number of reviews	k			
	0	1	2	3
100	1.0	14.3	71.9	89.3
200	2.0	26.2	84.0	92.7
300	3.0	35.9	87.8	93.8
400	3.9	43.8	89.5	94.1
500	4.9	50.7	92.0	95.4
600	5.8	56.4	92.8	95.6
700	6.8	61.3	93.6	95.9
800	7.7	65.6	94.4	96.2
900	8.6	68.6	94.2	96.0
1000	9.5	72.7	95.2	96.6
1100	10.4	74.7	95.5	96.8
1200	11.3	76.7	95.7	96.9
1300	12.2	79.7	96.0	97.0
1400	13.0	80.8	96.2	97.2
1500	13.9	82.5	96.5	97.3

Table 8.24: Network Coverage in % (ML_m^{10-20})

We can see that the coverage increases with the increasing number of references, given a fixed distance k and a fixed number of reviews. With 100 reviews and a distance of three, for instance, personalized TRE-visibilities can be computed in networks ML_m^{2-8} for around 50% of the documents, in networks ML_m^{6-14} for around 80% of the documents and in networks ML_m^{10-20} for around 90% of the documents. This increase in coverage holds true over all numbers of reviews and all $k \geq 1$. For $k = 1$ the coverage is identical over all types of networks because reviews are not propagated. The coverage increases because with more outgoing references per document, the reviews are propagated along more edges and represent thus indirect reviews for more documents. The indirect reviews have, however, a lower impact with increasing branching factor. The review contribution is split over all outgoing edges (in the path-based TRE-visibility, the outdegree is directly considered whereas in the distance-based TRE-visibility, λ estimates the outdegree) and thus the impact of the review decreases.

The coverage approaches 100% but does not reach them. This is due to the way the networks were generated. First of all, the documents from the newest generation are never cited (as older papers cannot update their references) and therefore do not benefit from indirect reviews. A personalized TRE-visibility can thus only be computed for those that were directly reviewed. There are also only few citations to the documents generated in the last few generations. Although selecting the documents to be referenced by Age PageRank favors those recently published, this does not mean that the documents from the previous generation are referenced exclusively as this would not hold true in reality. Therefore I used during network generation an adapted version of Age PageRank. The network coverage will thus never be 100% – unless all documents in the network are reviewed at least once, which is very unrealistic as this would mean having more reviews than documents. The TRE-visibility is identical with PageRank for a small proportion of documents.

I now look into more detail at the network coverage of networks with 6 to 14 references per document because I assume that this is realistic for many publication networks in computer science. With 100 reviews where approximately 1% of the documents have a review, a personalized TRE-visibility can already be computed for 81% of the documents. This is a very low number of reviews that can be provided without any difficulty by only ten users of the recommender system. Thus the TRE-visibility measures definitely do not have the ramp-up problem. Even limiting k to $k = 2$ means still being able to compute personalized visibilities for still around one half of the documents. With 400 reviews, the coverage is already greater than 90 percent. These results show that the joint propagation of information on the trust network and the document reference network as done by the TRE-visibility, offers a very effective means of personalizing document recommendations, even for a fairly small number of reviews. Certainly, the degree of personalization increases with the increasing number of reviews.

> ▶ **Result of the Study on the Network Coverage:** With propagating the reviews on the document reference network up to maximum three steps, a personalized TRE-visibility can already be computed for a large proportion of the documents when 1% of the documents is reviewed. A recommender

system that uses the TRE-visibility can thus provide fairly good results already in its starting phase when the number of reviews is still low. ◄

8.3.8 Summary

The simulation studies have shown that the TRE-visibilities obtained by the different TRE-visibility measures differ only slightly. Concerning the results, there is thus no preference for any of the TRE-visibility measures. I recommend to use the distance-based TRE-visibility as it can be computed efficiently. In the simulations, the TRE-visibility differed considerably from PageRank. This shows that the reviews, weighted with the requesting user's trust in the reviewers, have an impact on the recommendation. In order to analyze this impact, I have looked at how the TRE-visibility of a document changes for varying number of reviews and a varying average review value. Already a single trusted review $r = 1$ or $r = 0$ has much influence on the TRE-visibility. A positive review has especially strong impact on a document with a low reference-based visibility whereas the inverse holds true for adverse reviews. The more trustworthy reviews are available, the less impact has the reference-based part.

I have shown that TRE-visibilities differ for users who are members of two communities with a controversial view on documents. With five opposite reviews on the document from the respective communities, the difference in TRE-visibilities is already almost maximal. The TRE-visibilities are thus highly personalized from the perspective of a certain user. As the reviews are so important for the personalization, one might expect that in the starting phase of the recommender system when only few reviews are available, the TRE-visibility might often be based only on the reference-based part. In analysis, I could show that the TRE-visibility measures do not suffer from this ramp up problem. Personalized TRE-visibilities can already be computed for a quite low percentage of documents being reviewed.

8.4 Multi-Layer Networks for the ATE-Visibility Simulation Studies

The author-trust-enhanced visibility, the ATE-visibility, is computed on a two-layer network that comprises a document reference network and an author trust network. For the simulation studies concerning the ATE-visibility, I generate small and medium-sized document networks as described in section 8.2.1. However, the generation process of the networks is slightly modified: authors are attributed to the documents directly during the network generation. The authors are divided in three groups $\mathcal{A}$, $\mathcal{B}$ and

$\mathcal{C}$. Group $\mathcal{A}$ contains 90% of the authors, and groups $\mathcal{B}$ and $\mathcal{C}$ each contain 5% of the authors. Each document has exactly one author. So 90% of the documents are written by authors of group $\mathcal{A}$ and 5% by authors of groups $\mathcal{B}$ and $\mathcal{C}$. The exact number of authors in a group does not matter, I abstract thus from a concrete number of authors. Basically, the trust between all authors u_m and u_n is set to neutral; so $\forall u_m, u_n : t_{u_m \to u_n} = 0$. The basic trust is modified during the simulation when required. Table 8.25 shows the characteristics of the multi-layer networks with an author trust network.

	Small-Sized Networks (ML$_s$)	Medium-Sized Networks (ML$_m$)
document networks	D_m^{2-8}, D_m^{6-14}, D_m^{10-20}	D_s^{2-8}, D_s^{6-14}, D_s^{10-20}
authors	three groups of authors $\mathcal{A}$: contains 90% of the authors $\mathcal{B}$: contains 5% of the authors $\mathcal{C}$: contains 5% of the authors $\forall u_m, u_n : t_{u_m \to u_n} = 0$	
multi-layer networks	ML_m^{2-8}, ML_m^{6-14}, ML_m^{10-20}	ML_s^{2-8}, ML_s^{6-14}, ML_s^{10-20}

Table 8.25: Multi-Layer Networks with Authors and Trust

8.5 Evaluation of the ATE-Visibility

In order to evaluate the ATE-visibility measures, I perform two simulation studies. The first simulation deals with the personalization that is achieved by the different ATE-visibility measures. The second one again addresses the problem of faked papers and analyzes how the author-trust-based visibility measures modify the recommendations for such papers.

8.5.1 Parameterization of the ATE-Visibility Measures

In the simulation studies, I use the ATE-visibility measures that are based on Page-Rank. PageRank $vis_{p_d}^{PR}$ is computed with $\alpha = 0.85$ and the basic visibility is $\frac{1-\alpha}{k}$ with $k = 100$. In order to compute for the trust-weighted PageRank the edge weights based on the attributed trust edges, I use the mapping function I'_+ with $\Delta = 1$, so $w_{i \to j} = \frac{\Delta + \bar{e}_{i \to j}}{1 + t_{\max}} = \frac{1 + \bar{e}_{i \to j}}{2}$.

8.5.2 Personalization with ATE-Visibility and Personalized Weighted PageRank

In the first simulation, I am interested in the degree of personalization achieved by ATE-visibility $\mathrm{vis}_{p,u}^{\mathrm{ATE}}$, personalized trust-weighted PageRank $\mathrm{vis}_{p,u}^{\mathrm{WPR}}$ and their combination $\mathrm{vis}_{p,u}^{\mathrm{ATE}w}$. By comparing the results for three users with different trust in the authors of the documents, i.e. who represent a completely different view on the multi-layer network, we can see how strong the effect of each of the functions is. I aim to determine which of the measures - or which combination – is best suited for use in a trust-based document recommendation system. This simulation extends the simulation in Hess and Stein (2007b) by considering systematically different types of networks – different with respect to their size and with the number of references per document.

> ▶ **Aim:** Compare the personalized document rankings computed by ATE-visibility, weighted PageRank with personalized trust-based edge weights and the combined version, namely the weighted author-trust-enhanced visibility, for users who have assigned completely different trust values. If possible, give recommendations on which of the measures or which of the combinations to use. ◄

The different types of visibilities are computed on the small-sized and the medium-sized multi-layer networks. The trust between all authors remains set as neutral in order to avoid side effects. There are three users u^0, $u^{\mathcal{B},\overline{\mathcal{C}}}$ and $u^{\overline{\mathcal{B}},\mathcal{C}}$ who have a different personal trust in the authors of the documents:

- u^0 is neutral with respect to all authors, i.e.

$$\forall X \in (\mathcal{A} \cup \mathcal{B} \cup \mathcal{C}) : t_{u^0 \to X} = 0$$

- $u^{\mathcal{B},\overline{\mathcal{C}}}$ is neutral towards all authors from group $\mathcal{A}$, trusts all authors of group $\mathcal{B}$ and distrusts all authors of group $\mathcal{C}$, i.e.

$$\forall A \in \mathcal{A} : t_{u^{\mathcal{B},\overline{\mathcal{C}}} \to A} = 0, \quad \forall B \in \mathcal{B} : t_{u^{\mathcal{B},\overline{\mathcal{C}}} \to B} = 1, \quad \forall C \in \mathcal{C} : t_{u^{\mathcal{B},\overline{\mathcal{C}}} \to C} = -1$$

- $u^{\overline{\mathcal{B}},\mathcal{C}}$ has trust values that are absolutely contrary to $u^{\mathcal{B},\overline{\mathcal{C}}}$'s trust values: $u^{\overline{\mathcal{B}},\mathcal{C}}$ is neutral to all authors of group $\mathcal{A}$, trusts all authors of group $\mathcal{C}$ and distrusts all authors of group $\mathcal{B}$:

$$\forall A \in \mathcal{A} : t_{u^{\overline{\mathcal{B}},\mathcal{C}} \to A} = 0, \quad \forall B \in \mathcal{B} : t_{u^{\overline{\mathcal{B}},\mathcal{C}} \to B} = -1, \quad \forall C \in \mathcal{C} : t_{u^{\overline{\mathcal{B}},\mathcal{C}} \to C} = 1$$

The different author-trust-enhanced visibility measures are now computed for these three users. As they have a contradictory view on the author trust network, the resulting visibilities should be different. User u^0 is considered as baseline because he/she is neutral to all authors. The visibilities for users $u^{\mathcal{B},\overline{\mathcal{C}}}$ and $u^{\overline{\mathcal{B}},\mathcal{C}}$ should now differ both from the visibilities computed for u^0 as well as among each other. This should be visible in the document rankings generated for the three users based on the visibilities computed. For instance, documents written by authors of group $\mathcal{B}$ should have a higher position in the ranking computed for $u^{\mathcal{B},\overline{\mathcal{C}}}$ than in the ranking computed for u^0 due to $u^{\mathcal{B},\overline{\mathcal{C}}}$'s trust in authors from group $\mathcal{B}$. In the ranking generated for $u^{\overline{\mathcal{B}},\mathcal{C}}$, these documents should have a lower position than in the ranking for u^0 due to $u^{\overline{\mathcal{B}},\mathcal{C}}$'s distrust in authors of group $\mathcal{B}$. Table 8.26 gives an overview on the setting for this simulation study.

types of networks	ML_m^{2-8}, ML_m^{6-14}, ML_m^{10-20}, ML_s^{2-8}, ML_s^{6-14}, ML_s^{10-20}
# of networks	10 networks of each medium-sized network type, 10 networks of each small-sized network type
visibility measures	$\mathrm{vis}_{p,u}^{\mathrm{ATE}}$, $\mathrm{vis}_{p,u}^{\mathrm{ATE}'}$, $\mathrm{vis}_{p,u}^{\mathrm{WPR}}$, $\mathrm{vis}_{p,u}^{\mathrm{ATE}_w}$, $\mathrm{vis}_{p,u}^{\mathrm{ATE}'_w}$
comparison	percental difference in the average position in the ranking

Table 8.26: Personalization by ATE-Visibility Measures

Results of the Comparison of the ATE-Visibilities

I compute visibilities with the different ATE-visibility measures from the perspective of each of the three users. The documents are then sorted in descending order of their visibility. Based on the five author-trust-based visibility measures, this gives $\mathrm{vis} = \mathrm{vis}_{p,u}^{\mathrm{ATE}}, \mathrm{vis}_{p,u}^{\mathrm{ATE}'}, \mathrm{vis}_{p,u}^{\mathrm{WPR}}, \mathrm{vis}_{p,u}^{\mathrm{ATE}_w}, \mathrm{vis}_{p,u}^{\mathrm{ATE}'_w}$ the rankings $\mathcal{R}_{u^0}^{\mathrm{vis}}$, $\mathcal{R}_{u^{\mathcal{B},\overline{\mathcal{C}}}}^{\mathrm{vis}}$ and $\mathcal{R}_{u^{\overline{\mathcal{B}},\mathcal{C}}}^{\mathrm{vis}}$. For each set of three rankings $\mathcal{R}_{u^0}^{\mathrm{vis}}$, $\mathcal{R}_{u^{\mathcal{B},\overline{\mathcal{C}}}}^{\mathrm{vis}}$ and $\mathcal{R}_{u^{\overline{\mathcal{B}},\mathcal{C}}}^{\mathrm{vis}}$, I compute the average positions of documents written by authors from group $\mathcal{A}$, $\mathcal{B}$ and $\mathcal{C}$. I distinguish two types of documents, namely those documents that are written by authors from group $\mathcal{A}$, $\mathcal{B}$ or $\mathcal{C}$, respectively, and those documents that are cited by authors from the group $\mathcal{A}$, $\mathcal{B}$ or $\mathcal{C}$, respectively. The average positions of the documents are now compared: I compute how much the average positions of the documents written (cited) by authors from groups $\mathcal{A}$, $\mathcal{B}$ and $\mathcal{C}$ differ in the rankings $\mathcal{R}_{u^0}^{\mathrm{vis}}$ and $\mathcal{R}_{u^{\mathcal{B},\overline{\mathcal{C}}}}^{\mathrm{vis}}$ as well as in the rankings $\mathcal{R}_{u^0}^{\mathrm{vis}}$ and $\mathcal{R}_{u^{\overline{\mathcal{B}},\mathcal{C}}}^{\mathrm{vis}}$. Tables 8.27, 8.28 and 8.29 show the proportional change of the average position of all documents, computed over the each ten small-sized networks with branching factor 2 to 8, 6 to 14 and 10 to 20.

		$\mathcal{A}$	$\mathcal{B}$	$\mathcal{C}$	$\mathcal{A}$	$\mathcal{B}$	$\mathcal{C}$
			written			cited	
$\mathrm{vis}_{p,u}^{\mathrm{ATE}}$	$u^{\mathcal{B},\overline{\mathcal{C}}}$	-0.1%	20.0%	-20.0%	-0.8%	0.9%	-2.7%
	$u^{\overline{\mathcal{B}},\mathcal{C}}$	0.0%	-19.3%	20.7%	-0.8%	-2.6%	1.1%
$\mathrm{vis}_{p,u}^{\mathrm{ATE}'}$	$u^{\mathcal{B},\overline{\mathcal{C}}}$	1.1%	25.2%	-47.4%	-1.3%	0.0%	-5.8%
	$u^{\overline{\mathcal{B}},\mathcal{C}}$	1.3%	-48.9%	26.0%	-1.3%	-6.6%	-0.7%
$\mathrm{vis}_{p,u}^{\mathrm{WPR}}$	$u^{\mathcal{B},\overline{\mathcal{C}}}$	0.0%	-0.2%	0.2%	0.0%	3.0%	-4.1%
	$u^{\overline{\mathcal{B}},\mathcal{C}}$	0.0%	0.2%	-0.2%	0.0%	-4.1%	3.1%
$\mathrm{vis}_{p,u}^{\mathrm{ATE}w}$	$u^{\mathcal{B},\overline{\mathcal{C}}}$	0.0%	34.0%	-35.3%	-1.4%	3.7%	-5.6%
	$u^{\overline{\mathcal{B}},\mathcal{C}}$	0.1%	-35.6%	34.7%	-1.4%	-5.8%	3.9%
$\mathrm{vis}_{p,u}^{\mathrm{ATE}'_w}$	$u^{\mathcal{B},\overline{\mathcal{C}}}$	0.7%	38.3%	-47.8%	-1.8%	2.7%	-7.1%
	$u^{\overline{\mathcal{B}},\mathcal{C}}$	0.4%	-45.8%	36.3%	-1.7%	-7.2%	2.8%

Table 8.27: Comparison of the ATE-visibilities on ML_s^{2-8}

		$\mathcal{A}$	$\mathcal{B}$	$\mathcal{C}$	$\mathcal{A}$	$\mathcal{B}$	$\mathcal{C}$
			written			cited	
$\mathrm{vis}_{p,u}^{\mathrm{ATE}}$	$u^{\mathcal{B},\overline{\mathcal{C}}}$	0.0%	18.6%	-18.9%	-0.3%	0.4%	-1.6%
	$u^{\overline{\mathcal{B}},\mathcal{C}}$	0.0%	-19.0%	19.6%	-0.4%	-1.5%	0.4%
$\mathrm{vis}_{p,u}^{\mathrm{ATE}'}$	$u^{\mathcal{B},\overline{\mathcal{C}}}$	1.0%	26.2%	-49.3%	-0.6%	-0.6%	-4.0%
	$u^{\overline{\mathcal{B}},\mathcal{C}}$	1.4%	-47.5%	25.9%	-0.6%	-4.9%	-0.7%
$\mathrm{vis}_{p,u}^{\mathrm{WPR}}$	$u^{\mathcal{B},\overline{\mathcal{C}}}$	0.0%	0.0%	0.0%	0.0%	2.1%	-2.4%
	$u^{\overline{\mathcal{B}},\mathcal{C}}$	0.0%	0.0%	0.0%	0.0%	-2.4%	2.1%
$\mathrm{vis}_{p,u}^{\mathrm{ATE}w}$	$u^{\mathcal{B},\overline{\mathcal{C}}}$	0.0%	35.4%	-38.5%	-0.6%	2.0%	-4.2%
	$u^{\overline{\mathcal{B}},\mathcal{C}}$	0.2%	-36.4%	35.8%	-0.6%	-3.8%	2.2%
$\mathrm{vis}_{p,u}^{\mathrm{ATE}'_w}$	$u^{\mathcal{B},\overline{\mathcal{C}}}$	0.6%	39.6%	-46.8%	-0.7%	1.4%	-5.2%
	$u^{\overline{\mathcal{B}},\mathcal{C}}$	0.3%	-46.5%	38.8%	-0.8%	-4.9%	1.7%

Table 8.28: Comparison of the ATE-visibilities on ML_s^{6-14}

		$\mathcal{A}$	$\mathcal{B}$	$\mathcal{C}$	$\mathcal{A}$	$\mathcal{B}$	$\mathcal{C}$
			written			cited	
$\mathrm{vis}_{p,u}^{\mathrm{ATE}}$	$u^{\mathcal{B},\overline{\mathcal{C}}}$	0.0%	18.8%	-18.2%	-0.2%	0.1%	-1.2%
	$u^{\overline{\mathcal{B}},\mathcal{C}}$	-0.1%	-17.9%	18.4%	-0.2%	-1.2%	0.1%
$\mathrm{vis}_{p,u}^{\mathrm{ATE}'}$	$u^{\mathcal{B},\overline{\mathcal{C}}}$	1.1%	27.0%	-48.6%	-0.4%	-0.9%	-3.0%
	$u^{\overline{\mathcal{B}},\mathcal{C}}$	1.3%	-48.8%	26.3%	-0.4%	-2.8%	-0.9%
$\mathrm{vis}_{p,u}^{\mathrm{WPR}}$	$u^{\mathcal{B},\overline{\mathcal{C}}}$	0.0%	0.1%	0.1%	0.0%	1.4%	-1.6%
	$u^{\overline{\mathcal{B}},\mathcal{C}}$	0.0%	0.0%	-0.1%	0.0%	-1.6%	1.5%
$\mathrm{vis}_{p,u}^{\mathrm{ATE}_w}$	$u^{\mathcal{B},\overline{\mathcal{C}}}$	0.1%	37.6%	-37.5%	-0.5%	1.0%	-3.2%
	$u^{\overline{\mathcal{B}},\mathcal{C}}$	-0.1%	-36.1%	37.1%	-0.4%	-3.0%	1.0%
$\mathrm{vis}_{p,u}^{\mathrm{ATE}'_w}$	$u^{\mathcal{B},\overline{\mathcal{C}}}$	0.6%	39.2%	-47.5%	-0.5%	0.6%	-3.7%
	$u^{\overline{\mathcal{B}},\mathcal{C}}$	0.4%	-47.9%	39.3%	-0.5%	-4.0%	0.5%

Table 8.29: Comparison of the ATE-visibilities on ML_s^{10-20}

Interpretation of the Results from Comparing ATE-Visibilities

First of all, I can state that the results are absolutely consistent over the three types of small-sized networks as well as over the medium-sized networks and the networks used in Hess and Stein. This is to say that the ATE-visibility measures are not sensitive to the branching factor of the documents.

Over all measures, we can see that there are no differences in $u^{\mathcal{B},\overline{\mathcal{C}}}$'s and $u^{\overline{\mathcal{B}},\mathcal{C}}$'s ranking for documents written by authors from group $\mathcal{A}$. This is clear as both $u^{\mathcal{B},\overline{\mathcal{C}}}$ and $u^{\overline{\mathcal{B}},\mathcal{C}}$ have neutral trust in the authors from group $\mathcal{A}$.

ATE-Visibility $\mathrm{vis}_{p,u}^{\mathrm{ATE}}$ and $\mathrm{vis}_{p,u}^{\mathrm{ATE}'}$ Using $\mathrm{vis}_{p,u}^{\mathrm{ATE}}$ for the document rankings, the average positions of the documents written by authors of groups $\mathcal{B}$ and $\mathcal{C}$ differ in the rankings $\mathcal{R}_{u^0}^{\mathrm{vis}_{p,u}^{\mathrm{ATE}}}$ and $\mathcal{R}_{u^{\mathcal{B},\overline{\mathcal{C}}}}^{\mathrm{vis}_{p,u}^{\mathrm{ATE}}}$ ($\mathcal{R}_{u^0}^{\mathrm{vis}_{p,u}^{\mathrm{ATE}}}$ and $\mathcal{R}_{u^{\overline{\mathcal{B}},\mathcal{C}}}^{\mathrm{vis}_{p,u}^{\mathrm{ATE}}}$, respectively) by around 20%. That means that for $u^{\mathcal{B},\overline{\mathcal{C}}}$ who trusts the authors of group $\mathcal{B}$, the ranks of the documents written by authors of group $\mathcal{B}$ increase by around 20% compared with the "neutral" ranking computed for u^0. The positions of the documents by the distrusted authors from group $\mathcal{C}$ decrease analogously by around 20%. The inverse holds true for user $u^{\overline{\mathcal{B}},\mathcal{C}}$. Comparing the rankings for $u^{\mathcal{B},\overline{\mathcal{C}}}$ and $u^{\overline{\mathcal{B}},\mathcal{C}}$, the differences in positions is now around 40%.

The ATE-visibility $\mathrm{vis}_{p,u}^{\mathrm{ATE}}$ modifies only the basic visibility $1 - \alpha$ whereas $\mathrm{vis}_{p,u}^{\mathrm{ATE}'}$ modifies the complete PageRank-based visibility. This explains the differences between the results for both visibility measures. Using $\mathrm{vis}_{p,u}^{\mathrm{ATE}'}$, the ranks of documents written by authors of groups $\mathcal{B}$ and $\mathcal{C}$ are now increased or decreased in the ranking for $u^{\mathcal{B},\overline{\mathcal{C}}}$ (or $u^{\overline{\mathcal{B}},\mathcal{C}}$) between 25 and almost 50% compared with the ranking for u^0. The change of 50% in the ranks of the documents by distrusted authors means that these documents now have the lowest rank, because with neutrality they would have a position in the middle of the ranking.

Regardless of which version is used, the modified visibility of the documents written by authors from groups $\mathcal{B}$ and $\mathcal{C}$ also has some effect on the documents cited by them. This indirect influence, however, is quite low.

Personalized weighted PageRank $\mathrm{vis}_{p,u}^{\mathrm{WPR}}$ The average positions of the documents that are written by authors of group $\mathcal{B}$ and $\mathcal{C}$ do not differ in the rankings $\mathcal{R}_{u^{\mathcal{B},\overline{\mathcal{C}}}}^{\mathrm{vis}_{p,u}^{\mathrm{WPR}}}$ and $\mathcal{R}_{u^{\overline{\mathcal{B}},\mathcal{C}}}^{\mathrm{vis}_{p,u}^{\mathrm{WPR}}}$. This is clear when one looks at the definition of the measure: the trust in authors from group $\mathcal{B}$ (or group $\mathcal{C}$, respectively) modifies only the weights on the references from documents written by authors from group $\mathcal{B}$ ($\mathcal{C}$) to any other documents. Therefore we can see a difference in the ranks of the documents cited by users $u^{\mathcal{B},\overline{\mathcal{C}}}$ and $u^{\overline{\mathcal{B}},\mathcal{C}}$, respectively. These differences are around 2 to 4% to the average position in the ranking generated for u^0.

Combined Weighted ATE-Visibility   Combining the ATE-visibility and the personalized weighted PageRank increases the average differences in the rankings. The average positions of documents written by authors from group $\mathcal{B}$ and $\mathcal{C}$ are now increased by around 35% in $\mathcal{R}_{u^{\mathcal{B},\overline{\mathcal{C}}}}^{\mathrm{vis}_{p,u}^{\mathrm{ATE}w}}$ compared with $\mathcal{R}_{u^0}^{\mathrm{vis}_{p,u}^{\mathrm{ATE}w}}$, and decreased by around 35% in $\mathcal{R}_{u^{\overline{\mathcal{B}},\mathcal{C}}}^{\mathrm{vis}_{p,u}^{\mathrm{ATE}w}}$ compared with $\mathcal{R}_{u^0}^{\mathrm{vis}_{p,u}^{\mathrm{ATE}w}}$. In the rankings based on $\mathrm{vis}_{p,u}^{\mathrm{ATE}'_w}$, the average difference in the positions is around 40 to 45%. Both combined ATE-visibility measures certainly have an effect on the visibilities of the cited documents. This effect is much stronger than simply using only one of the measures.

▶ **Result of the Personalization Simulation Study**   The personalized document rankings generated with the different types of author-trust-enhanced visibility measures strongly reflect the user's personal preferences which show up in her or his web of trust. The visibility measures that are based on the trust between authors do not show any sensitivity to the network size nor to the branching factor. Thus, generally I can recommend using the ATE-visibility measures that affect the whole PageRank ($\mathrm{vis}_{p,u}^{\mathrm{ATE}'}$ or $\mathrm{vis}_{p,u}^{\mathrm{ATE}'_w}$) in order to achieve a stronger personalization. The analysis of the edge weights in the combined versions enhances the personalization even more. ◀

8.5.3 Downgrading Papers by Cheating Authors

The last study focuses on the evaluation of the author-trust-based visibility measures with respect to their ability to downgrade in the rankings those papers that are written by "cheating" authors, i.e. by authors who have written papers based on faked datasets etc.

> ► **Aim:** Analyze how the ATE-visibility measures and the personalized weighted PageRank decrease the ranks of papers written by "cheating" authors. ◄

I will discuss this question now separately for the ATE-visibility $\mathrm{vis}_{p,u}^{\mathrm{ATE}'}$ (which is to be preferred over $\mathrm{vis}_{p,u}^{\mathrm{ATE}}$ as discussed in the previous section), the (personalized) weighted PageRank and their combination. I'll perform a simulation study where a mathematical analysis is insufficient.

Decreasing Visibilities with $\mathrm{vis}_{p,u}^{\mathrm{ATE}'}$

ATE-visibilities are computed from the perspective of a user u, giving personalized rankings. In order to decrease the position of papers by a cheating author a in the ranking computed for u, it is sufficient that u provides a distrust rating on a (or that u changes trust in distrust, respectively). If $t_{u \to a} = -1$, then the reference-based visibility $\mathrm{vis}_p^{\mathrm{PR}}$ computed for a's papers p is multiplied with $t_a = 0$ (the interpersonal trust values are shifted by $+1$ in order to obtain author trust greater or equal zero). These documents have hence an ATE-visibility of 0, the lowest visibility possible. The ATE-visibility thus allows for efficiently excluding from the ranking such documents that are written by cheating authors. It is not necessary that any other authors change their trust in a in order to affect the ranks of a's documents in the ranking computed for u. Note that in contrast to the TRE-visibility measures in which adverse reviews affect only a certain paper, the distrust in the author affects the ATE-visibility of all papers written by this author.

The effect of downgrading papers in the ranking can also be seen in the results of the comparative study on the author-trust-based visibility measures in section 8.5.2. Comparing the average positions in the rankings computed for two users u_1 and u_2, with u_1 being neutral to an author a and u_2 distrusting a, the average change in positions of documents written by a is 50%. This means that for u_1, a's papers are on average in the middle of the ranking, whereas for u_2, a's papers have an ATE-visibility of 0 and are thus on the lowest ranks.

Decreasing Visibilities with (Personalized) Weighted PageRank $\mathrm{vis}_{p,u}^{\mathrm{WPR}}$

When using the unpersonalized weighted PageRank $\mathrm{vis}_p^{\mathrm{WPR}}$ for the computation of a document ranking, it is necessary in order to decrease the visibility of a's papers that the authors who cite the cheating author a set their trust in a to -1. The question on which percentage the ranks of a's papers decrease was addressed in Stein and Hess (2006). As the results of the above comparative simulation study were identical over the different types of networks, we can fairly assume that the results of this simulation can also be generalized.

This simulation comprised 10 runs on 10 distinct document reference networks. Each network contained around 3,500 documents written by around 100 authors. Documents were interlinked by 2–7 references. The visibility measures were parameterized as described above. We computed a first ranking $\mathcal{R}_+$ on the basis of $\mathrm{vis}_{p_d}^{\mathrm{WPR}}$ in which all users trusted each other, i.e., $t_{u_m \to u_n} = 1$ for all users in the network. Then, 80% of the other authors distrust author a. A second ranking $\mathcal{R}_-$ was computed on the basis of the modified trust network which led to modified weights on the references between documents. We compared the differences in the average ranks of all documents written by a in $\mathcal{R}_+$ and $\mathcal{R}_-$. On average, they decreased in their ranks by 22% (between 19 and 25% on the ten different networks). This means that a paper ranked at position 10 in $\mathcal{R}_+$, i.e. among the top papers, would be ranked at position 780 in $\mathcal{R}_-$. It would hence no longer be visible for a user doing a document search. This shows that weighted PageRank is appropriate for efficiently downgrading documents by distrusted authors.

In the case of the personalized weighted PageRank, the user u for whom the ranking is personalized cannot directly influence the visibility of documents written by a unless he/she cites a's papers. If this is not the case, u can only influence the edge weights on the references to a's papers. This means that u should trust the authors who are citing a only if they have changed their trust in a to distrust, otherwise u should distrust them. The personalized edge weights would thus also be 0 in those cases in which the citing author still trusts a. As no visibility is propagated via a reference attributed with 0, the visibility of a's papers decreases. This approach, however, also affects the visibilities of all other documents cited by those authors who cite documents by a. This effect is not desirable. Moreover, it assumes that u knows about the other authors' trust statements which will likely not be the case. Modulating the edge weights in this case is thus not reasonable.

Decreasing Visibilities with the Combined Weighted ATE-Visibility

If u directly distrusts the cheating author a, the documents by a obtain a visibility of $\mathrm{vis}_{p,u}^{\mathrm{ATE}'_w} = 0$. The degrees of trust of the other authors in the cheating author a

have no influence on this visibility. In the case that u has not yet changed her or his personal trust in a, the trust values set by the other users on a modify $\text{vis}_p^{\text{WPR}}$ (or $\text{vis}_{p,u}^{\text{WPR}}$, respectively), i.e. the part of the visibility which is based on the weighted PageRank. This visibility is decreased depending on how many of the authors who cite a also distrust a. Using the combined version thus means that the ranks of a's papers will be decreased if either u or some of the authors citing papers by a change their trust in a to distrust. User u obtains thus an appropriate recommendation for a's documents, even in cases in which he/she did not yet update his/her personal trust to a.

> **▶ Result of the Study on Downgrading Papers by Faking Authors** In order to set the ATE-visibility of a cheating author's papers to zero, from the perspective of any user u, it is sufficient that u distrusts the cheating author. In the case of weighted PageRank (personalized and non-personalized), it is necessary that authors who cite documents by the cheating authors a also distrust a. User u's distrust in a only influences the visibility of a's papers if u has cited any of them. If a certain number of the citing authors have changed their trust in a, the weighted PageRank considerably decreases the ranks of a's papers.
>
> By combining both approaches, the visibility of a's papers is either decreased by u's personal distrust in a or by the other authors' distrust in a. This combination is very efficient and also works well when u has not yet updated her/his personal trust in a. ◀

8.5.4 Summary

I analyzed the author-trust-based visibility measures with respect to two questions: the degree of personalization achieved and their ability to decrease the documents written by an author of faked publications in a ranking. In contrast to the TRE-visibility measures where I compared the different TRE-visibility measures, the author-trust-based measures are complementary to each other and can be used in combination. Concerning the personalization, I have shown by comparing the rankings generated for three users with completely different trust in the other authors, that the ATE-visibility measures offer a considerable personalization. Papers that show up in the first positions in the ranking generated for a user, who trusts the authors of these papers, are ranked for a user who distrusts these same authors in the last positions. The strongest personalization is achieved by combining the ATE-visibility measure with the personalized weighted PageRank, i.e. by $\text{vis}_{p,u}^{\text{ATE}'_w}$. This combined version is also very efficient at decreasing papers by cheating authors in their ranks. The visibility of such papers can be decreased down to zero; they are thus ranked at the last positions.

9 Conclusion

The starting point for my dissertation was the recent progress in research on trust-based recommender systems (see e.g. Golbeck, 2005; Ziegler, 2005). My central contribution to the research in this area was to extend the approach to trust-based recommendations, which up to now had been made for unlinked items such as products or movies, to linked resources, in particular documents. This means considering for the recommendation, apart from the trust network, a further type of network, such as the citation network of scientific publications or the hyperlink graphs of webpages and wikis. A setting in which these two networks are integrated to two-layer networks allows for extending the classical reference-based visibility measures on the linked documents, such as PageRank, with trust information.

9.1 Results

Based on the use cases for digital libraries and for wikis that I described in chapter 2, I could derive requirements for an architecture that combines different types of networks and for visibility measures that can be computed in such a setting (see section 2.3).

Multi-Layer Architecture

► **Requirement:** Specification of a multi-layer architecture that defines how networks are to be connected and that gives the framework for jointly analyzing the different layers. ◄

I defined such an architecture in chapter 4. The architecture is general: it allows for coupling different types of networks, and not only trust networks with document networks. I described how to connect different networks that are linked by some relationship (such as author networks being linked with document networks via the relationship 'is-author-of') to a multi-layer network which is then the basis for generating recommendations. In a multi-layer network, layers are connected by weighted or non-weighted edges only with the previous layer and with the subsequent layer. In order to exchange the information between the layers, I defined two basic propagation mechanisms: node-to-node and edge-to-edge propagation. The trust-enhanced visibility measures then build on these basic propagation mechanisms. I can thus say that the first requirement is met.

Trust-enhanced Visibility Measures

► **Requirement:** Definition of trust-enhanced visibility measures which should have the following properties:

(i) they are personalized depending on the user's personal preferences such as her or his reviews and her or his personal web of trust,

(ii) they allow for generating personalized rankings for all documents,

(iii) they decrease the visibility and thus also the ranks of faked papers,

(iv) they are efficiently computable at query time.

◄

In chapter 5, I defined two groups of measures. Firstly, the trust-review-enhanced visibility measures, the so-called TRE-visibility measures, work on a reviewer trust network and a document network. Secondly, the author-trust-enhanced visibility measures, the so-called ATE-visibility measures, use as a basis a two-layer network with an author trust network and a document network. I verify separately for both measures whether or not they meet the above stated criteria.

TRE-Visibility

(i) The TRE-visibility of a document is personalized on the basis of the trust-weighted reviews on this document. In section 5.1.3, I have defined how the trust in a review is determined on the basis of the trust statements given by the users. The influence of the trust-weighted reviews on the final recommendation depends on the trust in the reviewers. In the simulation study in section 8.3.4, I have shown that already with five trustworthy reviews on a document, the reference-based visibility has only minor importance: the recommendation is completely dominated by the trust-weighted reviews. The degree of personalization that is achieved by the trust-weighted reviews in comparison to a mere reference-based measure was analyzed in section 8.3.5 where I compared the TRE-visibilities for users with opposite opinions. I could show that the more such reviews were different and the more often they were given, the higher became the difference in the TRE-visibilities.

(ii) The TRE-visibilities computed are personalized for mostly all documents due to the joint propagation of information on the trust and the document reference network. On the one hand, users benefit from other users' reviews, and on the other hand, reviews indirectly influence the visibilities of the documents cited by the reviewed documents. As I could show in the simulation study in section 8.3.7, with 1% of the documents being reviewed and an indirect influence on documents at a maximum distance of three, already around 80% of the documents have at least one direct or indirect review; thus, their TRE-visibility is personalized based on the information from the trust layer. A small proportion of documents remains for which the TRE-visibility is identical with a simple reference-based measure because these documents are too recent to be cited or reviewed.

(iii) The TRE-visibility of a document is lower than its reference-based visibility if the average review values are below the reference-based visibility. As the simulation study in 8.3.6 has shown, this is easily achieved for a well-cited paper that has been detected as a fake and that consequently receives adverse reviews. The TRE-visibility measures thus decrease the visibility of faked papers and thus also their positions in a ranking.

(iv) In section 5.1.7, I addressed the task of defining an efficiently computable TRE-visibility that has the same properties as the integrated TRE-visibility which extends a reference-based measure such as PageRank in a very intuitive way. An efficient computation at query time is achieved by precomputing all non-personalized information. These pieces are personalized for the respective user at query time and then put together. The main question here was to determine the impact of indirect reviews. As shown in the comparative study on the TRE-visibilities, these efficient TRE-visibility measures, the so-called review-propagating TRE-visibility measures, give very similar results as the integrated TRE-visibility. They provide thus an efficient means of computing document recommendations while preserving the desired properties.

ATE-Visibility

(i) There are two personalization strategies for the author-trust-based visibility measures. On the one hand, the ATE-visibility of a document is personalized by modifying its reference-based visibility (e.g. PageRank or HITS) with the user's personal trust in the author (see section 5.2.1). On the other hand, edge weights on the references (which are derived from the trust network) are personalized based on the user's personal trust in the user who sets the reference (see section 5.2.3). As I could show in the simulation study in section 8.5.2, the strongest personalization is achieved by combining these two personalization strategies.

(ii) By combining both personalization strategies, the visibility is personalized not only on the requesting user's personal trust in authors but the user also benefits from the trust statements made by other users as these represent edge weights on the references.

(iii) It is again the combined version of ATE-visibility with weighted edges that is best suited for decreasing the visibility and thus also the ranks of papers by cheating authors. In contrast to the TRE-visibility which decreases the visibility of papers with adverse reviews, the ATE-visibility affects all papers by the cheating author.

(iv) In contrast to the TRE-visibility for which it is possible to precompute the distinct components, this is not feasible for the ATE-visibility. Its performance, however, can be improved by using well-suited initial values for the ATE-visibility so that only very few iterations are required until convergence.

Duplicate Documents

▶ **Requirement:** Duplicate documents should not distort the results of trust-enhanced visibility measures. ◀

In chapter 6, I addressed the problem of uncertainty caused by duplicate versions of the same document. I introduced a model for uncertainty. It deals with the problem that duplicates may have slightly diverging reference lists, so there is uncertainty on the edges in the graph of documents. This model allows for computing reference-based measures on document collections that contain duplicates. Due to this uncertainty, the visibility of a document is no longer a single value but is an interval with a minimum and maximum visibility. In order to make this computation more efficient, I discussed how to approximate this interval efficiently. As a concrete example, I showed this approximation for the TRE-visibility measures.

The main goal of the thesis, namely to show that the joint analysis of the different types of networks enhances recommendations for documents, is thus achieved.

9.2 Outlook

9.2.1 Trust-Based Recommendations in Future Publication Models

The TRE- and the ATE-visibility measures are well suited for computing recommendations and rankings based on the importance and the trustworthiness of documents.

This may be useful in future publication models. Over the last years, a radical change in scientists' publication behavior could be observed. Authors are more and more publishing their research results online in order to grant immediate access to them. The arXiv, for example, is extensively used by physicians for a pre-review dissemination of their scientific papers. A considerable number of the papers published there are later on printed in conventional peer reviewed journals (Ginsparg, 2003) because online publishing does not yet register the impact, in the same way that the publication in a prestigious journal does.

Recently developed publication models aim to combine the advantages of rapid online publishing, strong quality assurance, credentials as provided by peer reviewed journals and the possibility to discuss publications in a single system. Ginsparg proposes a two-tier system. Submitted publications would immediately be published in the first tier, the so-called standard tier, if they passed some preliminary automated checks. Carefully selected and peer reviewed papers are upgraded from the standard tier to the upper tier. Review commentaries and further information are made public in the form of an overlay guide to the upper tier which supports readers in the selection of papers and the navigation through the available literature. Pöschl (2004) discusses a publication model with a two-stage publication process. In the first stage, papers are published online in a scientific discussion forum where readers and reviewers can comment on them. Authors can directly answer on the reviews. The interactively peer reviewed papers are then published in a scientific journal.

These new publication models will have to deal with the problem that the amount of publications increases constantly because the number of papers represents an important measure for scientific productivity, hence for promotion. Therefore it is no longer possible to peer review all publications with the same high quality standards. Here the trust-based document visibilities come into play. In Ginsparg's two-tier system, positive reviews are the prerequisite for upgrade in the upper tier. The publication model by Pöschl already requires such positive evaluation before entering the first stage. The papers to be reviewed must be selected from a huge amount of submitted papers. This selection can be supported by classical citation-based measures and access statistics, e.g., the number of downloads (Ginsparg, 2003). Using the information available in a multi-layer architecture offers a new possibility for designing the review process. The idea is that readers actively participate in the publication process by providing reviews on papers. Papers can then be selected for the upper tier according to their trust-enhanced visibility with reviews by trusted users having a higher impact than reviews by less trusted users. In contrast to classical review processes, reviews are made not only by a selected group of referees but everybody is allowed to contribute. This was also intended by Ginsparg: he proposes to "collect confidential commentary from interested readers so that eventual referees would have access to a wealth of currently inaccessible information held by the community". This is in line with the ideas promoted in the context of the Social Web: users are no longer willing to simply accept what is presented to them on the web, but rather they want to participate actively.

Apart from supporting the reviewing process, the trust-enhanced visibility measures, however, would also support the readers in such a two-tier system. Based on the user's own web of trust, a personalized view on the upper tier and the overlay journal can be provided. This reflects that users from different scientific communities will consider different positions as valid. Users may have their personal instance of the overlay guide that assists them in the selection of the relevant papers for their queries and that provides additional information about the papers such as review commentaries.

9.2.2 Data Availability

When using the multi-layer-based recommendations in practice, such layered networks have to be available. Or at least, the required types of networks have to be separately available so that in future we can expect to have them in a form in which they can be jointly analyzed. Currently, the different types of networks, i.e. in particular, social trust networks and document reference networks, are separately available on the web. There are many social networking websites with millions of users, as for instance Friendster.com with its more than 40 million users. Considering the current success of social networking applications, it can be expected that they will continue growing in number and size. With respect to the document reference networks, there are many document collections online such as arXiv, PubMed and CiteSeer. Some of these document collections grant access to their metadata including the reference lists. For both types of networks, a set of measures, such as visibility measures for documents or centrality measures for users are already available and can be used for the evaluation of the information in the respective network (see chapter 3).

At present, trust networks and document networks are not available in a two-layered form in which the users in a trust network are the authors of the documents in the reference network, or in which the users in the trust network provide reviews on documents. In current trust networks, users rate different types of items which, however, are not linked to each other. Nevertheless, I think that it is fairly realistic to have such two-layered networks in the future. For instance, in the case of wikis, a first version of an author trust network might be automatically extracted from the interaction history between users: keeping the edits of the previous author means considering this contribution and thus this author as reliable, whereas removing this author's edits or changing them completely gives a hint on distrust. This author trust network could be refined by the contributors; for instance, they could fine-tune the degree of trust. This would give a two-layer network consisting of an author trust network and a document reference network. Methods for analyzing the network of wiki pages are currently in the focus of many research activities. This is a promising case of a two-layer architecture. In general, I expect that the interest in applications in which users actively participate and interact with other users, such as in the current Social Web applications, will further increase. A recommendation system in which the recommendation is based on the resources and the ratings provided by the community is also such a type of Social Web application and even goes a step further to the Semantic Web in the sense that the trustworthiness of information is evaluated.

Bibliography

Abdul-Rahman, A. (1997). The pgp trust model. *EDI-Forum: the Journal of Electronic Commerce*, **407**. 46

Abdul-Rahman, A. and Hailes, S. (1997). A distributed trust model. In *NSPW '97: Proceedings of the 1997 Workshop on New Security Paradigms*, pages 48–60. 49

Abdul-Rahman, A. and Hailes, S. (2000). Supporting trust in virtual communities. In *Proceedings of the 33rd Hawaii International Conference on System Sciences (HICSS '00)*, Washington, DC, USA. IEEE Computer Society. 47

Abrams, M. D. and Joyce, M. V. (1995). Trusted system concepts. *Computers & Security*, **14**(1), 45–56. 45

Adler, B. T. and de Alfaro, L. (2007). A content-driven reputation system for the wikipedia. In *Proceedings of WWW 2007*, Banff, Alberta, Canada. 29

Ali, K. and van Stam, W. (2004). Tivo: making show recommendations using a distributed collaborative filtering architecture. In *KDD '04: Proceedings of the tenth ACM SIGKDD international conference on Knowledge discovery and data mining*, pages 394–401. 41

Anderson, N. (2007). Citizendium: building a better wikipedia. Retrieved April 25, 2007, from `http://arstechnica.com/articles/culture/citizendium.ars`. 26

Andritsos, P., Fuxman, A., and Miller, R. J. (2006). Clean answers over dirty databases: A probabilistic approach. In *Proceedings of the International Conference on Data Engineering (ICDE)*. 125, 126, 127, 132

Anthony, D., Smith, S. W., and Williamson, T. (2005). Explaining quality in internet collective goods: Zealots and good samaritans in the case of wikipedia. 27

Avesani, P., Massa, P., and Tiella, R. (2005). A trust-enhanced recommender system application: Moleskiing. In *SAC '05: Proceedings of the 2005 ACM symposium on Applied computing*, pages 1589–1593. 42, 43, 59, 150, 151

Bachmann, R. (2003). The coordingation of relations across organizational boundaries. *International Studies of Management and Organization*, **33**(2), 7–21. Retrieved June 06, 2006, from www.bbk.ac.uk/manop/research/wpapers/mandocs/03_05_bachmann.pdf. 60, 62

Bachmann, R., Knights, D., and Sydow, J. (2001). Trust and control in organizational relations. *Organization Studies*, **22**(2), v–viii. 60

Barabási, A.-L. (2001). The physics of the web. *Physics Web - Physics World*. 52, 64

Barabási, A. L. and Albert, R. (1999). Emergence of scaling in random networks. *Science*, **286**. 51, 52, 64

Barber, B. (1983). *Logic and Limits of Trust*. Rutgers University Press, New Jersey. 46

Bedi, P. and Kaur, H. (2006). Trust based personalized recommender system. *INFO-COMP Journal of Computer Science*, **5**(1), 19–26. 42, 43, 44

Bell Labs (2002). Report of the investigation commitee on the possibility of scientific misconduct in the work of hendrik schön and coauthors. Retrieved April 04, 2006, from http://www.lucent.com/news_events/pdf/summary.pdf. 16

Benjelloun, O., Das Sarma, A., Hayworth, C., and Widom, J. (2006). An introduction to ULDBs and the trio system. *IEEE Data Engineering Bulletin*, **29**(1), 5–16. 124

Berners-Lee, T., Hendler, J., and Lassila, O. (2001). The semantic web. *Scientific American*, **284**(5), 34–43. 2

Beth, T., Borcherding, M., and Klein, B. (1994). Valuation of trust in open networks. In *Proceedings of the European Symposium on Research in Computer Security (ES-ORICS)*, LNCS 875, pages 3–18, Brighton, UK. Springer Verlag. 49, 54, 57, 59

Bharat, K. and Mihaila, G. A. (2001). When experts agree: Using non-affiliated experts to rank popular topics. In *Proceedings of the 10th World Wide Web Conference*, pages 597–602. 69, 70

Bollen, J., Rodriguez, M. A., and Van de Sompel, H. (2006). Journal status. *http://www.arxiv.org/abs/cs.GL/0601030*. 10

Boykin, P. O. and Roychowdhury, V. (2004). Sorting e-mail friends from foes: Identifying networks of mutual friends helps filter out spam. *Nature Science Updates*, **16**. 39, 44

Braendle, A. (2005). *Zu wenige Köche verderben den Brei. Eine Inhaltsanalyse der Wikipedia aus Perspektive der journalistischen Qualität, des Netzeffekts und der Ökonomie der Aufmerksamkeit; in english: "Too Many Cooks Don't Spoil the Broth".* Master's thesis, University of Zurich. 25

Breck, E., Choi, Y., and Cardie, C. (2007). Identifying expressions of opinion in context. In *Proceedings of the Twentieth International Conference on Artificial Intelligence (IJCAI 2007)*. 72

Brickely, D. and Miller, L. (2005). Foaf vocabulary specification. Retrieved September 07, 2005, from http://xmlns.com/foaf/spec/. 36

Börner, K., Maru, J. T., and Goldstone, R. L. (2004). The simultaneous evolution of author and paper networks. *Proceedings of the National Academy of Sciences*, **101**(suppl 1), 5266 – 5273. 64, 65, 78

Broder, A. Z. (2000). Identifying and filtering near-duplicate documents. In R. Giancarlo and D. Sankoff, editors, *Proceedings of the 11th Annual Symposium on Combinatorial Pattern Matching*, volume 1848 of *Lecture Notes In Computer Science*, pages 1–10. Springer-Verlag. 74

Broder, A. Z., Glassman, S. C., Manasse, M. S., and Zweig, G. (1997). Syntactic clustering of the web. *Computer Networks*, **29**(8-13), 1157–1166. 73

Brumfiel, G. (2002). Misconduct findings at bell labs shakes physics community. *Nature*, **419**, 419–421. 16

Budd, J. M., Sievert, M., and Schultz, T. R. (1998). Phenomena of retraction: Reasons for retraction and citations to the publications. *JAMA*, **280**(3), 296–297. 12

Buffa, M. (2006). Intranet wikis. In *Proceedings of the Intrawebs Workshop, WWW Conference 2006*, Edinburgh, Scotland, UK. 24

Burke, R. (2002). Hybrid recommender systems: Survey and experiments. *User Modeling and User-Adapted Interaction*, **12**(4), 331 – 370. 40, 42

Castelfranchi, C. and Falcone, R. (1998). Principles of trust for mas: Cognitive anatomy, social importance, and quantification. In *ICMAS '98: Proceedings of the 3rd International Conference on Multi Agent Systems*, page 72, Washington, DC, USA. IEEE Computer Society. 46

Castells, M. (1996). *The Rise of the Network Society*. Blackwell Publishers. 60

Cheng, R. and Prabhakar, S. (2003). Managing uncertainty in sensor databases. *Sigmod Record*, **32**(4), 41–46. 124

Chirita, P.-A., Diederich, J., and Nejdl, W. (2005). Mailrank: Using ranking for spam detection. In *CIKM '05: Proceedings of the 14th ACM International Conference on Information and Knowledge Management*, pages 373–380. 44

Cho, J., Shivakumar, N., and Garcia-Molina, H. (2000). Finding replicated web collections. In *SIGMOD '00: Proceedings of the 2000 ACM SIGMOD International Conference on Management of Data*, pages 355–366. 74

Ciffolilli, A. (2003). Phantom authority, self-selective recruitment and retention of members in virtual communities: The case of wikipedia. *First Monday*, 8(12). Retrieved May 12, 2007, from http://firstmonday.org/issues/issue8_12/ciffolilli/index.html. 28

Dalvi, N. and Suciu, D. (2005). Answering queries from statistics and probabilistic views. In *Proceedings of the 31st international Conference on Very Large Data Bases*, pages 805–816. VLDB Endowment. Trondheim, Norway. 124

de Rougemont, M. and Vieilleribière, A. (2007). Approximate data exchange. In *Proceedings of ICDT 2007*, pages 44–58. 75

Deutsch, M. (1962). Cooperation and trust: Some theoretical notes. In M. Jones, editor, *Nebraska Symposium on Motivation*. Nebraska University Press. 46

Ding, L., Kolari, P., Ganjugunte, S., Finin, T., and Joshi, A. (2004). Modeling and evaluating trust network inference. In *Seventh International Workshop on Trust in Agent Societies at AAMAS 2004*. 49, 54

Dong, P., Loh, M., and Mondry, A. (2005). The "impact factor" revisited. *Biomedical Digital Libraries*, 2(7). 9

Dumbill, E. (2002). Finding friends with xml and rdf. IBM's XML Watch. 36

Erdös, P. and Rényi, A. (1959). On random graphs. *Publicationes Mathematicae*, **6**, 290–297. 52

Etzioni, O. (1996). The world-wide web: Quagmire or gold mine? *Communications of the ACM*, **39**(11), 65–68. 63

Galaskiewicz, J. (1985). *Social Organization of an Urban Grants Economy: A Study of Business Philanthropy and Nonprofit Organizations*. Academic Press. 80

Gambetta, D. (1990a). Can we trust? In Gambetta (1990b). Retrieved October 10, 2004, from http://www.sociology.ox.ac.uk/papers/trustbook.html. 46

Gambetta, D., editor (1990b). *Trust: Making and Breaking Cooperative Relations.* Electronic edition, Department of Sociology, University of Oxford. Retrieved October 10, 2004, from `http://www.sociology.ox.ac.uk/papers/trustbook.html`. 46, 206

García-Barriocanal, E. and Sicilia, M.-A. (2005). Filtering information with imprecise social criteria: A foaf-based backlink model. In *Fourth Conference of the European Society for Fuzzy Logic and Technology EUSFLAT*, Barcelona, Spain. 78, 79

Garfield, E. (1965). Can citation indexing be automated? In M. E. Stevens, V. E. Giuliano, and L. B. Heilprin, editors, *Statistical Association Methods for Mechanized Documentation (National Bureau of Standards Miscellaneous Publication 269)*, pages 189–192. National Bureau of Standards. Reprint: Essays of an Information Scientist,vol. 1, p. 84–90, 1962–73. Current Contents, no. 9, March 4, 1970. 11

Garfield, E. (1972). Citation analysis as a tool in journal evaluation. *Science*, **178**, 471–479. 9, 66

Garfield, E. (1999). Journal impact factor: a brief review. *Cmaj*, **161**, 979–980. 9

Garfield, E. (2003). The meaning of the impact factor. *International Journal of Clinical and Health Psychology*, **3**(2), 363–369. 9

Getoor, L. and Diehl, C. P. (2005). Link mining: A survey. *SIGKDD Explorations*, **7**(2), 3–12. 64

Gibson, D., Kleinberg, J., and Raghavan, P. (1998). Inferring web communities from link topology. In *Proc. 9th ACM Conference on Hypertext and Hypermedia.* 69

Giles, C. L., Bollacker, K., and Lawrence, S. (1998). CiteSeer: An automatic citation indexing system. In I. Witten, R. Akscyn, and F. M. Shipman III, editors, *Digital Libraries 98 - The Third ACM Conference on Digital Libraries*, pages 89–98. ACM Press. 73, 146

Giles, J. (2005). Internet encyclopaedias go head to head. *Nature*, **438**, 900–901. 25

Ginsparg, P. (2003). Can peer review be better focused? Retrieved November 05, 2004 from `http://arxiv.org/blurb/pg02pr.html`. 199

Golbeck, J. (2005). *Computing and Applying Trust in Web-Based Social Networks.* Ph.D. thesis, Faculty of the Graduate School of the University of Maryland. 46, 50, 58, 195

Golbeck, J. (2006). Generating predictive movie recommendations from trust in social networks. In *Proceedings of the Fourth International Conference on Trust Management*, Pisa, Italy. 44, 45

Golbeck, J. and Hendler, J. (2004). Reputation network analysis for email filtering. In *Proceedings of the First Conference on Email and Anti-Spam*. 44, 54, 58

Golbeck, J. and Hendler, J. (2006). Filmtrust: Movie recommendations using trust in web-based social networks. In *Proceedings of the IEEE Consumer Communications and Networking Conference*. 42, 43, 44

Golbeck, J., Parsia, B., and Hendler, J. (2003). Trust networks on the semantic web. In *Proceedings of Cooperative Intelligent Agents*, Helsinki, Finland. 58

Gray, E., Seigneur, J.-M., Chen, Y., and Jensen, C. (2003). Trust propagation in small worlds. In *Proceedings of the 1st International Conference on Trust Management*. 54

Griffiths, N. (2005). Task delegation using experience-based multi-dimensional trust. In *AAMAS '05: Proceedings of the fourth international joint conference on Autonomous agents and multiagent systems*, pages 489–496. 47

Guha, R. (2003). Open rating systems. Technical report, Stanford Knowledge Systems Laboratory, Stanford, CA, USA. 51, 54, 57

Guha, R., Kumar, R., Raghavan, P., and Tomkins, A. (2004). Propagation of trust and distrust. In *WWW '04: Proceedings of the 13th international conference on World Wide Web*, pages 403–412, New York, NY, USA. ACM Press. 54, 56, 57, 59

Gyöngyi, Z., Garcia-Molina, H., and Pedersen, J. (2004). Combating web spam with trustrank. In *Proceedings of the 30th International Conference on Very Large Data Bases (VLDB)*, pages 271–279. 68

Hagmann, M. (2000). Scientific misconduct: Panel finds scores of suspect papers in german fraud probe. *Science*, **288**(5474), 2106 – 2107. 16

Haveliwala, T. H. (1999). Efficient computation of pageRank. Technical Report 1999-31, Stanford University. 67

Haveliwala, T. H. (2002). Topic-sensitive pagerank. In *Proceedings of the Eleventh International World Wide Web Conference*, Honolulu, Hawaii. 71

Herlocker, J. L., Konstan, J. A., Terveen, L. G., and Riedl, J. T. (2004). Evaluating collaborative filtering recommender systems. *ACM Trans. Inf. Syst.*, **22**(1), 5–53. 40

Hess, C. (2005). Trust-based recommendations for publications - a multi-layer network approach. Doctoral Consortium at the 9th European Conference on Research and Advanced Technology for Digital Libraries (ECDL 2005), Vienna, Austria. 7, 79

Hess, C. and de Rougemont, M. (2007). A model of uncertainty for near-duplicates in document reference networks. In *Proceedings of ECDL 2007*. 131

Hess, C. and Stein, K. (2007a). Efficient calculation of personalized document rankings. In *Proceedings of the Twentieth International Conference on Artificial Intelligence (IJCAI 2007)*. 93, 95, 98, 99, 163, 174

Hess, C. and Stein, K. (2007b). Personalized document rankings by incorporating trust information from social network data into link-based measures. In *Proceedings of the IJCAI 2007 Workshop on Text Mining & Link Analysis*. 103, 187, 190

Hess, C., Stein, K., and Schlieder, C. (2006). Trust-enhanced visibility for personalized document recommendations. In *Proceedings of the 21st Annual ACM Symposium on Applied Computing*, Dijon, France. 84, 179

Jeh, G. and Widom, J. (2003). Scaling personalized web search. In *WWW '03: Proceedings of the 12th international conference on World Wide Web*, pages 271–279. 71

Jøsang, A. and Pope, S. (2005). Semantic constraints for trust transitivity. In *APCCM '05: Proceedings of the 2nd Asia-Pacific conference on Conceptual modelling*, pages 59–68, Darlinghurst, Australia. Australian Computer Society, Inc. 49

Jøsang, A., Gray, E., and Kinateder, M. (2003). Analysing topologies of transitive trust. In T. Dimitrakos and F. Martinelli, editors, *Proceedings of the First International Workshop on Formal Aspects in Security & Trust (FAST2003)*, pages 9–22, Pisa, Italy. 49

Kamvar, S. D., Haveliwala, T. H., Manning, C. D., and Golub, G. H. (2003). Extrapolation methods for accelerating pagerank computations. In *Proceedings of the Twelfth International Conference on World Wide Web*. 67

Kautz, H., Selman, B., and Shah, M. (1997). The hidden web. *AI Magazine*, **18**(2), 27–36. 39

Kinateder, M. and Rothermel, K. (2003). Architecture and algorithms for a distributed reputation system. In *Proceedings of the First International Conference on Trust Management*, volume 2692, pages 1–16. Springer Verlag. 42, 48, 49, 54

Kleinberg, J. M. (1999). Authoritative sources in a hyperlinked environment. *Journal of the ACM*, **46**(5), 604–632. 66, 69

Kochan, C. A. and Budd, J. M. (1992). The persistence of fraud in the literature: the darsee case. *Journal of the American Society for Information Science*, **43**(7), 488–493. 12

Kohlenberg, K. (2006). Die anarchische Wiki-Welt. *Die Zeit,* **37**. Only available in German; "The anarchic world of wikis". 26

Korfiatis, N. and Naeve, A. (2005). Evaluating wiki contributions using social networks: A case study on wikipedia. In *First on-Line conference on Metadata and Semantics Research (MTSR'05).* 29, 78, 79

Korfiatis, N., Poulos, M., and Bokos, G. (2006). Evaluating authoritative sources using social networks: an insight from wikipedia. *Online Information Review,* **30**(3), 252–262. 29

Korfiatis, N., Sicilia, M., Hess, C., Stein, K., and Schlieder, C. (in print). Social network models for enhancing reference-based web eankings. In D. H. Goh and S. Foo, editors, *SocialInformation Retrieval Systems: Emerging Technologies and Applications for Searching the Web effectively.* IDEA Group Publishing. 79

Kosala, R. and Blockeel, H. (2000). Web mining research: a survey. *ACM SIGKDD Explorations Newsletter,* **2**(1), 1–15. 63

Lane, C. (1998). Introduction: Theories and issues in the study of trust. In Lane and Bachmann (1998). 61

Lane, C. and Bachmann, R., editors (1998). *Trust Within and Between Organizations: Conceptual Issues and Empirical Applications,* New York. Oxford University Press. 60, 210, 213, 215

Lawrence, S., Giles, C. L., and Bollacker, K. (1999a). Digital libraries and autonomous citation indexing. *IEEE Computer,* **32**(6), 67–71. 73

Lawrence, S., Bollacker, K., and Giles, C. L. (1999b). Indexing and retrieval of scientific literature. In *CIKM '99: Proceedings of the eighth international conference on Information and knowledge management,* pages 139–146. 73

Lee, D., Kang, J., Mitra, P., Giles, C. L., and On, B.-W. (2006). Are your citations clean? new challenges and scenarios in maintaining digital libraries. In *In ACM Comm. of the ACM (CACM).* 73, 74

Leuf, B. and Cunningham, W. (2001). *The Wiki Way: Collaboration and Sharing on the Internet.* Addison-Wesley. 22

Levien, R. (2003). *Attack Resistant Trust Metrics.* Ph.D. thesis, UC Berkely, Berkeley, CA, USA. 55

Levien, R. and Aiken, A. (1998). Attack-resistant trust metrics for public key certification. In *Proceedings of the 7th USENIX Security Symposium,* San Antonio, Texas, USA. 54

Leydesdorff, L. (1998). Theories of citation? *Scientometrics*, **43**(1), 5–25. 8, 9

Leydesdorff, L. and Wouter, P. (1999). Between texts and contexts: Advances in theories of citation. *Scientometrics*, **44**(2), 169–182. 8

Lih, A. (2004). Wikipedia as participatory journalism: Reliable sources? metrics for evaluating collaborative media as a news resource. In *Proceedings of the 5th International Symposium on Online Journalism*. 23

Linden, G., Smith, B., and York, J. (2003). Amazon.com recommendations: item-to-item collaborative filtering. *IEEE Internet Computing*, **7**(1), 76–80. 41

Linden, G. D., Jacobi, J. A., and Benson, E. A. (2001). Collaborative recommendations using item-to-item similarity mappings. US Patent 6,266,649 (to Amazon.com), Patent and Trademark Office, Washington, D.C. 41

Luhmann, N. (1979). *Trust and Power*. John Wiley & sons, Chichester. 46

Malsch, T. and Schlieder, C. (2002). Communication without agents? from agent-oriented to communication-oriented modeling. In G. e. a. Lindemann, editor, *Regulated Agent-Based Social Systems: First International Workshop, RASTA 2002*, pages 113–133, Bologna, Italy. Springer-Verlag. 8, 65

Malsch, T., Schlieder, C., Kiefer, P., Lübcke, M., Perschke, R., Schmitt, M., and Stein, K. (2007). Communication between process and structure: Modelling and simulating message reference networks with com/te. *Journal of Artificial Societies and Social Simulation*, **10**(1). 8, 9, 67, 70

Marsh, S. (1994a). Optimism and pessimism in trust. In J. Ramirez, editor, *Proceedings of the Ibero-American Conference on Artificial Intelligence*, Caracas, Venezuela. 47, 48

Marsh, S. and Dibben, M. R. (2005). Trust, untrust, distrust and mistrust - an exploration of the dark(er) side. In P. Hermann, V. Issarny, and S. Shiu, editors, *Proceedings of Third iTrust International Conference (iTrust 2005)*, pages 17–33, Rocquencourt, France. 46, 47, 48, 50

Marsh, S. P. (1994b). *Formalising Trust as a Computational Concept*. Ph.D. thesis, University of Stirling. 46, 48

Massa, P. and Avesani, P. (2005). Controversial users demand local trust metrics: An experimental study on epinions.com community. In *AAAI 2005*, pages 121–126. 54

Massa, P. and Hayes, C. (2005). Page-rerank: using trusted links to re-rank authority. In *Proceedings of Web Intelligence Conference*. 72, 73

Matsuo, Y., Tomobe, H., Hasida, K., and Ishizuka, M. (2004). Finding social network for trust calculation. In *Proceedings of the ECAI 2004*, pages 510–514. 39

Mayer, R. C., Davis, J. H., and Schoorman, F. D. (1995). An integration model of organizational trust. *Academy of Management. The Academy of Management Review*, **20**(3), 709–735. 91

McEvily, B., Perrone, V., and Zaheer, A. (2003). Introduction to the special issue on trust in an organizational context. *Organization Science*, **14**(1), 1–4. 60

McGuinness, D., Zeng, H., Pinheiro da Silva, P., Ding, L., Narayanan, D., and Bhaowal, M. (2006). Investigations into trust for collaborative information repositories: A wikipedia case study. In *Workshop on the Models of Trust for the Web (MTW06)*. Edinburgh, Scotland. 28

Menczer, F. (2002). Growing and navigating the small world web by local content. *Proceedings of the National Academy of Sciences of the United States of America (PNAS)*, **99**(22), 14014–14019. 64

Mika, P. (2005). Flink: Semantic web technology for the extraction and analysis of social networks. *Journal of Web Semantics*, **3**(2). 39

Milgram, S. (1967). The small world problem. *Psychology Today*, **2**, 60–67. 52

Montaner, M., López, B., and Lluís de la Rosa, J. (2002). Opinion-based filtering through trust. In S. Ossowski and O. Shehory, editors, *Proceedings of the Sixth International Workshop on Cooperative Information Agents*, volume 2446 of *LNAI*, pages 188–196, Madrid, Spain. Springer Verlag. 42, 43, 44, 54

Newman, M. E. J. (2003). The structure and function of complex networks. Retrieved September 07, 2004, from http://arxiv.org/cond-mat/0303516. 50, 51

Newman, M. E. J. (2004). Coauthorship networks and patterns of scientific collaboration. *Proceedings of the National Academy of Sciences*, **101**(suppl 1), 5200 – 5205. 80

news@nature.com (2005). Stem-cell brothers divide. Retrieved April 04, 2006, from http://www.nature.com/news/2005/051114/full/438262a.html. 14

news@nature.com (2006a). Schatten in the spotlight. Retrieved April 04, 2006, from http://www.nature.com/news/2006/060109/full/060109-7.html. 15

news@nature.com (2006b). Timeline of a controversy. Retrieved April 04, 2006, from http://www.nature.com/news/2005/051219/full/051219-3.html. 14, 89 news@nature.com (2006c). Verdict: Hwang's human stem cells were all fakes. Retrieved April 04, 2006, from `http://www.nature.com/news/2006/060109/full/439122a.html`. 14

"Not-so-deep impact" (2005). *Nature*, **435**, 1003–1004. 10

O'Donovan, J. and Smyth, B. (2005). Trust in recommender systems. In *IUI '05: Proceedings of the 10th International Conference on Intelligent User Interfaces*, pages 167–174. 43, 45

Opthof, T., Coronel, R., and Piper, H. M. (2004). Impact factors: no totum pro parte by skewness of citation. *Cardiovascular Research*, **61**, 201–203. 10

O'Reilly, T. (2005). What is web 2.0: Desing patterns and business models for the next generation of software. Retrieved March 21, 2007, from `http://www.oreillynet.com/pub/a/oreilly/tim/news/2005/09/30/what-is-web-20.html`. 1

Osareh, F. (1996a). Bibliometrics, citation analysis and co-citation analysis: A review of literature i. *Libri*, **46**, 149–158. 66

Osareh, F. (1996b). Bibliometrics, citation analysis and co-citation analysis: A review of literature ii. *Libri*, **46**, 217–225. 66

Page, L., Brin, S., Motwani, R., and Winograd, T. (1998). The pagerank citation ranking: Bringing order to the web. Technical report, Stanford Digital Library Technologies Project. 10, 66, 67, 71, 107

Pfeifer, M. P. and Snodgrass, G. L. (1990). The continued use of retracted, invalid scientific literature. *JAMA, The Journal of the American Medical Association*, **263**(10), 1420–1423. 12

Pinski, G. and Narin, F. (1976). Citation influence for journal aggregates of scientific publications: Theory, with application to the literature of physics. *Information Processing & Management*, **12**, 297–312. 10, 66, 67

Porter Liebeskind, J. and Lumerman Oliver, A. (1998). From handshake to contract: Intellectual property, trust, and the social structure of academic research. In Lane and Bachmann (1998). 117

Powell, W. W., Koput, K. W., and Smith-Doerr, L. (1996). Interorganizational collaboration and the locus of innovation: Networks of learning in biotechnology. *Administrative Science Quarterly*, **41**(1), 116–145. 62

Pöschl, U. (2004). Interactive journal concept for improved scientific publsihing and quality assurance. *Learned Publishing*, **17**(2), 105–113. 199

Rabin, M. (1981). Fingerprinting by random polynomials. Technical Report TR-15-81, Harvard University, Department of Computer Science. 75

Rateike, V., Rösner, J.-M., Denks, L., and Eberts, C. (2007). Die Entwicklung exzellenter Artikel in der deutschsprachigen Wikipedia - Keine Qualität ohne Küchenchef? Retrieved April 24, 2007, from `http://141.13.22.238/mediawiki/index.php/Die_Entwicklung_exzellenter_Artikel_in_der_deutschsprachigen_Wikipedia`. Only available in German; "The development of excellent articles in the German Wikipedia – No quality without a chef?". 25

Re, C., Dalvi, N., and Suciu, D. (2006). Query evaluation on probabilistic databases. *IEEE Data Engineering Bulletin*, **29**(1), 25–31. 124

Reiter, M. K. and Stubblebine, S. G. (1997). Toward acceptable metrics of authentication. In *Proceedings of the IEEE Symposium on Security and Privacy*, pages 10–20. 54

Resnick, P. and Varian, H. R. (1997). Recommender systems. *Communications of the ACM*, **40**(3), 56–58. 40

Resnick, P., Iacovou, N., Suchak, M., Bergstrom, P., and Riedl, J. (1994). Grouplens: An open architecture for collaborative filtering of netnews. In *CSCW '94: Proceedings of the 1994 ACM Conference on Computer Supported Cooperative Work*, pages 175–186. 40

Richardson, M., Agrawal, R., and Domingos, P. (2003). Trust management for the semantic web. In D. Fensel, K. P. Sycara, and J. Mylopoulos, editors, *Second International Semantic Web Conference (ISWC 2003)*, volume 2870 of *Lecture Notes in Computer Science*, pages 351–368, Sanibel Island, FL, USA. Springer Verlag. 46, 48, 55, 57

Sanger, L. (2007). Why the citizendium will (probably) succeed. Retrieved April 25, 2007, from `http://www.citizendium.org/whyczwillsucceed.html`. 26

Schafer, J. B., Konstan, J., and Riedl, J. (1999). Recommender systems in e-commerce. In *EC '99: Proceedings of the 1st ACM Conference on Electronic Commerce*, pages 158–166. 40

Schiff, S. (2006). Know it all. *New Yorker*. includes the editor's note; Retrieved April 17, 2007, from `http://www.newyorker.com/archive/2006/07/31/060731fa_fact`. 22

Seglen, P. O. (1992). The skewness of science. *Journal of the American Society for Information Science*, **43**(9), 628–638. 10

Seglen, P. O. (1997). Why the impact factor of journals should not be used for evaluating research. *BMJ*, **314**(7079), 497–. 9, 10

Shivakumar, N. and Garcia-Molina, H. (1998). Finding near-replicas of documents on the web. In *Proceedings of Workshop on Web Databases (WebDB'98)*. 73

Sinha, R. and Swearingen, K. (2001). Comparing recommendations made by online systems and friends. In *Proceedings of the DELOS-NSF Workshop on Personalization and Recommender Systems in Digital Libraries*, Dublin, Ireland. 42

Sox, H. C. and Rennie, D. (2006). Research misconduct, retraction, and cleansing the medical literature: Lessons from the poehlman case. *Annals of Internal Medicine*, **144**(8). 12, 16

Stallings, W. (1995). The pgp web of trust. *Byte.* online available at `http://www.byte.com/art/9502/sec13/art4.htm`. 45

Stein, K. and Hess, C. (2005). Information retrieval in trust-enhanced document networks. In *Workshop Proceedings of the European Web Mining Forum 2005*, Porto, Portugal. 103

Stein, K. and Hess, C. (2006). Information retrieval in trust-enhanced document networks. In M. Ackermann, B. Berendt, M. Grobelnik, A. Hotho, D. Mladenic, G. Semeraro, M. Spiliopoulou, G. Stumme, V. Svatek, and M. van Someren, editors, *Semantics, Web, and Mining. European Web Mining Forum, EMWF 2005, and Knowledge Discovery and Ontologies, KDO 2005, Porto, Portugal, October 2005, Revised Selected and Invited Papers*, LNAI 4289. Springer. 103, 193

Stvilia, B., Twidale, M. B., Smith, L. C., and Gasser, L. (2005). Assessing information quality of a community-based encyclopedia. In *Proceedings of the International Conference on Information Quality - ICIQ 2005*, pages 442–454. 27

Swartz, A. and Hendler, J. (2001). The semantic web: A network of content for the digital city. In *Proceedings Second Annual Digital Cities Workshop*, Kyoto, Japan. 2, 46

Sydow, J. (1998). Understanding the constitution of interorganizational trust. In Lane and Bachmann (1998). 61, 62

University of Pittsburgh (2006). Summary investigative report on allegations of possible scientific misconduct on the part of gerald p. schatten, ph.d. Retrieved April 04, 2006, from `http://newsbureau.upmc.com/PDF/Final%20Public%20Report%202.08.pdf`. 15

Viégas, F., Wattenberg, M., and Dave, K. (2004). Studying cooperation and conflict between authors with history flow visualizations. In *Proceedings of CHI 2004*, Vienna, Austria. 27, 29

Wales, J. (2007). Wikipedia and the future. Talk at DGPuK, Bamberg. 23

Wasserman, S. and Faust, K. (1994). *Social Network Analysis*. Cambridge University Press, Cambridge. 50, 53, 80

Watts, D. J. (1999). Networks, dynamics, and the small-world phenomenon. *American Journal of Sociology*, **105**(2), 493 – 527. 52

Watts, D. J. and Strogatz, S. H. (1998). Collective dynamics of 'small world' networks. *Nature*, **393**, 440–442. 52

Widom, J. (2005). Trio: A system for integrated management of data, accuracy, and lineage. In *Second Biennial Conference on Innovative Data Systems Research (CIDR 05)*, pages 262–276. 124

Wilson, T., Wiebe, J., and Hwa, R. (2006). Recognizing strong and weak opinion clauses. *Computational Intelligence*, **22**(2), 73–99. 72

Wu, B., Goel, V., and Davison, B. D. (2006). Propagating trust and distrust to demote web spam. In *Models of Trust for the Web (MTW'06)*. 68

Ziegler, C.-N. (2005). *Towards Decentralized Recommender Systems*. Ph.D. thesis, Albert-Ludwigs-Universität Freiburg, Freiburg i.Br., Germany. 195

Ziegler, C.-N. and Golbeck, J. (2006). Investigating correlations of trust and interest similarity. *Decision Support Services*, **to appear**. 42

Ziegler, C.-N. and Lausen, G. (2004a). Paradigms for decentralized social filtering exploiting trust network structure. In R. Meersman and Z. Tari, editors, *Proceedings of the DOA/CoopIS/ODBASE Confederated International Conferences*, volume 3291 of *LNCS*, pages 840–858, Larnaca, Cyprus. Springer-Verlag. 42

Ziegler, C.-N. and Lausen, G. (2004b). Spreading activation models for trust propagation. In *Proceedings of the IEEE International Conference on e-Technology, e-Commerce, and e-Service*, Taipei, Taiwan. IEEE Computer Society Press. 46, 54, 55, 57

Ziegler, C.-N. and Lausen, G. (2005). Propagation models for trust and distrust in social networks. *Information Systems Frontiers*, **7**(4-5), 337–358. 57